Bi

Notes for a
Bisexual Revolution

Shiri Eisner

SEAL PRESS

BI
Notes for a Bisexual Revolution

Copyright © 2013 Shiri Eisner
Published by Seal Press
An imprint of Perseus Books
A Hachette Book Group company
1700 Fourth Street
Berkeley, California
www.sealpress.com

Library of Congress Cataloging-in-Publication Data

Eisner, Shiri.
Bi : notes for a bisexual revolution / by Shiri Eisner.
pages cm
ISBN 978-1-58005-474-4
1. Bisexuality. I. Title.
HQ74.E35 2013
306.76'5—dc23
2012047200

10 9 8 7 6 5 4 3

Cover design by Erin Seaward-Hiatt
Interior design by Domini Dragoone
Printed in the United States of America

Contents

Introduction

"I hope they're revolting against our methods. I think it's the duty of every generation to revolt against the older generation and to go further. My expectation is that they ought to have a higher level of consciousness than I did, because they're standing on our shoulders."
—David Lourea, bisexual activist (1945–1992)

I started doing bisexual activism in 2009, after many years of being active with the radical queer, feminist, and Palestine solidarity movements. Up until then, I had no idea that these two places in my head—bisexuality and activism—could connect. I (as well as my bisexual friends) were all active in those movements, organizing and participating in projects that changed events and politics. Throughout this time, we kept talking about our bisexuality, about erasure and biphobia in our communities, and wondered why no one was doing anything about it. I remember waiting for years for something to start, all the while never thinking about bisexual activism as an option.

In 2008, the first bisexual support group in Tel Aviv was started by Elad Livneh, a long-time bisexual activist and one of two people running Bisexuals in Israel, a Jerusalem-based organization active between 2004 and 2007. From the moment I heard about the new support group (while marching with the first transgender block in the Jerusalem pride march), I became so excited that the two dots had finally connected. Very quickly I found myself writing about bisexuality, distributing fliers, promoting the support group, and organizing groups and events of my own. Within a year I had published an article in a book (*Getting Bi: Voices of Bisexuals Around the World*, second edition), was regularly publishing texts online, had founded a bisexual film club, organized the first bi/pan block in the Tel Aviv pride parade, started an Israeli bisexual online mailing list, and formed the second-ever bisexual and pansexual organization in Israel/Occupied Palestine, Panorama—Bi and Pansexual Feminist Community.

At around the same time, my learning about bisexuality started as well. I swallowed up anything I could get my hands on: anthologies, articles, books—both academic and political. As my knowledge expanded, my bisexual politics deepened with it. Very soon I found that I needed to explain it to everyone else. I knew why *I* did bisexual activism, but if I wanted to encourage others to join me, I had to elaborate. I opened a bisexual blog in Hebrew, and later in English. But one of the first things I discovered was that no matter how much I wrote, everything seemed partial, like fragments of a bigger whole. I also discovered that I not only had unique *views* about bisexuality, but also unique *knowledge*—since I had read so much about bisexual politics and theory, I was able to draw on information that most people didn't have access to.

For a very long time, I had a vague idea that one day I would write a book about bisexuality. At first, I didn't know what it would be about, but later it grew into an outline. One day I sat in the kitchen with my girlfriend, Lilach, and told her (for what must have been the millionth time) that I had a book in my head. Unlike the previous times, this time her response was: "Write it." And I did.

This book is about why I do bisexual activism. It's the full explanation that I could never quite provide on either of my blogs. Everything written in this book, no matter how theoretical or academic, informs everything I do as a bisexual activist. As such, I view this book as a field guide. No matter how theoretical it is at times, the theory doesn't—and shouldn't—remain on the pages alone.

This is the first book to attempt a distillation of a coherent radical, rather than liberal, bisexual politics. The word *radical* stems from the Latin *radix* ("root"), and denotes anything relating to the root. In the case of politics, this signifies an examination of the roots of oppression in society. As opposed to liberal politics, whose goal is to *gain access* to social power structures, radical politics criticizes these very structures and ultimately seeks to take them apart. As opposed to liberal politics, which prioritizes hegemonic viewpoints and "top to bottom" change, radical politics prefers marginalized points of view and "bottom to top" solutions. While liberal politics presumes that the system (whether social, political, economic, and so on) is basically okay and simply needs a few corrections, radical politics recognizes it as the very source of oppression. According to radical politics, liberation can't be gained by further contributing to these systems or by requesting them to extend their control. Rather, what needs to be done is minimize their control and finally tear them down. Radical politics is not about receiving rights, protection, or privilege; it is not about inserting small changes in the system so that it "works better"; it is not about changing legislation and waiting for the effects to "trickle down." Instead, radical politics is about the revolution.

What a radical viewpoint might offer for bisexual politics is an opportunity to examine and oppose bi people's oppression, as it pertains to the roots rather than the surface. So far, the main goal of mainstream bisexual movements in North America and Western Europe has been to become "accepted" by society and to "gain rights." But instead of looking at things from a bird's-eye view, as liberal politics does, this book attempts to shed light on how things look "down below" in people's lives. It also tries to uncover the reasons these things happen, and show

how, rather than being isolated, they relate to other forms of oppression. Rather than trying to normalize bisexuality, this book tries to extract its enormous subversive potential, and utilize it to break down social order and create a revolution.

In keeping with radical politics' preference for marginalized viewpoints, this book is also strongly queer, feminist, antiracist, and trans-inclusive. Where it can, and where appropriate, it reaches out to those and other groups, examining intersections between them and bisexuality. This comes from the understanding that no one struggle is complete without connection to others. Oppression of any one group doesn't happen in isolation, but parallels, draws from, and intersects with that of others. Further, these types of oppression don't only exist in the "outside" world, separate from various communities and movements, but also affect them from within. For this reason, ignoring other types of oppression in favor of "single issue" politics means reinforcing them. This is why the book constantly takes care to make these connections alongside examinations of monosexism and biphobia.

This book is very much influenced by academic theories, and takes the time to explain them. Being both an activist and an academic, I find in theory the language and tools needed to understand how things work. It allows me to examine how oppression is created and maintained, and then provides the antidote for taking it apart. In writing about academic theories, I hope to achieve two things: first, bringing this inaccessible knowledge back to people who might not have the financial or educational access to it; and second, allowing people to use these theories to take a hard look at monosexism and biphobia, how they work and why. Following these understandings, I hope the theories I use can also supply the antidote for resisting oppression.

By now you've probably noticed my insistence on the word *bisexuality* rather than *pansexuality, omnisexuality,* or *queerness,* identities that hold more currency within radical queer communities and politics. A full explanation for why I insist on keeping the word "bisexual" can be found at the end of chapter 1. Having said that, one can also view this book as an attempt to radicalize bisexuality, and thereby also reclaim it. Though I support the identities mentioned above and consider them part of my community, I must also acknowledge that this book is not (fully) about them. This is not meant to erase, disregard, or exclude them, but rather to acknowledge existing differences and points of view. That said, I also hope that this book might serve as a resource for other nonmonosexual groups, that they find inspiration and empowerment within, perhaps enough to join extended bisexual movements as part of an umbrella struggle for all of us.

This book is also limited in perspective mostly to North America and Western Europe (with some references to Israel/Occupied Palestine). While I acknowledge that other cultures have multiple, complex, and different systems of sex, gender, and sexual practice, I must also acknowledge my own limited viewpoint. As a result of white cultural imperialism, despite my living in the Middle East, I was not taught, nor do I know much about gender and sexuality in cultures other than the ones I discuss. The colonial project that is Zionist Israel imagines itself as an extension of the "enlightened" white world in the "primitive" East, and draws its cultural influences from minority-world cultures (North America and Western Europe). Ironically, though I, as a Middle Easterner, might have more in common with majority-world bisexuals than American or European ones, I nonetheless don't know enough about them—certainly not enough to write a book about them. I realize that in writing a book about white cultures, I might be reinscribing the same kind of cultural imperialism. However, I must also acknowledge my own limitations, and allow myself the space to research the cultures that I *am* informed about. That said, I hope that my staunch antiracist and anticolonial position balances out this initial bias.

Some readers might find the radical perspective of this book challenging. In fact, the book often makes a point of challenging readers to
examine their own privileges and oppressive behaviors, alongside examining their shared oppression. In this I do not mean to alienate my readers or to make them feel attacked. Rather, the criticism contained herein
is done in the spirit of community support, recognizing that calling out
our friends and communities is an important part of the learning process in which we all partake. Debate, dissent, and conflict are the living
fire of a community's heart. They allow us to learn, teach, form opinions, develop concepts and language, and ultimately grow and change.
To criticize a movement from within is to express solidarity with it, to
contribute to it, and support it on its way to the revolution.

Another very different challenge contained in this book is that it
sometimes discusses difficult topics such as violence, sexual violence,
and other issues. For this reason, the book contains *trigger warnings*
throughout its length. A trigger warning is a statement coming up before
a text or an image that might cause extreme emotional responses, such
as post-traumatic flashbacks, anxiety, panic, and so on (that is, it might
"trigger" such a response). The purpose of trigger warnings is to allow
people to choose whether or not to expose themselves to potentially trig-
gering content. They are about being attentive to our own, as well as
others', emotional state. Their goal is creating a safer space for everyone, acknowledging that many people are survivors of violence, sexual
violence, and other traumatizing experiences. When you encounter a
trigger warning in this book, please consider whether or not the content
following it might trigger you. If so, please consider reading it somewhere that feels safe for you, and at a time when you have emotional
support available should you need it.

Writing this book has been a long, often fun but sometimes difficult
process. While I owe much of it to my own abilities as well as to my

friends' support, I also need to acknowledge the privileges that enabled me to begin this pursuit in the first place. First and foremost, as a Jewish citizen of apartheid Israel/Occupied Palestine, I have access to many privileges: I am a citizen of the country rather than "resident" or refugee; I am allowed to reside in my home without being expelled from it or having to fight for my right to live there; I live in relative safety rather than under siege or the constant threat of military attack; I have regular access to clean food, water, and medicines; I enjoy freedom of movement as well as freedom of speech, being able to participate in political struggles, to read and to write about politics. These are only a few of the benefits that I hold directly on account of Palestinians, as well as of non-Jewish migrant workers and asylum seekers. The racist apartheid system of Israel directly benefits me for the sole "virtue" of my Jewishness while oppressing others for the "crime" of wanting to live here.

In addition to this, I hold various other privileges that enabled me to write this book: I'm an English speaker, meaning that I could choose to write a book in this language and expand my potential circle of readers; I have academic education, as well as access to books, articles, and other resources about bisexual and queer politics. This means that I've had access to the necessary knowledge required to write a book; I work at a steady job that pays enough for me to be able to afford housing, clothes, and food; it also enables me to own a computer and to have enough spare time to use it for writing; I have the knowledge and ability to operate a computer. This includes physical ability, as computers are built to cater to those who can move their hands and see the screen. In addition, I'm in the "right age" to be considered an "edgy, young writer" on the one hand, and to be taken seriously on the other. This contributes to my status as a writer, and consequently to the status of the book. While these are not all of the privileges that I enjoy, they are nonetheless the main ones. Most people in the world do not have them, and in taking advantage of my relative privilege I do not mean to forget or dismiss those on whose backs this privilege exists. I stand shoulder to shoulder with all these groups and people, and I strive for their liberation alongside my own.

If I could ask any one thing of my readers, it's that they don't leave this book on the shelf but take it to the streets. Use this book to inform and create your own radical bisexual movements with which to take apart oppression and work toward liberation. The purpose of this book is to serve as inspiration for activism, for getting out there and changing the world.

In addition, I hope this book will influence a change within existing bisexual movements in North America and Western Europe. Though these bi movements have had fiercely radical, feminist, antiracist, and trans-inclusive histories, they have also suffered from problems that the book takes the time to address. I hope it could also plant a seed of change within these existing movements, leading to a more radical, less assimilationist path, to creating new alliances—and to revolutionizing our bi communities.

The bisexual revolution is there waiting for us. Let's start making it happen.

CHAPTER 1:

What is Bisexuality?

Too many books are written about bisexuality without first asking, or indeed explaining, what bisexuality means. As with many other concepts in **minority world** cultures (such as feminism, for example, or radical politics), it seems as though many people are sure that they know what bisexuality means, when there is far more to the concept. Many assume that bisexuality has a single, straightforward definition with little to no added meanings. This leads to a situation in which many people are at best convinced that they already know all about it and at worst sure that it's so simple that there's nothing to talk about, think about, or (in the activist field) organize around.

So let me be the first to say this: *I have no idea what bisexuality means.* Thinking about this section of the book, I got so confused that it took me a while to realize that I didn't need to—and couldn't possibly—cover all the possible meanings that bisexuality can have. To do that would

Minority world is a term denoting the geographical areas and countries usually imagined as the "West" (west of what?). It corresponds with the term **majority world**, which comes to replace the use of the problematic term "third world." It allows us to keep in mind that, while minority-world thinkers have been busy pathologizing sex, gender, and desire, many majority-world societies have long had mainstream, socially acceptable patterns of practices and behaviors that minority-world people might understand as "queer."

take a whole other book, and even that wouldn't be close to comprehensive.

I do have a few guesses, though.

SOME HISTORY

Bisexuality, as a term and as a concept, was born around the end of the nineteenth and beginning of the twentieth century, a time when minority-world men (mostly Europeans) first started their all-encompassing project of categorizing (and pathologizing) the world around them—and specifically, where it came to bodies, sexualities, and desire. Researchers such as Richard von Krafft-Ebing, Henry Havelock Ellis, and Magnus Hirschfeld considered bisexuality either a physical or a psychological condition, having traits of what was once thought of as "both sexes."

At the time, one of the popular theories about sexuality was that of **inversion.** According to inversion theory, gay men and lesbians were "inverts"—people who were physically male or female, but internally the "opposite sex." Same-gender desire was explained as latent heterosexuality: gays and lesbians were really just heterosexual people born in the wrong bodies. Inversion theory understood sex, gender, and desire as one and the same, imagining homosexuality and transgender as expressions of one another, and creating the still-standing myth that gay men are necessarily "internally feminine," that lesbians are necessarily "internally masculine," and that transgender people are actually "gay men" (when applied to trans women) or "lesbian" (when applied to trans men).

According to this theory, "bisexuality" was used to describe what we now call **intersexuality** (formerly *her-maphroditism*, meaning bodies with nonbinary genitals and other sexual traits). Bisexual desire was called *psychosexual hermaphroditism*, linking the concepts of bisexuality as both a physical state and desire. Bisexual people were seen as psychologically intersex, bringing the logic of inversion (latent heterosexual attraction) into the field of bisexual desire. In other words, a bi person's "male" part desires women, whereas her "female" part desires men.

> **Transgender** is anyone whose gender identity is not "appropriately" aligned with the sex one was assigned at birth. In addition to being an adjective, "transgender" can also be used as a noun in place of "transgenderism," which bears negative connotations.

You might notice that this theory is at once incredibly gender-binary *and* androgynous. Despite its **binarism** and heterosexism, I like the way that this theory connects bisexuality to intersexuality and opens a sort of "third space" for both bodies, genders, and desires. In minority-world societies, both intersex bodies and bisexual identities are perceived as an aberration. They are perceived as needing immediate "correction" to fit the binary standards of society: intersex babies are treated as a medical emergency and undergo imposed sex-reassignment surgeries, often immediately after birth and without consent. In a similar, though certainly less violent and more symbolic way, bisexual identity is often treated as a sexual emergency: bisexual individuals face strong resistance and social pressure to immediately change our sexual identity into something else (often *anything* else, just as long as we don't use the "B-word").

Freud was one of the first minority-world thinkers to use the word *bisexuality* in order to describe desire (instead of a physical or psychological state). The way Freud described it, bisexuality (also named "polymorphous perversity") was the ground from which ("normal") heterosexuality and ("pathological") homosexuality developed. Very few remember to mention bisexuality as the basis for Freud's oedipal theory: According to Freud, the (male) child is born bisexual, desiring both his mother and his father, overcoming and repressing his bisexual desire through the oedipal process. Success in this process would leave the child heterosexual (read: "healthy"), while failure would make the child homosexual (read: "sick"). Bisexuality, in itself, ceases to be an option for the child, and is relegated to a "primitive" psychological past.[1] In Freud's theory, then, bisexuality can't be thought of as a sexual orientation (such as hetero- or homosexuality), but only the repressed basis for the development of other sexualities.

As a result of this, Freud's theory is responsible for several of the popular beliefs generally associated with bisexuality in minority world societies:

- Everyone is "actually bisexual" or "born bisexual."
- No one is, in fact, bisexual.
(These first two are different sides of the same coin.)
- Bisexuality is a passing phase.
- Bisexuality is an unfinished process.
- Bisexuality is immature.

(Note, by the way, that I don't necessarily agree or disagree with the three latter meanings, and I intentionally refrained from calling them *myths*. In fact, I think many of these so-called myths can be very helpful in building radical bisexual political thought—more on that later.)

The first important minority-world researcher to have treated bisexuality as an existing sexuality, and as a viable option, was Alfred Kinsey in his landmark research *Sexual Behavior in the Human Male*, first published in 1948. Kinsey, bisexual himself, famously wrote:

Males do not represent two discrete populations, heterosexual and homosexual. The world is not to be divided into sheep and goats. Not all things are black, nor all things white. It is a fundamental of taxonomy that nature rarely deals with discrete categories. Only the human mind invents categories and tries to force facts into separated pigeon-holes.

Kinsey was also responsible for creating the now-famous Kinsey Scale, categorizing different degrees of homosexuality and heterosexuality, using numbers from zero (exclusively heterosexual) to six (exclusively homosexual). On Kinsey's scale, the "true bisexual" was imagined to be a three, equally attracted to both males and females (other sexes and genders were not regarded). In this way, Kinsey is responsible for the popular concept that we all experience desire on a sliding scale, adding to the Freudian-based myth that very few people are actually **monosexual** (a homophobic notion that disrespects monosexualities and erases unique bisexual identity and experience).

Monosexual means someone who is attracted to people of no more than one gender.

Cisgender is someone whose gender identity is "appropriately" aligned with the sex one was assigned at birth, i.e. men who were assigned a male sex at birth, and women who were assigned a female sex at birth.

Discourse is a term coined by French philosopher Michel Foucault. It means everything spoken, written, or otherwise communicated about a certain topic. An important derivative is **dominant discourse**, meaning a discourse created by those in power and which dominates social understandings about a given topic.

You will notice that so far, the only people who talked about bisexuality in minority-world cultures were the white **cisgender** of the medical and psychological institutions and schools. This means that the people who controlled the definition, concept, and **discourse** about bisexuality were people representing the system, medicalizing and often pathologizing our desires and ways of life. By this, of course, I don't mean to insinuate that these people didn't make important contributions to our understanding of sexuality in

Hegemony means dominance, power, and control.

Symbolic capital is a term coined by French sociologist Pierre Bourdieu. It refers to the symbolic (intangible) resources that a certain person has, such as prestige, reputation, and acknowledgement, all of which give a person more value in the eyes of society and culture.

Racialized means someone perceived as having a "race." This term comes to replace "people of color," which presumes whiteness as default (as white people are rarely imagined to be "of color" or to have a "race").

Disability should not be understood as relying on physical "impairment," but rather as referring to a situation of being actively disabled by social standards of able-bodiedness and the "failure" to achieve them.

general, and bisexuality in particular, or that their importance is to be dismissed. I also do not mean to insinuate that they meant to harm bisexual people or operated maliciously. What I do mean is to highlight that, much like many other LGBT and queer identities, bisexuality, too, was first invented and scrutinized by **hegemonic** powers under the mass project of categorizing and then pathologizing various human experiences and behaviors, only later to be reclaimed by the bisexual movement. Bisexual people themselves served as research objects, the ground upon which to base theories about bisexuality and, indeed, about the entire continuum of bodies, gender, and desire. This means that bisexual people served as the "raw material" for theories that they could not control. Researchers gained their prestigious reputations and **symbolic capital** on the backs of bisexual research subjects, their lives and experiences, while distributing none of their gains—symbolic or material—back to the community. This problem is shared by many marginalized groups (including LGBTs, women, intersex people, **racialized** people, **disabled** people, and many, many more), and is indeed widespread to this day in many ways.

However, it's also worth noting that in many ways, this categorization and **pathologization** of bisexuality was one of the things that eventually gave rise to the creation of a bisexual movement. To adapt from French philosopher Michel Foucault: After the medical insti-

Pathologization means imposing a medical viewpoint on certain human feelings, thoughts, or behaviors (which are otherwise normal), in a way which views these things as pathological.

tution's project of categorization, "the [bisexual] was now a species." Before this bout of sexuality research, what we now call bisexuality was a series of sexual acts, which in and of themselves had nothing to do with a bisexual person or her self-identity. Medical and psychological research first created the category of bisexuality (while also controlling its contents and definitions). From the moment that bisexuality became a category, it also became adoptable as a personal identity, a mark for a type of person rather than a series of isolated acts. What remained, then, for the bisexual movement, was to reclaim bisexuality—as a term, an identity, and a concept—back into the hands of bisexual people, in a way that would benefit bisexual populations and give something back to them.

It is somewhat surprising, then, that a minority-world bisexual movement took until the 1970s—and then again until the 1990s—to do that very thing. Very little research is available regarding the lives of bisexuals in those intermediate years, but from what can be gleaned, it seems as though many bisexuals in the 1950s and 1960s were part of gay or lesbian communities, as well as taking part in the very first gay rights organizations in the United States ("homophile" organizations, as they were called). Despite the fact that bisexuality was even then considered a subset of homosexuality (a biphobic notion that erases the uniqueness and specificity of bisexuality), bisexuals still suffered from biphobic treatment within gay and lesbian communities.[2] However, it seems as though LGBT communities, as a whole, were at such risk and were so intent on survival that there was little freedom for anyone to speak about or create different identities or spaces. Although biphobia had been present even then, only once the gay movement (and later the lesbian movement) gained enough ground was there enough breathing room to found a separate bisexual movement. (Interestingly, this process was shared, in many ways, by the transgender movement, which came out as a movement of its own at around the same time as the bisexual movement).

In the 1970s, and again in the 1990s,[3] the bisexual movement reclaimed bisexuality both as an identity and as a subject for research and political thought, in what appeared—and to this day appears—to be a mass project for proving the existence, validity, and the normativity of bisexuality (all problematic concepts that I criticize below). This movement normally defined bisexuality as attraction to "both men and women" (following the medical institution), with variations as to what kinds of attraction might constitute bisexuality (emotional, sexual, behavioral, etc.). Between the 1990s and the 2000s, bisexuality's definition gradually changed in order to accommodate nonbinary gender identities that found themselves erased from the language of desire. Today most bisexual movements use the expanded definitions of bisexuality: attraction to people of more than one sex or gender; attraction to people of genders similar to our own, and to people of genders different from our own; or attraction to people of multiple genders.

However, timelines are limited. They create the illusion that time, movements, and definitions and their development move forward on a straight line. Do not be fooled by this: There is no one definition to bisexuality, and all the definitions I mentioned above (including the medical ones) are still used in some form. This chapter, then, will be an attempt to explore some of the meanings of bisexuality that are often invoked in minority-world culture.

DEFINING BISEXUALITY

In this part, I'll try to define bisexuality as a contemporary identity, diverging from traditional medical definitions and instead seeking new ways of observing it. Bisexuality isn't only a form of desire but also a carrier of multiple meanings (a concept that I will go deeper into later). Bisexuality can be defined and politicized on all or any of three axes that I will describe: desire, community, and politics.

It's important to mention that, though I suggest definitions for bisexual identity, I won't be trying to define bisexuality for everyone, rather describing the way that I see it and why I connect to it, hoping that it resonates with you. However, if you identify as bisexual, the only person who can define what your bisexual identity means is you.

It's also important to note that this section is about definitions that I *like*, which means it does not include binary definitions of bisexuality, despite their (unfortunate) popularity. By this I do not mean to ignore or gloss over them—I will discuss them, at length, in chapter 6.

DESIRE

The first type of meaning I'd like to give bisexuality is that of desire. I'd like to examine two definitions of this type, and extend their political and personal implications: *more than one* and *same and different.* The first definition is wide and enabling, giving us tools to think of bisexuality as a continuum. The second definition brings hierarchical differences to the forefront and enables us to address power relations in our intimate relationships as well as our communities.

More than One

My favorite definition for bisexuality so far is the one popularized by (the wonderful) bisexual activist Robyn Ochs. Ochs says, "I call myself bisexual because I acknowledge that I have in myself the potential to be attracted—romantically and/or sexually—to people of more than one sex, and/or gender, not necessarily at the same time, not necessarily in the same way, and not necessarily to the same degree."

This is by far the broadest and most enabling definition of bisexuality that I've found to date. Its strength is in the way it enables anyone

Cissexism is the social system according to which everyone is, or should be, cisgender (i.e. non-transgender), including the social system of privilege for those who are cisgender, and punishment for those who are not.

The gender binary refers to the minority-world gender system, in which only two opposing and mutually exclusive genders are recognized (woman and man).

who wants to identify as bisexual to do so. (In other words, it reassures people.) In a world in which bisexuality is usually very narrowly defined, many people who experience bisexual desire, and want to identify as bi, often feel afraid to start (or keep) identifying as such, as they feel as though they "don't qualify." The role that an enabling definition for bisexuality can fulfill to counter these feelings of internalized biphobia is invaluable—and I feel that Ochs's definition does just that. It reassures people that they are "allowed" to identify as bisexual if they wish to do so.

Though this definition is already quite popular, having been in use for many years, it still remains innovative and challenging in several ways: First, it challenges the gender binary system, pointing out that bisexual desire can work toward any number of genders beyond one. This gives space for people to identify as bisexual even when they are attracted to more than the mythological "both genders," as well as removing the **cissexist** emphasis on partners' genitals for determining bisexuality. Second, by specifying that bisexual desire can be either romantic, sexual, or both, this definition assures people who only feel one of those things, without the others, that they are not lacking in anything for their bisexual identity. Third, this definition's acknowledgment that attraction to more than one sex or gender doesn't necessarily happen at the same time opens up space to consider lifelong stories and narratives.[4] Through this, people who experience shifts in their desire over time are again given space to identify as bisexual. Lastly, acknowledging that bisexual desire does not necessarily happen in the same way or to the same degree reassures people that they do not necessarily need to desire (or have experience with) every gender on their palate equally in order to "qualify" as bisexual. This enables the option to identify as bisexual for people who prefer one gender over others, who have had more experience with one gender than with others, or who have felt differently about their desires toward each gender that they like.

To continue from the starting point marked by this definition, bisexual desire can be seen as a continuum. But not the Kinsey-scale kind of continuum, bordered by a gender binary system, sexual behavior, and the hetero-homo divide. Instead, we can imagine bisexual desire more like Adrienne Rich's lesbian continuum. In her seminal essay, "Compulsory Heterosexuality and Lesbian Existence," Rich defines lesbian existence as "not simply the fact that a woman has had or consciously desired genital sexual experience with another woman," but rather as "a range— through each woman's life and throughout history—of woman-identified experience." She continues:

> If we expand it to embrace many more forms of primary inten-
> sity between and among women, including the sharing of a rich
> inner life, the bonding against male tyranny, the giving and
> receiving of practical and political support; if we can also hear
> in it such associations as marriage resistance and the "haggard"
> behavior identified by Mary Daly (obsolete meanings intrac-
> table, willful, wanton, and unchaste, a woman reluctant to
> yield to wooing)—we begin to grasp breadths of female history
> and psychology that have lain out of reach as a consequence of
> limited, mostly clinical, definitions of lesbianism.

Similarly, I would like to think about bisexual desire not only as romantic and/or sexual attraction toward people of more than one gender (i.e. not simply by the fact that a person has had or has consciously desired people of more than one gender), but as a range—through each person's life and throughout history—of mixed-gender experience. Similar to Rich's proposal that we expand lesbian existence to other forms of "primary intensity between and among women," bisexuality can also be seen as an expanse of forms of "primary intensity" with people of more than one gender. Among other things, this gives way to political bisexual identification by anyone who experienced intimacy, emotional bonding, or any other form of "primary intensity" with people of more than one gender. Also, similar to Rich's readings of marriage resistance or "haggard" behavior as lesbian, we can also read *closet cases, fence sitters, traitors, sluts,* and *sexually ambivalent types* as bisexual. These readings could provide a social context for the realities of bisexual lives. They could also expose the ways in which our lived experiences and desires have been compartmentalized, pathologized, medicalized, and erased by dominant discourses.

Note that by suggesting these things, I do not mean to reiterate the hated familiar notion that "everyone is actually bisexual." Saying that would indeed diffuse the meaning of bisexual existence, leaving it to drown in the mire of Freudian bisexuality: infantile, pre-oedipal, primitive, and nonexistent in the present. I also do not mean to desexualize bisexuality and render it abstract, pretending that specific bisexual desire and sexuality are nonexistent or marginal. I believe that bi sexuality and bi sexual culture are central to the power of bisexuality as a political concept as well as a personal identity or experience (for those who are sexual).[5] Instead, this working definition can be a tool or a window through which to look at—and identify—bisexuality in everyday life, as well as in society, culture, and history. It might mark those moments that we consider (bisexually) significant wherever we can find them. It also means that this tool can be used to open an additional space for a political—albeit not necessarily sexual—bisexual identity and encourage such political identification, even for people who don't experience bisexual desire.

Same and Different

This definition was popularized around 2009 by *The Bisexual Index* website and by the blog *Bi Furious!* It relies on the "classical" definition of bisexuality as a "combination" or "unification" of homosexuality and heterosexuality. If homosexuality is understood to mean *attraction to people of genders similar to one's own*, and heterosexuality is understood to mean *attraction to people of genders different from one's own*, then bisexuality can just as well mean attraction to people of genders similar to and different from one's own.

What I love about this definition is how it invokes the topic of gender, but without limiting its options—pertaining to two categories, but leaving their contents open. As an inherent effect, this definition gently questions people about their own gender identities and how their own gender is related to their desires toward others. In other words, it manifests difference.

This definition opens up significant questions about things that many people regard as obvious nonissues: How do I define gender? What is my gender identity? What are the genders that are different from mine? How would I define similarity in terms of gender? How would I define difference? Which differences do I eroticize, and how? Which similarities? Do I eroticize mixed gender traits when they exist in one person, or am I more attracted to clear differentiation? How does my gender influence my desire and my relationships? How do they interact? How do my desire and my relationships influence my gender identity?

The answers to these questions are never trivial, and whichever conclusions one might end up with, their importance is in the questioning of gender identities, gender binaries, and gender-based interactions. In fact, many people might, through these questions, think about things they'd never thought of before, find angles through which they'd never examined themselves. These questions might enable us to examine the social context for our personal interactions, as well as provide tools for more specific descriptions of our experiences of bisexuality.

This definition also identifies hierarchies. In a society that is **patriarchal** and cissexist, gender differences always carry the baggage of hierarchy with them. Male or masculine-spectrum people occupy a higher place

Patriarchy literally means "male rule." It reflects a social structure in which men have both material and symbolic control over every sphere in life.

Genderqueer is a name for gender identities other than "woman" or "man." For example, people who identify as both man and woman, neither man nor woman, fluid, third gender, etc., might identify as genderqueer.

in the social order than female and feminine-spectrum people. Cisgender people likewise occupy a higher hierarchical place than transgender and **genderqueer** people. Even cisgender femininities and masculinities are different from culture to culture, and white (cis)gender expression is considered superior to any other. Think, for example, about the differences— and the differences in perception— between white, black, Latino, Jewish, Middle Eastern, and Asian masculinities (to name just a few). Each carries its own weight, each is perceived differently, yet it's clear that the only type of masculinity that is wholly validated in white/minority-world society is the white kind (and the same, of course, goes for femininity). In addition, these hierarchies don't only apply outside in the public sphere; they exist in our homes, in our relationships, and in every aspect of our personal lives, creating power imbalances within our intimate relations. Recognizing difference in gender (in all its multiplicity and complexity) might also inform us about the hierarchies at work in our intimate interactions, and encourage us to work at deconstructing them.

Recognizing gender hierarchies, in turn, might help us also identify other kinds of hierarchies that might be present in our relationships and influence them: race, class, ability, age, education, sexuality (straight/ queer, monosexual/bisexual, etc.), and many more. Indeed, these factors might also function as components of sexual desire of the kind questioned above. Recognizing each of these things and attempting to deconstruct the power relations that go along with them might also serve as a tool for revolutionary bisexual relationships, changing and reconstructing what it means to be in intimate interactions with each other.

Do note that I am not advising erasure or deconstruction of the differences themselves. Diversity and difference are wonderful, and, if anything, should be celebrated. Also, I would not want to contribute to the notion that the way to get over these hierarchies is to ignore them. A utopian world in which everyone is already perfectly equal might be a noble idea indeed, but in order to get there we first need to do some serious work to make it happen. To quote a famous text by Israeli radical queer group, Black Laundry:

> *Love without borders? Ignoring borders won't make them go away. Borders of poverty, of war, and of social labels surround us wherever we go, cutting through the flesh. Our race turns from a source of joy into a suffocating limitation; rules of sexuality and gender prevent us from being who we are and loving whom we want; biological diversity is locked behind the bars of cages that imprison other animals. The borders always surround us. But we can climb over them and gnaw at them, slip and help others slip under the barbed wire, deceive the guards and paint the walls with bold graffiti. We must struggle because every border surrounds someone chained, someone who is our ally in struggle, love, and liberation.*
>
> *Cross borders of gender. Betray borders of nation. Overcome borders of species. Break through racial borders . . .*

Using this type of definition might help us do just that: become aware to differences, hierarchies, and borders, and to start working at pulling them apart.

COMMUNITY

This type of definition looks at bisexuality as a community identity. It marks an identification with bisexual communities and movements, in addition to—or separately from—bisexual desire.

"You Can Stand Under My Umbrella"

Recently the word *bisexual* has been assigned a new use with increasing popularity: that of an umbrella term for multiple bi-spectrum identities, those that involve attraction to people of more than one sex and/or gender. This works similarly to the word *transgender*, which is not only a name for a specific identity, but also a general term encompassing many identities that deviate from cisgender norms. Just as the word *transgender* can refer to a specific identity (as a synonym for *transsexual*), as well as to multiple identities on the transgender spectrum (including transsexual, cross dresser, androgyne, genderqueer, butch, femme, bigender, and many more), so can "bisexual" denote a specific identity as well as a multiple-identity umbrella. Some bisexual-spectrum identities are:

Bisexual: as defined above, and throughout this chapter.

Pansexual/omnisexual: people who are attracted (sexually, romantically, and/or otherwise) to people of all genders and sexes, or to multiple genders and sexes, or regardless of sex and gender, and who identify as pan/omni. Pansexuality and omnisexuality differ from each other by their Greek and Latin roots (*pan* meaning *all* in Greek, and *omni* the same in Latin).

Polysexual: people who are attracted (sexually, romantically, and/or otherwise) to people of many genders and sexes (but not all), and who identify as poly.

Queer: a nonspecific identity that describes anyone diverging from heterosexuality, monogamy, and vanilla (non-kink) sexuality. In a bi-spectrum context, it's used to denote attraction to people of more than one, or of many, gender(s).

© SHIRI EISNER

and many more...

dyke AC/DC fluid multisexual versatile
heteroflexible omnisexual humansexual
pansexual nonmonosexual homoflexible
bidyke bisexual pomosexual anthrosexual down low
switch hitter msm bi-curious polysexual queer
trisexual lesbian gender blind
biromantic bi-furious yestergay panromantic
ambisexturous wsw

Fluid: describes attraction that changes or might change over time (toward people of various genders).

Homoflexible/Lesbiflexible: people who are usually attracted to people of genders similar to their own, but might occasionally be attracted to people of genders different from their own.

Heteroflexible: people who are usually attracted to people of genders different from their own, but might occasionally be attracted to people of genders similar to their own.

Bi-curious: people who are usually heterosexual, lesbian, or gay, and who are curious about experimenting with people of genders different from their usual preference.

Other bi-spectrum identities include biromantic, panromantic, bisensual, pansensual, bidyke, byke, bisexual-lesbian, ambisextrous, anthrosexual, multisexual, gender-blind, pomosexual, and many more. Where appropriate, it might also include *questioning* and *unlabeled.*

It's important to note that though some people might feel uncomfortable identifying with the word *bisexuality,* even through its umbrella use, many others often do consider themselves part of the bisexual community/movement and thus identify under the broad term. It is with respect to these people that I offer the usage of the umbrella term. I include under it only those people who want to be included under it. However, as an alternative term for inclusion of those who feel uncomfortable with the bisexual umbrella, Julia Serano (in her blog post "Bisexuality and Binaries Revisited") has suggested the acronym "BMNOPPQ", "where B = bisexual, M = multisexual, N = no label, O = omnisexual, P = pansexual, P = polysexual, and Q = experientially bisexual folks who primarily identify as queer (arranged alphabetically)."

Notwithstanding, I also mean this as a suggestion for solidarity between the various groups under the bi umbrella. This would allow us to examine the enormous common ground that we all share by virtue of our attraction to people of more than one gender. In addition to conditions and oppression specific to each of these groups, we all certainly share the effects of biphobia and monosexism. We have many common goals toward which we can work. In addition, many of the social meanings associated with bisexuality (which I'll soon examine) are also shared by the other bi-spectrum identities. We also share the full scale of bisexuality's subversive and revolutionary potential (only augmented by the many identities that might be found under it).

The idea of bisexuality as an umbrella term emphasizes one of the greatest meanings often associated with bisexuality: that of multiplicity.

Whereas bisexuality as *desire* as well as a cultural idea might invoke a multiplicity of attractions, objects choices, and sexual or romantic partners, the idea of bisexuality as an *umbrella term* can emphasize a multiplicity of identities, forms of desire, lived experiences, and politics. What it means is that an umbrella definition of bisexuality might give us more space for what I enjoy thinking about as the three Ds: difference, diversity, and deviation.

What it means is that bisexuality under this definition enables us to resist a single standard. To be different from each other as well as from the norm, to be diverse and diversify ourselves, to deviate from paths we've been pushed into by society and by oppression. It means that bisexual communities and movements can resist standardization imposed upon us by straight society, gay communities, or even the mainstream bisexual movement itself. Our communities can refuse to toe the lines, to police or impose order upon bisexual people or anyone at all. It means no one gets thrown overboard, rather that our differences can serve as a source of power.

In her article "Sexual Diversity and the Bisexual Community" (written fifteen years ago and still no less relevant), Carol Queen writes:

> *And all the while [that bisexuals are stereotypically sexualized,*
> *and are organizing ourselves in response to those biphobic*
> *beliefs], busy bisexuals are having sex: with women, with men,*
> *with both at once; with partners whose gender is unclear, fluid*
> *or mixed;[6] in and out of committed relationships; a lot or a*
> *little; in groups and alone; for love, for fun and for money;*
> *safely and unsafely; drunk and sober; in every possible combi-*
> *nation, location and variation . . . But too many of us, when*
> *faced with a sexual stereotype we cannot relate to, would like to*
> *vociferously deny that "they" (the swingers, the transgenderists,*
> *the closeted husbands) are part of our community. . . .*
>
> *Let us make [diversity] a strength, not a failing, of our*
> *movement. If we begin to reify bisexual (as if in saying the*

word we agree to the specifics of its meaning—already a mistake, in my opinion, and not yet possible at this stage of our community development), we may be tempted to leave out the wonderful, difficult complexity of acknowledging the diverse spectrum our community holds. I would prefer us to mindfully write it in—we may not fuck anything that moves, but, in our rainbow of difference, we practically are *everything that moves, and if we welcome each other in these differences as well as in our similarities, we will weave community of strong cloth indeed.*

Difference, diversity, and deviation are not only sexual, however. They mean recognizing and drawing strength from the fact that along with cisgender, monogamous, vanilla, HIV-, nondisabled, white, middle class citizens of the country and community, the bisexual community is also shared by transgender and genderqueer people; nonmonogamous, **polyamorous**, slutty or promiscuous people; sex workers; BDSM practitioners; drug users; HIV+ people, disabled, chronically ill and mentally disabled people; working class people, migrants, illegal immigrants, refugees, racialized people, and many, many more. This does not mean that we should encourage or glamorize social oppression or unsafe behaviors. It means that our political struggle needs to reflect the interests of everyone, address everyone's needs, and endeavor to attain resources for and empower people of all groups—not just the ones who fit a certain palatable standard.

This also does not mean creating a new "inverted" standard for people in bisexual communities; nor does it mean erasing differences or ignoring them. It means that each identity and group within the

Polyamory is a nonmonogamous practice or lifestyle, which involves being open to more than one (sexual or romantic) relationship at the same time, with the knowledge and consent of everyone involved.

community is uniquely celebrated, accepted, and empowered, no matter who they are. It means every different perspective is listened to and honored. It means acknowledging hierarchies and making sure that every group gets its voice and that no one group takes up space, resources, or attention at the expense of any other. It means dismantling the single standard currently operating, breaking it into a million little pieces and giving solidarity to each and every piece. This usually entails specifically working from the bottom, to empower the groups that are the most marginalized, both within the community and in general.

Tradition

The bisexual movement, though certainly not perfect, carries many traditions that make me really proud to consider myself part of it. I'd like to describe some of them, hoping that they resonate with you and add additional depth to the community definition of bisexuality.

The bisexual movement is a feminist movement, having been led and headed by women and other feminists through most of its existence. From Maggi Rubenstein (who founded the San Francisco Bisexual Center in the seventies) through Naomi Tucker, Lani Ka'ahumanu, and Loraine Hutchins, to Robyn Ochs and many many others, the leaders of the bisexual movement in the United States (and outside of it) have always expressed their commitment to feminism. These leaders have insisted on emphasizing the importance of feminism to the bisexual movement, as well as bisexuality's feminist potential.

Bisexuals also comprise such a huge part of the sex radical feminist movement of the United States that it may very well be considered a bisexual movement in its own right. With activists and writers such as Carol Queen, Susie Bright, Patrick Califia, Betty Dodson, and many others, bisexuality and bisexual identity constitute a significant part of sex-radical culture and thought, and vice versa.

The bisexual movement is also one of the only mixed-gender movements I know of in which men have thought, spoken, and written about feminism, masculinity, sexism, and patriarchy. This means that the bisexual movement has also served as a space for men to participate in feminism and to critically examine their lives and our society. This makes the bisexual movement one of the cutting-edge social sites for men's pro-feminism.

The bisexual movement has also always insisted upon inclusion of—and alliance with—transgender people, often serving as one of the most accepting communities for trans and genderqueer people. In the 1990s—a period when transgender people needed to fight and insist on inclusion even when it came to the name of the community (then, LGB)—most bisexual anthologies and zines, representing the "face" of the movement, contained essays by transgender people and insisted on the inclusion of the transgender community. In fact, inclusion, alliance, and intersections with transgender people and issues have been among the most central topics in the bisexual movement and research even to this day.

The bisexual movement has also been one of the most race-aware movements that I know of. It is often aware of the importance of inclusion of racialized people in the movement, and takes measures to create a more welcoming space for racialized bisexuals. Similar to the inclusion of trans people described above, most bisexual anthologies also contain many essays by racialized people and advocate race awareness within the movement and in general.

The bisexual movement has been one of the most inclusive toward disabled and chronically ill people, setting a unique standard for accessibility to conventions and events. This has been so unique that people from other communities often attend simply to learn more about accessibility, disability, and neurodiversity (as is the case, for example, with the U.K. BiCons).

The bisexual movement has had a long tradition of grassroots organizing, independent activism, support, and consciousness-raising groups. A seminal example of this is the Bi Women Boston organization, which, throughout its almost-thirty years of existence, has maintained its grassroots, non-hierarchical structure and still keeps its diverse activities related to bisexuality.

While many of these endeavors failed to completely work out (as I shall point out throughout the book), it is still important to acknowledge these lines of political thought, action, and tradition within the bisexual movement. All these things have certainly made the bi movement one of the most radical movements among LGBT communities and in minority-world cultures. Regardless of results, its ideology of inclusion, diversity, and political awareness is nearly beyond compare, rivaled only by that of the anarchafeminist, queer anarchist, and disability justice movements.

POLITICS, OR: THE TRUE MEANING OF BI

Bisexuality is much more than just an identity. Like with every concept in society, bisexuality carries many associations and connotations—not only about itself, but also about the world in general. As opposed to the popular belief I mentioned in the beginning, not only is bisexuality worth talking about, but it offers us a very rich array of connotations and knowledge, with enormous political and activist potential. These meanings that accompany bisexuality are independent of bisexual identity and are not linked to any specific bisexual person. Rather, these ideas and connotations are a result (or a reading, if you will) of the way that bisexuality is, and was, imagined in culture. These ideas are reflected in the arts, literature, media, history, and any other record of society in which the concept of bisexuality is invoked.

In academic language, this way of looking at things is called **epistemology**. The questions that bisexual epistemology asks are:

> *[What are] the ways in which [bisexual] meanings accrue;*
> *. . . and what strategies can be used to effect a more useful or*
> *enabling range of meanings?—Bi Academic Intervention*

*How [does] bisexuality [generate] or [how] is [it] given mean-
ing in particular contexts[?]—Clare Hemmings*

*[W]hat other functions does bisexuality perform in discourses
on sexuality? When does it get invoked, and how? When and
why does it disappear, and with what effects? What other issues
seem to attach to it; what questions does it perennially raise?
—Stacey Young*

Looking at bisexuality as an identity to be reinforced and nothing
more is politically limiting, leaving us with only one concept and one purpose on our hands. The straightforward idea that bisexuality is a valid and
normal (though erased and silenced) sexual orientation very easily leads
us to the idea that all we need to do is validate bisexuality, validate bisexual people, validate bisexual identity, validate bisexual community . . .
These are all true things—but this is where this approach ends.

It is difficult to grasp why this limiting concept of bisexuality was
the main one to gain prominence in the movement. It is high time to
expand upon it. Therefore I want to take an epistemological approach to
bisexual politics, to examine how bisexuality is thought of or imagined
and contemplate why. By connecting these things to a political agenda, I
hope to expand the ideology, options, and scope of the bisexual movement
as a whole. It needs to be noted that this is not done in vain, nor simply as
an intellectual game: Connecting between different struggles is one of the
cornerstones to radical political thinking. To acknowledge that all forms
of oppression are interrelated is to acknowledge that we all have a stake in
each other's liberation, that none of us is free until everyone is free.

I'd like to examine two contradicting ways in which bisexuality is
imagined: first within society as a whole, and then within the dominant
discourse of the bisexual movement. I will then offer a third way of reading these imagined meanings of bisexuality in a way that I believe would

benefit radical bisexual political thought: I would like to do all this by referring to bisexual stereotypes.[7]

More than anything, stereotypes are the immediate meanings attached to bisexuality and bisexual people. When people think about bisexuality, stereotypes are what they think about—this is what they "know." These stereotypes comprise a body of (imagined) knowledge about bisexual people, about the meaning of bisexuality, and of the way it works. A reading of biphobic stereotypes can be enlightening for our understanding of the social and cultural meanings given to bisexuality. Afterward we could proceed to ask: How can we, as bisexuals, use these meanings to our benefit?

Some Hegemonic Thought

Here is a basic list of commonly cited stereotypes about bisexuality. If you've traveled through a patch of life carrying a bisexual identity, there's a pretty good chance you'd find these familiar:

Bisexuality doesn't exist

Perhaps the most popular belief about bisexuality. According to this stereotype, there is no such thing as bisexuality—and people who do claim to be bisexual are simply wrong or misguided. Needless to say, this notion both feeds and is fed by bisexual erasure. It creates the impression that bisexuality doesn't appear in popular culture (or indeed anywhere) because it really doesn't exist. This also causes people to ignore (erase) bisexuality where it does appear for that very same reason. (What you know is what you see.)

Bisexuals are confused, indecisive, or just going through a phase

A "natural" extension of the first one, this stereotype explains how it happens that some people actually do identify as bisexual—they simply have it all wrong. This stereotype also invokes the idea of alternating between partners of different genders, meaning: a perceived failure of consistency. If a "true choice" can only be defined as a single gender preference, then structurally, bisexuality is impossible by definition.

Bisexuals are slutty, promiscuous, and inherently unfaithful

If a single gender preference is the only choice imaginable, then anything exceeding that number would automatically be perceived as excess. The idea of excessive sexuality then naturally leads to a notion of promiscuity. According to this stereotype, by virtue of having more than one gender preference, bisexuals are indiscriminate about their choice of partners and are therefore slutty or promiscuous. The idea of inherent unfaithfulness comes from the widely held belief that bisexuals are incapable of being satisfied with only one partner (since, evidently, they can't be satisfied with only one gender).

Bisexuals are carriers or vectors of HIV and other STIs

Relying on the previous stereotype, bisexuals are often thought to be more likely than monosexual people to carry and spread HIV and other STIs. Often combined together, this stereotype and the previous one both imagine bisexuals—bisexual men in particular—as people who engage in indiscriminate sex with multiple partners, collecting various STIs as they go along and spreading them on as they go. This stereotype, of course, leans heavily upon the assumption that having sex is infectious in and of itself, conveniently dismissing information about safer sex practices as well as other, nonsexual ways of contracting these diseases.

Another component of this stereotype is **ableism,** as it is heavily charged with negative views toward disabled and chronically ill people. It draws on severe social stigma working against people with HIV, AIDS, and other STIs, as well as the notion that STIs are in fact a punishment for promiscuity or for certain sexual practices.

Bisexuals are actually gay or actually straight

This stereotype draws upon the second cluster of stereotypes that I listed above, according to which bisexuals are confused—that we are actually anything other than bisexual. In hegemonic discourse, this "anything" is usually imagined as the narrow option of either gay or straight. Interestingly, for bisexual women the presumption is that we're really straight, while bisexual men are often presumed to be really gay. This suggests a presumption that everyone is really into men—a **phallocentric** notion testifying to this stereotype's basic reliance on sexism.

Ableism is the social system according to which everyone is, or should be, nondisabled, including social rewards for nondisabled people and punishments against disabled people.

Phallocentrism is a cultural and social system privileging masculinity and the phallus (the symbolic erect penis), and granting it power and value above other things.

Bisexuals can choose to be gay or straight

This stereotype envisions bisexuals as people who can choose between gay or straight identities and lifestyles. The stereotype couples bisexuality together with an idea of "privilege," and in this way is used to decrease the legitimacy of unique bisexual identity as well as politics. It disqualifies bisexuals from participating in gay movements by implying that bisexuals will always leave their gay or lesbian partners for an "opposite sex" relationship. (Relationships with nonbinary-gender people never seem to be part of this popular imagination).

All of these stereotypes are personalized, relating to particular people (who identify as bisexual), and are taken literally and at face value. They imagine bisexual people—and bisexuality itself—as inauthentic, unstable, predatory, infectious, and dangerous. Implicitly, these stereotypes also entail a demand for normalcy because they present bisexuality as a deviation from the norm, and therefore inherently perverse.

In light of that, it is odd to see that the mainstream bisexual movement's rebuttals, or, more popularly, "myth busting," generally remain within this literal and personalized framework. In addition to being personalized and literal, they also hearken to the demand for normalcy presented therein.

"But That's Not True!"

In the overwhelming majority of cases, the bisexual movement's rebuttals have been based on a single-value reading and denial of these stereotypes, using a "that's not true!" formula for any such stereotype (or: "that's not *necessarily* true" for those who consider themselves more progressively minded). Lists of such stereotypes, coupled with rebuttals/ denials, abound both on the Internet and in the bisexual activist field. In addition, they have become characteristic of bisexual political discourse in many other contexts as well.

Here is my list again, this time with rebuttals (or "myth busting" replies) typical to the bisexual movement (and including one or two grains of salt):

Bisexuality doesn't exist

Yes, it does! Many studies and statistics exist that attest to the existence of bisexuality. I'm bisexual myself, and I'm not imaginary, right? Also, there's a whole bisexual movement for people who feel or identify as such. Bisexual people definitely exist; so no more denial.

Bisexuals are confused, indecisive, or just going through a phase

No, we're not! We know who we are and have decided that we are bisexual. Many bisexuals have identified as such for many, many years and couldn't possibly be accused of being unstable or going through a phase. In addition, research says that many bisexuals have gone through phases of identifying as gay or lesbian—however, gay and lesbian people aren't accused of going through a phase. Plus, research says that if you change your sexual identity, most chances are that you'll be changing it from monosexual to bisexual, not the other way around. So really, bisexuality isn't a phase at all. It's just as stable as any other sexual identity.

Bisexuals are slutty, promiscuous, or inherently unfaithful

No, we're not! We are perfectly capable of being monogamous, and we are just as likely to cheat on our partners as anyone else. Many bisexual people have succeeded in maintaining happy, long-term, exclusive relationships for years. Just because we like more than one gender doesn't mean we have sex indiscriminately. I mean, seriously, we have taste too! (Oh, and some of us might be polyamorous or enjoy sex with multiple partners, but that means nothing about the rest of us!)

Bisexuals are carriers or vectors of HIV and other STIs

No, we're not! What gives people HIV and other STIs is sexual behavior, not sexual identity. People get infected with HIV through unsafe sex, needle sharing, and infected blood transfusions. Being bisexual doesn't make you infected or infectious.

Bisexuals are actually gay or actually straight

No, we're not! We really are bisexual and are truly attracted to people of more than one gender. Even if some of us have a preference for one gender over others, that still doesn't make us any less bisexual. It's enough to have any portion of attraction to more than one gender to qualify. Also, don't be temped to think that we're just closeted and cowardly or just experimenting: We're out and proud!

Bisexuals can choose to be gay or straight

No, we can't! You can't choose to be gay, right? So how can you choose to be bisexual? Bi people can't choose who to fall in love with or who to be attracted to. Yes, we can choose with whom we have relationships, but giving up on one part of our sexuality is just as painful as being in the closet. Gays and lesbians can choose a heterosexual lifestyle just as well, yet bisexuals are the only ones who get scapegoated for it.

This outright denial of the stereotypes creates a mirror image of the bisexual imagined therein. While the bisexual person imagined by the stereotypes was threatening, dangerous, infectious, and unstable, this bisexual is reassuring, harmless, stable, and safe. To further look at this rebuttal would show bisexuality (or a bisexual person) that is *very* authentic, *very* stable, monogamous, and nonsexual (or at least "appropriately sexual"[8]), unthreatening and normative, as well as docile and unproblematic. As opposed to the negatively stereotyped bisexual(ity), this one doesn't pose a threat to society, but is a harmless and benign sexual citizen. In fact, this entire rebuttal comprises a reassurance for bisexuality's—and bisexuals'—safety to society, answering each and every call for normativity with enthusiastic consent, thereby reinforcing it. In short—it takes the sting out, making bisexuality seem more like an agent of normativity than an agent of social change.

In addition, taking all the stereotypes at face value and as personalized attitudes also successfully throws overboard any bisexual person who *does* fit these stereotypes: Many bisexuals might indeed feel comfortable and well represented by this "myth busting," but what of the many people who don't fit in this standard of the "normal" or "good" bisexual? Some bisexuals are sluts (read: sexually independent women), some bisexuals are just experimenting, some like people of certain genders only sexually and not romantically, some like to have threesomes and perform bisexuality for men, some are HIV and STI carriers, some don't practice safer sex, some are indecisive and confused, some cheat on their partners, some do choose to be bi, as well as many other things that the "myth busting" tries to cast off. A very long list of people is being thrown overboard in the effort to "fight biphobia." In this way, the rebuttal in fact imposes biphobic normative standards on the bisexual community itself, drawing a line between "good" and "bad" bisexuals.

Either way, benign docility and unthreatening citizenship are not exactly what I would want my bisexuality to be associated with.

No Myths, No Busting

> *"I want to have adventures and take enormous risks*
> *and be everything they say we are."*
> —Dorothy Allison, lesbian activist

Taken from an epistemological perspective, these stereotypes should not be taken literally at all, but rather read as metaphors about the subversive potential of bisexuality. What I mean is that bisexuality as an idea is something that society finds threatening to its normal order. This has nothing to do with bisexual individuals. I certainly do not mean to suggest that being bisexual is subversive or radical in and of itself (if only it were). Being politically subversive or radical takes a lot of work, thought, and effort, which a simple identity label is insufficient to achieve. I also do not mean to set a whole new standard for bisexual behavior that might alienate large portions of the bisexual community. And I do not mean to imply that the stereotypes are correct as far as the personal behavior of bisexual people goes. What I do mean to do is to examine why society places bisexuality on the side of anxiety, threat, and subversion. And how can we use these very things to disrupt social order and create social change?

In so doing, what I'm attempting to do is step away from the binary discourse of Yes versus No, True versus False, or Good versus Bad, and open a third, radical choice of transgression, subversion, and multiplicity. Such a move, in my opinion, is also bisexual in character, marking a resistance to binaries, a collapse of boundaries, and a subversion of order. (You'll see what I mean in just a bit).

So here is a third reading of the same stereotypes—this time, trying to understand why they're there and what we can do with them:

Bisexuality doesn't exist

This is by far the simplest: Society routinely tries to deny subversive ideas out of existence. Bisexuality is charged with meanings that attest to society's various anxieties. The attempt to eliminate bisexuality's existence is an attempt to eliminate the subversive potential that it holds. Simply put, if society gets so hysterical around a certain idea that it tries to eradicate its existence in any way possible, it affirms that this idea is perceived as threatening. Bisexuality has a lot of revolutionary potential. Society recognizes this. It's time for us to start as well.

Bisexuals are confused, indecisive, or just going through a phase

Confusion, indecision, and phases indicate a state of instability, fluidity, and process. Confusion points to instability as well as doubt, marking bisexuality as a vantage point for questioning, as well as marking a radical potential for change. Bisexuality can be thought of as a destabilizing agent of social change, promoting doubt in anything, starting with our own sexual identities, going through the structure of sex, gender, and sexuality; heteropatriarchy, and racism; and ending with such oppressive structures as the state, law, order, war, and capitalism.

The indecision, that is, fluidity associated with bisexuality can be used as a refusal to conduct ourselves through society's narrow constrictions. It is a refusal and deconstruction of any socially dictated boundaries at all. This marks a collapse of both binaries and boundaries, and a collapse of separation and isolation (embedded in us by both capitalist culture and internalized biphobia). It gives us the opportunity to call for difference, solidarity, and connection. It also comprises a powerful tool for looking into hierarchical social structures (which so often come in the form of binaries) and opposing them from a uniquely bisexual standpoint.

The idea of a phase associated with bisexuality implies the option of process, allowing us to think about sexuality not as a fixed, unmoving, complete thing, but

> **Hypersexualization** means imposing an exaggerated sexuality on a person or a group.

rather as an open-ended, complex, multiple, and continual process of learning, feeling, and experiencing. It allows us the opportunity to learn attention and sensitivity, to ourselves as well as others—and not only on a personal level, but also a political one: sensitivity to oppression and encouragement of processes, which facilitate change.

Bisexuals are slutty, promiscuous, or inherently unfaithful
This marks minority-world society's fear of sexuality. Bisexuality is here being **hypersexualized** under the presumption that sex is bad, that wanting too much of it is bad, that wanting any of it is bad, that wanting people of more than one gender is bad, and that wanting more than one person is bad. The concept of infidelity or unfaithfulness might help us think about monogamy as one of society's oppressive structures. Monogamy has been used historically and currently as a capitalist and patriarchal tool for controlling women, and for keeping all people in small, docile units where they are isolated and unable to connect and organize (especially in minority-world cultures). This keeps resistance to a bare minimum. In a society based on sexual fear and a **culture of rape**, the sexualization of bisexuality can open a window to a different kind of sexual culture, encouraging sexual independence, exploration, and enjoyment of our bodies, our sexualities, our various genders, and our sexual interactions. It can subvert and transgress boundaries of identity, body, sexuality, and gender. It can give us a vantage point of opposing patriarchy and heterosexism, and to creating a sexually radical culture.

> **Rape culture** means dominant cultural attitudes that promote rape and sexual violence against women.

In addition and on the other hand, it can allow us to look into the ways in which sexuality is imposed on us, without consent and to the satisfaction of others. It can allow us to examine—and oppose—rape culture, sexual harassment, and asexuality-phobia, pointing out the ways that sexuality is imposed on all of us.

The idea that bisexuals are indiscriminate about their choice of partners also echoes society's anxiety about subversion of cissexist norms. It is often said that "a bisexual is the kind of person who can reach down someone's pants and be happy with whatever they find." This emphasizes the fact that we can never actually know what's "down" anyone's "pants." This marks bisexuals as "accomplices" to transgender and genderqueer people, and it connects bisexuality and transgender as two intertwining ideas, both of which deviate society's rules about normative gender and its enforcement.

The idea of unfaithfulness also brings into light the metaphor of the bisexual as traitor (one of my personal favorites). The dictionary defines treason as "a betrayal of trust," or as "an attempt to overthrow the government . . . or to kill . . . the sovereign," a definition that *betrays,* if you will, bisexuality's function as an agitator. We can think about bisexuality as betrayal of the trust imposed on us by power structures, as well as embodying an attempt to overthrow or "kill" hegemonic order. We can then use this as a gateway to betraying monogamy, patriarchy, governments, countries, and wars, betraying the "LGBT" (meaning, the **GGGG**) movement, for promoting the assimilation of our communities and cooperating with oppressive structures. We can be traitors to anything that confines us, and to anything that stands in our way: all power structures, all oppression.

Bisexuals are carriers or vectors of HIV and other STIs

Taken metaphorically, AIDS is always imagined as the "queer disease," being both a "punishment" for being queer and the embodiment of the straight population's fear of being "infected" by queerness. Bisexual men are always imagined as contagious agents of disease, having unprotected bisex only to return home and infect their innocent, straight wives and children. In this way, bisexuality destabilizes the clear-cut border between gay and straight, symbolizing anxiety of the invasion of queerness into straight populations. We can envision bisexuality as the carrier of queerness into the straight population, having the potential to infect—that is, disrupt and queer up—**heteronormative** structures.

Heteronormativity is a set of cultural and social norms, according to which there are only two binary sexes and genders (man and woman), and the only acceptable form of sexuality or romance is between one cisgender man and one cisgender woman. According to heteronormative standards, any lifestyle or behavior deviating from the above is abnormal and should change to fit.

Taken from another angle, this image of bisexuality also destabilizes the border between sickness and health, calling society's ableism into question and marking disabled and chronically ill bodies as yet another site of transgression and resistance.

Bisexuals are actually gay or actually straight

This stereotype can be thought of as yet another way of trying to redraw the borders threatened with transgression, and once again deny bisexuality out of existence. However, more central to this one is the presumption I mentioned in the first part, that bisexual women are actually straight, while bisexual men are actually gay. The idea presented here is that of the immaculate phallus, suggesting that phallic adoration is the one true thing uniting all bisexual people. It projects society's own phallocentrism onto the idea of bisexuality. This permits us to critically reflect this phallocentrism back into society, exposing the underlying system of sexism and **misogyny** as we do so. It might also help us explore alternative ways of relating to the penis itself, as well as to masculinity, subverting sexist connotations of the penis as an all-powerful,

4 8 BI: Notes for a Bisexual Revolution

> **Misogyny** means hatred of women.
>
> **Hypermasculinization** means imposing an exaggerated masculinity on a person or a group of people.

all-forceful, all-domineering, hyper-sexualized, and **hypermasculinized** phallus. Instead, we can reconstruct the male body and masculinity and create new visions of subversive and feminist masculinities.[9]

Bisexuals can choose to be gay or straight

The idea that bisexuals can choose their sexuality stems from a standpoint that sees choice as negative or as a mark of illegitimacy. In a movement where the dominant discourse relies on lack of choice as its political path to equal rights, this lack of choice (the "born this way" argument) becomes a "tool" for attaining legitimacy and acceptance by society.

The way this argument usually goes is: "We were born this way; we can't help it; if we could choose then we would never have chosen to be gay. Now give us rights because we can't change." Internalized homophobia aside, this argument marks immutability—that is, "nature"—as authentic and therefore legitimate, while marking choice—that is, "culture"—as inauthentic and illegitimate. Bisexuality's place as an "unnatural" choice is a point of strength in my opinion, opening a space for bisexuality to challenge notions of authenticity, legitimacy, and normalcy (as the "natural" is also always imagined as "normal"). We can also think about a challenge to the very concept of nature and the politics of the "natural," as well as human exploitation of "nature" (in symbolic and material ways). Bisexuality can offer an alternative politics of inauthenticity, the unnatural, the illegitimate, and the chosen: the rejection of nature, natural categories, human exploitation of nature, and the politics of the natural. Promoting a politics of the inventable, the unimaginable, the possible, and the impossible: everything we can be and everything we can't.

What this reading offers, I hope, is a new way of reading and creating bisexual politics. The political weight that society places on bisexuality (as seen through bisexual stereotypes) can be levered by us and used as a force. While these readings represent only tiny fragments of the radical potential of bisexuality, they will also serve the basis for my standpoint throughout this book. For now, though, the most important thing is to realize this is the starting point: We have immense revolutionary potential.

THE QUESTION OF BINARY
(OR: WHY "BI" IS BINARY BUT "FTM" IS NOT)

Yet another way in which bisexuality has been recently imagined is as inherently binary, and therefore intrinsically **transphobic**. As this is one of the central ways in which bisexuality is defined and imagined today, I'd like to take some time in order to examine and deconstruct it.

Bisexuality, it's been claimed, is a gender binary, and therefore oppressive, word. As the argument classically goes, since the word *bisexuality* has *bi* (literally: *two*) in it, it inherently refers to a two-gender structure. This means it erases nonbinary genders and sexes out of existence. Those subscribing to this approach usually suggest the use of alternative identity categories that convey attraction to more than two genders, such as pansexual, omnisexual, polysexual, queer, etc.[10] While I find these additional identities helpful and positive in promoting discussion about different gender identities, I also feel that the binary allegations against bisexuality are less than helpful. This section will, then, offer a criticism of the *bi is binary* discourse in hopes of countering it and suggesting an alternative point of view about it.

Similar to discourse about stereotypes, the bisexual movement in general has responded to the binary allegations with its catch-all response, "But that's not true!" mostly without attempting to look into the politics and power relations underlying them. In this form, the counterarguments seem to be no more than apologetics, attempts to defend bisexuality's "damaged reputation." For the sake of the argument, I will

include them here. However, remember that I'm including them here for
the purpose of background only.

The counterarguments claim that:

- similar to *homosexuality* and *lesbianism*, bisexuality is a
  word reclaimed by the bisexual movement from the medical
  institution. The bi community itself had therefore little to no
  influence over the formation and structure of the word, but
  has since reclaimed it to mean "potential attraction to more
  than one sex or gender."

- linguistically, the "two" in *bisexual* might refer to attraction
  to genders like our own (homosexuality) and attraction to
  genders different from our own (heterosexuality).

- the bisexual movement started gaining momentum at around
  the same period as the transgender movement. In its early
  stages, no language was available for the description of
  attraction to nonbinary sexes and genders. However, throughout the history of the movement, the word has constantly been
  used for describing it, using such terms as *third gender(s),
  androgynous people, those in between*, etc.

- historically, bisexual communities have always been some of
  the most accepting places toward transgender and genderqueer people, and the two communities have always shared a
  strong alliance.

- a discussion focusing on bisexuality solely in relation to
  transgender politics performs structural bisexual erasure, as
  it prioritizes transgender politics over bisexual politics, in a
  discussion about bisexual identity. Since I've only heard myself
  voicing this argument, I would give it a few more lines just to
  clarify my intention (quoting myself from an online discussion
  on the topic):

It often feels to me as if bisexuality is never really about our own sexual identity(ies), i.e., our experiences, our desires, our lives as bisexuals, the oppression we experience as such, the cultural, social, and political systems working to shape the experience of bisexual people, institutional oppression experienced by bisexuals, etc., etc. Instead I feel that my sexual identity (i.e., whether I should identify as bisexual, pansexual, queer, etc.) is expected to be determined according to other people's gender identity.

The question of whether bisexuality is more or less helpful in reducing gender binarism poses this quite clearly. It implies that bisexual people should determine their identification according to transgender politics as opposed to bisexual politics. Taken from that perspective, then of course the answer would be: "Yes, definitely pan/queer." But lately I've been questioning this very outset as influenced by internalized biphobia. The fact that we (as a movement) have been focusing on this question as a central one implies a political hierarchy that prioritizes transgender issues over bisexual issues.

To stress this point even further, a reverse argument might sound something like: "Which words should transgender people use to identify their genders, in order to help bisexuality gain legitimacy and visibility?" A question which no one with the least of political sensitivity would accept, and which I hope illustrates how ridiculously inappropriate this question—and argument—is.

INTERLUDE

The great majority of this debate is being perpetuated and developed by bisexual-identified transgender and genderqueer people on the one hand, and non-bi-identified transgender and genderqueer people on the other. I need to draw attention to this, as the "binary" side of this debate often seems to frame it as a transgender-cisgender debate. This locates the "bisexual" side not only as linguistically transphobic, but also as external to the transgender community and politics—in other words, privileged.

A painful example of this was a debate between one American transgender blogger and me in the responses section of one of his posts. Throughout the debate, my genderqueer identity and position were completely ignored and dismissed in light of my bisexual identification. He even went as far as saying "if your concern for trans issues seemed to be equal to your concern that people be allowed to use a word that erases large categories of trans people, I would not have spoken like that" (addressing me as if I was cisgender). By saying that, he was insinuating that bisexual identification and politics are inherently transphobic, and are therefore in opposition to genderqueer and trans identification and politics.

SLIPPAGE

As implied through this blogger's position, bisexuality is no longer critiqued simply as a term, but is rather experiencing a slippage of meaning: from a problem with words, it becomes a problem with people. If: *bisexuality* equals *transphobia,* then: *bisexual* equals *transphobic* as well. It's not a huge jump, and I'm both unsurprised and brokenhearted to see it happening. I've once had someone argue to me that the "bad binary reputation" that bisexuality is increasingly receiving is happening because of bisexual people's actual transphobia. I've also noticed that, notwithstanding bisexual erasure, the only instances in which bisexual people or movements are mentioned in some transgender writings are as oppressors of transgender people.

While writing this text, I was reading Susan Stryker's *Transgender History,* a book summarizing the history of the American transgender movement starting from the 1950s and up to this day. Upon reaching the '90s I realized that up until now, only one mention of bisexuality was made in the entire book: one sentence at the introduction, explaining the meaning of the word (as *attraction to any gender*). From here until the 1990s, bisexuality and bisexual people fade away from historical attention, despite the fact that gay and lesbian people are mentioned in abundance (both favorably and unfavorably). Just to stress my point, bisexuals were erased in the book even from where they were undoubtedly present: demonstrations, the Stonewall rebellion, pride marches, the gay liberation movement, etc. Mentions of the bisexual community resurface, however, when we reach into the nineties, but solely in the context of transgender exclusion.

Another example is the acronym LGB that some transgender writers use in the same context of transgender exclusion. In his (otherwise fantastic) article "Fighting to Win," from the wonderful anthology *That's Revolting!*, transgender activist Dean Spade constantly uses the form LGBfakeT—situating bisexual people not only as oppressors of transgender people, but also as those who benefit from assimilationist gay privilege. This wrongfully presumes that assimilationist gay campaigns include the needs and the agenda of bisexual people (and do not, in fact, trample all over us on their golden way to heteronormative white privilege).

The blogger I debated with also used the acronym "LGB community" in contrast to the T (very aptly commenting that "the LGB community wants nothing to do with us. T is for tokenism"), only correcting it to cisLGB after my comment on his blog. However, even this correction fails to challenge this basic structure: bisexuality is still only invoked, in this context, in relation to oppression of transgender people.

SO WHERE IS ALL THIS COMING FROM?

I find this debate exceedingly suspicious: If transphobia was truly the matter at hand, then why focus on bisexuality alone? Or if it's binary terms that we're concerned with, wouldn't it make more sense to first address the hetero-homo binary, a far more prevalent and oppressive structure? Or if it's inner-LGBT community transphobic approaches that we want to address, shouldn't we first see the white gay cisgender men? Or the lesbian movement, with its long-time and long-established exclusionary practices? Why the bisexual community, historically and currently the least transphobic of the three, as well as the one with the *least resources from which to exclude* transgender and genderqueer people?

To be fair, transphobia is indeed a problem in many bisexual communities. I have seen evidence of this myself and will give it ample attention further on in the book. However, for now I need to say that I feel that the scope given, within this debate, to addressing transphobia in bisexual communities is not only excessive in relation to actual amounts of transphobia (which says a lot, because transphobia abounds everywhere), but also that the content of the arguments in this debate fails to address any real problems existing within actual bisexual communities. Simply put, it feels less like community work and more like slander.

I THINK I KNOW THIS SONG

The argument claiming that bisexuality is binary situates bisexuality as an oppressive identity that promotes hegemonic ideas. More simply put, to say that bisexuality is binary is to say that bisexuality is an oppressive identity contributing to dominant social order. Now, where have I heard that before?

It seems as though the first people to make this binary claim weren't people from the transgender movement, but rather academics: one gay male and one straight female (gay-male-identified). The former is Lee Edelman and the latter is Eve Kosofky-Sedgwick, both very high-profile queer theorists. A quote of Edelman in his 1994 book, *Homographies,* says:

> *the hetero/homo binarism (a binarism more effectively rein-forced, than disrupted by the "third term" of bisexuality)*(con-fining bisexuality to the small space inside his parentheses).

Sedgwick wrote something similar at around the same time.

And so, while these dignified scholars have probably picked up this line from activist communities, they greatly contributed to popularizing it. I don't mention this in attempt to erase the importance of activist-based discourse, but rather to emphasize standpoints within this debate. As an academic gay white cisgender man and an academic straight cisgender woman, both theorists had a political and academic interest in eliminating bisexuality from their theory and studies.[11]

SO WHAT DOES THIS REMIND ME OF?

Claims of bisexuality as an oppressive or privileged identity are not new. As most anyone who identifies as bisexual knows, we are often accused of bearing heterosexual privilege—especially by, but not limited to, lesbian communities. These accusations—classical by now—rely on the presumption that bisexual people are, in fact, straight. They also assume that by refusing to relinquish our "attachment" to male-identified people, we are perpetuating heterosexual and sexist hegemony and oppression of women and queers.

The "perpetuating X hegemony" trope, then, seems to be a recurring one. Here's a little experiment:

- Bisexuals are a privileged group perpetuating heteropatriarchal hegemony and oppressing gay and lesbian people.
- Bisexuals are a privileged group perpetuating cisgender hegemony and oppressing transgender and genderqueer people.

Could it be possible that the second one has been inherited from the first?

In any case, as eloquently pointed out by Julia Serano in her article "Bisexuality does not reinforce the gender binary," this idea is suspicious to say the least:

> For me, the word "reinforcing" is a red flag: Whenever somebody utters it, I stop for a moment to ask myself who is being accused of "reinforcing" and who is not. There is almost always some double standard at work behind the scenes.

And given the turbulent history of who gets to be considered inside and outside of the gay/lesbian/queer community, it does not surprise me that the only people who are never accused of "reinforcing" the hetero-patriarchal-gender-binary are non-feminine, cisgender, exclusively homosexual folks.

ANOTHER REMINDER

A fact that is often neglected in the context of this debate is that these very same arguments were (and in some cases, still are) used against transgender people as well.

Here is what bisexual transgender activist and scholar Jillian Todd Weiss writes about transphobia in her essay "GL vs. BT":

Although "male to constructed female" transsexuals claimed to be against the stereotyped gender system by virtue of their escape from stereotypical masculinity, they in fact added force to the binary system by merely escaping from one stereotype to another, or at most mixing together different stereotypes, rather than advocating true gender freedom. They were not political radicals, as they claimed, but reactionaries seeking to preserve a stereotypical gender system that was already dramatically changing due to the political action of '60s and '70s feminists and gays.

Similar claims, of course, have been made throughout the years against transgender men as well, trying to paint them not only as per-petuating the oppressive gender binary, but also as opportunistic seekers of male privilege. As Julia Serano writes:

While the reasons for bisexual and transgender exclusion from lesbian and gay communities during the '70s and '80s may be somewhat different, the rhetoric used to cast us away was eerily similar: We, in one way or another, were supposedly "buying into" and "reinforcing" heteronormativity. Transsexuals, transvestites, drag artists, butches and femmes were accused of aping heterosexist gender roles. Bisexuals were accused of purposefully seeking out heterosexual privilege and (literally) sleeping with the enemy.

WHY THIS? WHY NOW?

For a brief explanation of this, I'll quote my online discussion again:

Another thought regarding the origin of those allegations is what Julia Serano calls the masculinism of the transgender movement, which I think comes into play on this issue as well. Serano says, and I agree, that the transgender movement consistently prefers masculine-spectrum viewpoints and ideas, while marginalizing those of feminine-spectrum trans and genderqueer people. Specifically regarding the issue of increased criticism toward the bi community and relative lack of criticism toward the lesbian community about transphobia, I think this is heavily influenced by the fact that the transgender movement is mainly controlled by trans men who emerged and were influenced by lesbian communities.[12] That is, the reason why they don't criticize lesbians is that very often, these are their home communities. However, criticizing bisexuals is very much in keeping with the often-present biphobia of many lesbian communities.

In addition, the transgender movement has a clear interest in the disownment of bisexuality: an acceptance of, or alliance and association with, bisexuality would doubtlessly cause the popularity of the transgender movement to be "dragged" even further "down" within the assimilationist gay movement as well as the public mainstream. Considering both widespread transphobia and bisexuality's lack of popularity and huge invisibility within both these populations, everything is to be gained by a transgender movement dissociating itself from bisexuality, everything to be lost by alliance.

However, what makes it truly necessary for the transgender movement to rid itself of the connection to the bisexual movement is not to be found in any quality intrinsic to the trans community or its politics. Instead it seems that often, the gay and lesbian movement makes it out as though there's "only one spare place" at their proverbial table. The idea of only three imaginary chairs, where two are marked "gay" and "lesbian" creates the inevitable (and oh-so-convenient) antagonism between the other erased and repressed groups competing for that one extra spot. Of course, this practice is inherited by the gay and lesbian movement from heterosexual society, when heteronormativity makes it clear that it cannot "make room" for all of us. This is how those in privilege secure their own places, by having all our movements step over each other, rather than fighting the real enemy together. In this way, the heteronorm, and in turn the GGGG movement, can stop worrying about how to hinder our ways to threatening their positions of power—setting us against one another makes sure that we'll do that job for them.

Of course I think that much more can be gained through a radical alliance between bisexual and transgender movements. In fact, I've written a whole chapter about it. For now, however, I will just conclude and leave the "what's next" for later. The allegations of binarism have little to do with bisexuality's actual attributes or bisexual people's behavior in real life. Instead, these allegations stand in keeping with dominant power structures within the GGGG movement, imagining bisexuality as inherently oppressive. It is a political method to keep the bisexual movement clear of the power centers and to keep the bisexual and the transgender movements separated.

CHAPTER 2:

Monosexism and Biphobia

Oddly enough, the issue of biphobia, or monosexism, is one of the most hotly contested territories in bisexual politics, and certainly one of the least understood. A term much-feared and slightly frowned upon, biphobia has often been dismissed even by the most avid bisexual scholars and activists. Some insinuate that bisexuals don't actually suffer oppression that is separate from homophobia or lesbophobia. In fact, very often, simply raising the issue of biphobia (in any setting) is perceived as an affront to gay and lesbian politics and is ridiculed, often with the ubiquitous "bisexuals are privileged" argument (an argument which will be given copious attention in the next chapter).

Before I refute the argument that bisexuals don't suffer from a unique type of oppression (biphobia), let's examine where this argument places bisexuality and bisexual people: To look at the first part of this argument, we will soon discover the old and familiar "bisexuality doesn't exist" trope. To claim that bisexuals do not experience oppression differently from gays or lesbians is to subsume bisexual experience into homosexuality, thus eliminating its unique existence. For if no unique bisexual experience is to be found, then certainly the category of bisexuality itself is null. The second half of the argument ("privilege") acknowledges the existence of bisexuality, but connects it with the notion of privilege and thus oppressor status, again nullifying the unique oppression that bisexuals experience and the need for specific attention to it. In this way, bisexuality is here spoken about on two levels: first as a nonexistent other, and second as an oppressor (presumably of gays and lesbians). The notion that bisexuals are only oppressed as a result of homophobia and lesbophobia erases the need for a unique bisexual liberation struggle and places bisexuals as "halfway" add-ons to the gay and lesbian movement.

I feel the need to emphasize this, as people often see (when they do see) biphobia as a series of straightforward, direct personal attitudes and behaviors, rather than as a structure. In fact, biphobia is often defined in exactly that way—for example, the Wikipedia entry on biphobia defines it as an "aversion felt toward bisexuality and bisexuals as a social group or as individuals," and the *STFU Biphobia* blog defines it as "fear or hatred of bisexuals, pansexuals, omnisexuals, and anyone who doesn't otherwise fall within the binary gay or straight." In her article "Biphobia: It Goes More Than Two Ways," Robyn Ochs cites prejudicial behavior, discrimination, and stereotyping as characteristics of (biphobic) oppression. A widely publicized online list titled "What Does Biphobia Look Like?" (but perhaps more accurately described as "biphobic things that people do") cites a list of biphobic behaviors, such as "*assuming* that everyone you meet is either heterosexual or homosexual," "*thinking* bisexual people haven't made up their minds," and "*feeling* that you can't trust a bisexual because they aren't really gay or lesbian, or aren't really heterosexual" (all emphases mine).

Another problem with discussions of biphobia is that they

overwhelmingly focus on biphobic stereotypes, as if stereotyping (and stereotypical thinking) is the only biphobic phenomenon in existence and the end-all of biphobia in general. For example, Ochs dedicates much of her article to discussing the ways in which bisexuals are *perceived* by biphobic people (in other words, stereotyping), the Wikipedia entry on biphobia likewise patterns itself on listing biphobic stereotypes, and the "What Does Biphobia Look Like?" online list also consists of descriptions of behaviors or beliefs that are likewise based on stereotypes. A Google search I performed for the word "biphobia" showed fifty links over the first five pages, of which 60 percent focused on stereotypes (or other such "people think bad things about us" varieties), whereas only 20 percent dealt with other forms of biphobia (mainly bisexual erasure).[13] This overwhelming reference to stereotypes in the context of biphobia creates the impression that stereotypical beliefs are the near-only origin and form of biphobia, and that direct personal mistreatment is the only (or main) result thereof.

Studied accounts of biphobia also overwhelmingly focus on personalized attitudes or mistreatment experienced by bisexual people (for example, in anthologies such as *Bi Any Other Name: Bisexual People Speak Out* or *Bisexual Politics: Theories, Queries, and Visions*) and *especially* by gay or lesbian communities. For example, out of five studies of biphobia cited by Ochs, only two deal mainly with heterosexual (or "general") biphobia. Even Ochs herself dedicates *four times* as much space in her article to discussing biphobia in lesbian and gay communities as to discussing biphobia in heterosexual communities. Considering the fact that the overwhelming majority of biphobia and monosexism originates not from gay and lesbian communities but from heterosexual structures, it seems like the bisexual movement, as a whole, is focused on the wrong aspect.

This overwhelming focus on gay and lesbian biphobia creates a false impression that, as a commentator recently put it on my blog, "[bisexuals are] perfectly justified saying we get worse treatment in the gay community [than in straight ones]." In turn, this notion contributes to the beliefs that bisexuals do not, in fact, experience (as much?) oppression by heterosexual society and that our "real problem" lies not within heteropatriarchy but within gay and lesbian communities (that is, scapegoating). Another side effect of this unfortunate cluster of meanings is the phenomenon I mentioned above, in which talking about biphobia is perceived as an affront to gay and lesbian politics, community, and movements.

On a side note: To answer the question of why bisexual discourses, as a whole, have maintained such a focus on gay and lesbian biphobia, one need only look at bisexual people's (and especially bisexual activists' and writers') lived experiences. Most bisexuals come out not to bisexual communities but to gay or lesbian ones, seeking the same acknowledgment, acceptance, and support that gay and lesbian people expect to—and indeed do—receive there. However, as opposed to gays and lesbians, bisexuals often encounter erasure, exclusion, and biphobic responses within those communities. This experience is particularly painful, since gay and lesbian communities are where we often come seeking help, and where we subsequently become heartbroken and even betrayed, as this rejection seems to come from where we least expect it—where we came for support. This feeling of pain and heartbreak is not only real but might also be thought of as a central component in many bisexuals' lived experiences, in the formation of bisexual identities, and certainly in forming bisexual politics, as evidenced above.

In her article "GL vs. BT," Jillian Todd Weiss criticizes the terms *biphobia* and *transphobia* for being too clinical and implying a psychological and personal problem rather than a social structure.[14] Instead she suggests the use of the term *heterosexism* to imply structural oppression working against all LGBT people. While I perfectly agree with the first part of Weiss's criticism, the latter part unifies four types of oppression into a single mold and erases the differences between them. Though all LGBT people are indeed oppressed by heterosexism, using it as a single term leaves out the structures of heteropatriarchy, cissexism, and monosexism—all equally shared by LGBT people but often erased as a result of these power structures themselves. As an alternative to Weiss's suggestion, then, within the frame of discussion on biphobia, the term "monosexism" is a tool that can be used to examine and deconstruct the underlying power structure at the basis of biphobia.

On par with other terms such as heterosexism, cissexism, sexism, or racism, I define *monosexism* as a social structure operating through the presumption that everyone is, or should be, monosexual, a structure that privileges monosexuality and monosexual people, and that systematically punishes people who are nonmonosexual. I define *monosexuality* as attraction to only one sex and/or gender.

The use of *monosexism* is not meant to completely replace the use of *biphobia,* nor indeed deny the reality of biphobia in people's lived experiences. Nor is it meant to locate gay and lesbian people as oppressors of bisexuals. In fact, my goal is quite reverse: to look upon monosexism as a social structure first and foremost originating from and upholding heteropatriarchal structures, to examine it as a form of oppression shared by everyone (not just bisexual people), and to add an additional perspective through which to examine biphobia. Using the concept of monosexism might provide us the option to examine a structure not necessarily or directly linked with named bisexual identity or with explicitly biphobic behavior. It might allow us to read between the lines of culture in order to delineate where it is that bisexuality is forbidden, denied, or erased, and why. It might also allow us to examine how monosexual people are themselves influenced—and indeed oppressed—by monosexism, as well as to examine what privileges they might enjoy by virtue of this structure, all by way of deconstructing it.

Monosexism can viewed as a social system that works in many ways, both direct and indirect, material and symbolic. Monosexism, as I see it, is no less significant and no less overbearing than any other oppressive structure. It is both sad and unsurprising that even the topics of monosexism and biphobia themselves undergo vehement erasure on many levels, as demonstrated above: On the level of speech, they are rarely mentioned or seriously engaged with when addressing bisexuality and bisexual issues; on the level of content, when they do come to be mentioned, they undergo many kinds of delegitimation; and finally, even when they do appear and are validated, they are only spoken of in the narrow context of stereotypes and personal mistreatment. Concurrently, this kind of discourse creates the impression that biphobia and monosexism don't actually exist, that if they do then they are overrated, and that even if they do exist and deserve attention, they are limited only to personalized negative attitudes—hardly comparable to wide and overbearing social structures such as heterosexism, cissexism, and heteropatriarchy. However, this erasure, delegitimation, and limited extent only serve as evidence of the very existence of the structure.

Monosexism kills. Biphobia kills. Bisexual people commit suicide, bisexual people get sick, bisexual people lose our homes, our families, our friends, our communities, our support, our jobs, our money, our education; bisexual people suffer violence and sexual violence; we are beaten, brutalized, bullied, bashed, raped, and sexually assaulted; we get STIs, no information, and no treatment; we get exploited, alienated, marginalized, disempowered, dismissed, erased, derided. And after all of this, we are told that it's all in our heads, that monosexism and biphobia do not exist, that those problems are our personal problems: We are pathologized. Our experiences, our lives, our pain, and our oppression are written out and wiped clean of history, culture, and community. But this is not our "personal" problem, this is not "just in our heads." It is not a figment of the imagination. It is real, and we see it and feel it in our bones, as we struggle to survive and as we struggle to live. We testify as we also remember those gone: Monosexism kills. Biphobia kills.

In 1963, American feminist writer Betty Friedan published a book called *The Feminine Mystique,* in which she spoke about "the problem that has no name." At the time of her writing, little to no language, tools, or analysis existed for looking into women's oppression. Women's issues were all considered personal and private problems, and women themselves had difficulties naming the reasons they felt as they did: Many were depressed and unhappy, feeling stuck and miserable. The feminist writing done by Friedan (and many others) at that time helped many women put their experience to words, to expose power structures, and to speak about their oppression.[15] In writing about monosexism, in many ways I write about a problem that has no name. The tools and language available for addressing, analyzing, and deconstructing monosexism and biphobia are meager; and just like women's oppression at the time of Friedan's writing, bisexuals' oppression is everywhere and nowhere, a problem without a name. Therefore when I write now about monosexism, I am merely scratching the surface. However, I hope that what I have to say will aid further development of language, tools, and concepts with which to engage with, recognize, and deconstruct monosexism and biphobia.

There are three main perspectives through which one might begin to discuss monosexism's impacts on bisexuals' lived experience: bisexual erasure, the material faces of monosexism, and statistical evidence. In speaking about monosexism as a structure and in material ways, I also hope to remind my readers that no discussion of bisexuality—no matter how theoretical or academic—is ever only theoretical. As a reality and a lived experience, theories of bisexuality and of monosexism are deeply interlinked with bisexual politics and activism, as the former contains enormous potential to inspire and instigate the latter.

Before I begin my description, it is important for me to note that whereas I will pay equal attention to both heterosexual and gay and lesbian monosexism and biphobia, I most certainly do not wish to equate the two groups as oppressors of bisexuals. Gay and lesbian communities may well be *collaborators* in the oppression of bisexual people; however, both groups do not carry equal weight in the oppression of bisexuals.

Rather, the overwhelming majority of oppression against bisexual people is performed by heterosexual power structures. While I believe that both groups' monosexism deserves attention, it is important to remember that heterosexual society is far more powerful, prevalent, and oppressive than gay and lesbian communities have ever been, and that heterosexual society is the main source and field of monosexism, biphobia, and oppression of bisexuals.

BISEXUAL ERASURE

In 2000, New York University professor Kenji Yoshino published "The Epistemic Contract of Bisexual Erasure," one of the most important and groundbreaking bisexual theory texts to have been overlooked (until very recently) both by the academia and within the bisexual movement. That the text has been so widely overlooked for so many years is odd to say the least, and might be explained both by the theory presented in the text itself, as well as by the bisexual movement and theory's general aversion to directly engaging with biphobia and monosexism.

Yoshino begins his theory by claiming that invisibility is not a natural quality inherent to bisexuality, rather a result of active social and cultural construction, performed and perpetuated by and within both heterosexual, and gay and lesbian, discourses. He suggests that the structures of homosexuality and heterosexuality share a common interest in the erasure of bisexuality. He calls this the "epistemic contract of bisexual erasure," meaning a contract of production, generation, or maintenance of cultural knowledge that erases bisexuality.

I define bisexual erasure as the widespread social phenomenon of erasing bisexuality from any discussion in which it is relevant or is otherwise invoked (with or without being named). As I've already mentioned above, bisexual erasure is all-encompassing, in a way that makes it into the most significant aspect of the monosexist structure.

Bisexual erasure is present on every level and sphere of our lives, from the public and cultural level, through the social and community level, and to the private level. Bisexual erasure means, among other things, a lack of representations, lack of communities, lack of awareness, lack of speech, and lack of acknowledgment. It means that most of the time, most of our culture operates under the presumption that bisexuality doesn't—and cannot—exist.

For example, in the public and cultural spheres, there's an enormous lack of bisexual representation. According to a study made by the U.K. organization Stonewall called *Unseen on Screen*, out of nearly 127 hours of British television examined, only five minutes and nine seconds were devoted to depicting bisexual characters. (For the sake of comparison, four hours and twenty-four minutes were devoted to gay men and forty-two minutes to lesbians; transgender representations weren't examined.) Also according to the report, "at no point in this coverage were bisexuals portrayed in a positive or realistic manner." In a U.S. study, prominent researcher Gregory Herek found that heterosexual viewers stated that—with the exception of intravenous drug users—bisexuals are their least favorite film characters, a factor which may well influence the film and television industries. Even when there are historical, popular, and other personalities who are or were known to be bisexual, they are generally spoken of as either heterosexual or gay/lesbian (for example, Freddie Mercury, Virginia Woolf, or Lady Gaga).

In the social/community sphere, bisexuals are generally presumed to be either straight or gay/lesbian, and bisexual issues and people are left unaddressed. Bisexuals experience pressure to change their identity to anything other than bisexual (usually gay, lesbian, or straight, though not always) and experience social isolation in both heterosexual and lesbian and gay communities.

In the private sphere, upon coming out as bisexual, bi people's families often keep presuming that they are actually heterosexual (or that they're really gay or lesbian, depending on the situation) and continue to pressure them to "choose" heteronormativity.

Yoshino refers to the first type of erasure (social) when he says that bisexuality suffers three levels, or layers, of erasure in Western culture: first, the general erasure of anything pertaining to sexuality. This layer of erasure is shared by all sexual orientations and pervades over any discourse on sexuality as a whole.[16] The second layer is cultural erasure of same-gender desire, related to minority-world conservatism and affecting all discourses involving queer sexualities. The third layer is specific to bisexuality and is related to the politics of bisexual erasure (namely, the "epistemic contract"). This layer influences any discourse describing desire toward more than one gender, and in particular, the ones that are or might be named as bisexual.

He also refers to the latter two types (social and personal) when he says that bisexual erasure "prevents the articulation of bisexual identity at every phase of bisexual development" (also attempting to counter the notion that bisexual people benefit from their own erasure, also known as the "bisexuals enjoy straight privilege" accusation). When coming out to oneself, says Yoshino, bisexual erasure prevents the naming of bisexual identity, since many times people are unaware of the term, or if they are, might not consider it a viable option. After coming out to some others, as mentioned above, bisexuals experience considerable pressure to change their identity to *anything other than bisexual*, and especially to monosexual identities. In addition, bisexuals also experience pressure to remain selectively closeted in contexts where they might experience biphobic treatment (for example, dating, activism, or work). And finally, even bisexuals who are "all the way out"[17] continue to be read as monosexual, according to their social surroundings, their relationships, their sex lives, or any other factor, having people imposing monosexual (and other) identities on them regardless of their own identification.

Yoshino mentions three ways in which bisexual erasure is enforced within both heterosexual and homosexual discourses:

> **Categorical erasure,** meaning the erasure of bisexuality
> as a category. A famous example of this kind of discourse

on the heterosexual side might be the infamous Bailey study, widely publicized in the media under the title "Gay, Straight, or Lying," which denied the existence of bisexual men. In gay and lesbian discourses, a good example might be American queer theorist Judith Butler's theory of gender melancholy, according to which heterosexuality and homosexuality are both manifested by rejection of one another, leaving no room to think about a possibility of bisexuality.

Individual erasure, by which bisexuality as a category is acknowledged but, at the same time, the particular *person* in question is deprived of her bisexuality. An example of this from the heterosexual side is mentioned in U.K. scholar Kate Chedgzoy's article "'Two Loves I Have': Shakespeare and Bisexuality." Chedgzoy explains how various Shakespeare scholars have attempted to deny the bisexuality evident in his sonnets and to instead present them as heterosexual. Yoshino presents an example from the gay and lesbian side from American scholar Terry Castle's film research, *The Apparitional Lesbian*, in which she describes 1920's film star Greta Garbo as a lesbian, even after mentioning that Garbo desired men as well as women.

Delegitimization, under which bisexuality and bisexual people are attributed negative meanings. According to Yoshino, the clearest expression of this is biphobic stereotypes. Delegitimization and stereotyping is done, in heterosexual discourses, when bis are described as promiscuous or treacherous, or as vectors of STIs. In gay and lesbian discourses, this is done when bisexuals are described as closet cases, fence sitters, traitors of the community, and so on.

According to Yoshino, the reason for the existence of the epistemic contract is that both structures of heterosexuality and homosexuality are threatened by bisexuality, creating a shared interest in its erasure.[18] He describes three ways in which bisexuality threatens both these structures:

STABILIZATION OF SEXUAL ORIENTATION

Yoshino argues that an acknowledgment of bisexuality as a viable option would render it impossible to prove either heterosexuality or homosexuality. This is because currently, in order to receive recognition of either homo- or heterosexuality, all one needs do is to prove their attraction either to a member of "their own" gender or to a person of "the other" gender.[19] However, social recognition of bisexuality would render these proofs impossible, since attraction to any single gender would not be considered contradictory to attraction to any other gender(s)—they could coexist.

Both heterosexual and homosexual structures have a stake in maintaining this clear borderline. The heterosexual stake is, of course, to maintain privilege. As a hegemonic identity, heterosexuality—and heterosexual people—enjoy many privileges in all spheres of life. Recognition of bisexuality might destabilize heterosexual people's ability to prove their heterosexuality and thus hinder their access to privilege. In addition, creating a distinct line between heterosexuality and homosexuality allows heterosexual people to "exorcise" their personal doubts about same-gender desire and thus helps them maintain their personal heterosexual identity. Recognition of bisexuality as an option would render this impossible.

Yoshino attributes the gay and lesbian stake to the immutability ("born this way") claim. This argument, commonly used to justify "equal rights" for gay people, is hindered by bisexuality's disruption to proving homosexual identity, as well as by the common perception of bisexuality as something that encapsulates choice. The perception of a choice between homosexuality and heterosexuality means that acknowledging bisexuality causes a disruption to the "born this way" claim—turning bisexuality itself into a hindrance to assimilationist gay goals.

MAINTAINING THE PRIMACY OF GENDER AS A SOCIAL CATEGORY[20]

According to Yoshino, bisexuality has the potential to subvert the structure of the gender binary, since bisexuality is perceived as a type of desire that doesn't distinguish between people based on their genders. In Yoshino's words, "without a clear and privileged distinction between 'man' and 'woman,' there is no clear and privileged distinction between 'straight' and 'gay.'" This challenge to the primacy of gender is threatening to homosexuality and heterosexuality for two reasons: Firstly, the lack of distinction between genders destabilizes monosexual identity (and is threatening for the same reasons described in the previous section). Secondly, it emphasizes the tension between public and private attitudes toward gender. Moreover, Yoshino claims that this lack of distinction threatens not only the gender binary, but also the definition of humanity itself. Yoshino here is relying on Judith Butler, who argued that people are never acknowledged as human until they have a gender (in other words, until the moment when the question "is it a boy or a girl?" can be answered).

Bisexuality emphasizes the tension between public and private attitudes toward gender because in the public sphere, gender-based discrimination is not only frowned upon but illegal. As widely practiced as sexism might be, the dominant cultural notion about it says that you're not supposed to be overtly sexist. However, when it comes to monosexual identities, gender-based discrimination not only is encouraged but also constitutes the basis on which monosexual identities are created and withheld. In this way bisexuality exposes inconsistencies within the system, pointing out social sexism and patriarchy.

Yoshino attributes the heterosexual interest in this matter to maintaining heterosexual gender performance. He says:

When (as now) heterosexuality is the prevailing code of desire, women will be encouraged to perform their sex in a way that is attractive to men (and vice versa, although the symmetry is not complete). To be a "woman" is to be attractive to men; to be a "man" is to be attractive to women.

Yoshino claims that bisexuality's subversive potential in relation to this straight gender performance is greater than that of homosexuality, since bisexuality can't be heterosexualized by being imagined as inversion. In the popular mind, gays and lesbians are still often thought of as inverted heterosexuals: effeminized men and masculinized women. However, bisexuality can't be heterosexualized in that way, since desire toward more than one gender becomes unintelligible in a framework of single-aim gender performance and gender essentialism. (Despite this, it should be noted that, although less popular or apparent, bisexuality can still be imagined in this way, as in the inversion theories mentioned in the first chapter.)

Yoshino ties the gay and lesbian interest in this regard to lesbian separatism. While acknowledging that separatism might be practiced by both gay men and lesbians, he explains that lesbians' oppression as women has made their need for feminism—and, by extent, separatism—more urgent than that of gay men. In a situation where "feminism is the theory, lesbianism is the practice," bisexuality might come to symbolize a potential "invasion" and "contamination" of the movement by people other than cisgender women (notably, cisgender men and trans people). Likewise, it might be said that male bisexuals can invoke some gay men's misogyny and transphobia by their association with attraction to more than one gender.

PRESERVATION OF MONOGAMY

It's no news that bisexuality is closely associated with nonmonogamy. According to Pepper Mint, "because our society conceptualizes bisexuality as inherently nonmonogamous, a single set of associations [is] drawn directly from bisexuality to cheating, instead of being drawn from bisexuality to nonmonogamy to cheating." Yoshino links this to the social perception of bisexuality as excessive: In popular imagination, the "one," "complete" sexuality is monosexual, and any addition to it becomes excess.

Yoshino attributes heterosexual and homosexual discourses' shared interest here to romantic jealousy that might arise in relationships between monosexuals and bisexuals, and monosexuals' fear that their bisexual partner might leave them for a person of a different gender category. One might add to this claim that this fear represents anxiety of disruption of the structure of romantic couplehood, as a practice and as a culture that presides over our lives and thus controls them.

The heterosexual stake in this is based on the stereotype of bisexuals as carriers of HIV and STIs. Yoshino quotes Robyn Ochs, who writes:

In the minds of many heterosexual Americans, bisexuality has come to be strongly identified with images of married, dishonest, closeted men sneaking out on their unsuspecting wives, contracting AIDS through unsafe sex with other men, then infecting their innocent wives and children.

Simply put, since bisexuals are perceived as promiscuous vectors of disease, bisexual existence becomes a threat to the structure and the safety of monogamy.

The gay male stake is linked to the assimilationist gay movement and its attempts to disprove the stereotype of gay men as promiscuous. Acknowledgment of bisexuality as a part of the assimilationist gay movement might "spoil" the "respectable" image that this movement attempts to create. Another stake is related to lesbian discourse, in which bisexuality is perceived similarly to the heterosexual stance: bisexual women often being seen as "AIDS-carrying high-risk parasite[s] on the movement" (as one commentator is quoted as saying in Yoshino's article). Thus, in lesbian discourses, bisexuality might again symbolize contamination of the lesbian community.

Of course, more interests might be listed, as demonstrated in my discussion of stereotypes in the first chapter. Bisexuality is perceived as threatening in manifold ways, shared by both structures of heterosexuality and homosexuality. However, this not only provides society with reasons to erase bisexuality, but also charges bisexuality with a myriad of political meanings, giving it the power to subvert these very structures by taking them on their own terms. While we address monosexism, biphobia, and bisexual erasure, we must also keep in mind that the very powers that oppress us also give us the crack through which to break the system.

In the beginning of this section, I mentioned some of the ways in which monosexism, through bisexual erasure, influences bisexual people's lives: It disrupts the articulation of a bisexual identity at all levels of development. However, the influence of bisexual erasure isn't limited to the field of sexual identity alone. Other influences of monosexism go far deeper than that, encompassing many fields of our lives and influencing us in dispersed, often counterintuitive and unrecognized ways.

DECONSTRUCTING BIPHOBIA

A shiny, new theory about biphobia was published in 2011 by Miguel Obradors-Campos under the name of "Deconstructing Biphobia," offering new tools with which to observe monosexism. Obradors's text describes biphobia as I would describe monosexism: a social structure that affects the lives of bisexual people in ways that are often invisible, making it impossible to trace a single "source" to explain the phenomenon. In order to uncover some of the aspects of this structure, Obradors adapts the "five faces of oppression" model offered by Iris Marion Young in her book *Justice and Politics*, and he adds three additional ones also relevant to monosexism. The main importance of this tool is not only that it points out a structure rather than a series of personal attitudes, but also that it highlights the often-overlooked material consequences of monosexism on bisexual people's lives and experiences.

It's important to note that although these tools are incredibly useful for the analysis of monosexism as a whole, Obradors only provides anecdotal instances of biphobia in gay communities. Therefore, in order to expand the broad potential that these tools hold, I'll provide additional examples, as well as some from heterosexual contexts. It's again important to remember that although I pay equal attention to lesbian/gay and straight contexts, my main focus is institutional and heterosexual oppression of bisexuals (while still acknowledging that gay and lesbian communities are often complicit in this). The eight faces of bisexual oppression are:

EXPLOITATION

Obradors uses Young's definition of exploitation as a situation where "people exercise their capabilities under the control, according to the purposes, and for the benefit of other people." According to Obradors, many bisexual activists' work is exploited by the gay movement. The products of the work of bisexual activists are often used for the benefit of gay people, without reflecting back on the bisexual community for either visibility, symbolic capital, or various material gains. Indeed, bisexuals have been some of the founders and leaders of the gay liberation movement, yet have either had their importance and contributions dismissed or their bisexuality erased. As a classic example of this, Obradors mentions bisexual activist Brenda Howard, who thought up and initiated the first pride march after the Stonewall rebellion, and whose seminal donation to the LGBT movement has been all but erased from community history.

On the heterosexual side of things, bisexuals and bisexuality have routinely been exploited in symbolic and material ways, in many contexts. For example, in the academic field, Freud's theory of sexuality was based on interviews with his patients, using their bisexual lived experiences as ground not only for his theories, but also for his fame, reputation, and symbolic capital. Another prominent example might be mainstream pornography, in which the bodies and sexualities of bisexual women are exploited as a spectacle for the satisfaction of straight men. One more example might be film, in which bisexuality is often used to represent anything but itself (often to underline characteristics such as murderousness, duplicitousness, hedonism, etc.), while erasing bisexuality as a topic in its own right.

CULTURAL IMPERIALISM

In Obradors's words:

> *Cultural imperialism . . . has a paradoxical meaning . . . . On the one hand, cultural imperialism invisibilizes a group of people by denying its very existence. On the other hand, this group of people is anyway described through a number of prejudices that creates a clear (and biased) image of them.*

In relation to bisexuality, such is the case of bisexual erasure. Obradors mentions the famous "Gay, Straight, or Lying?" study, which denied the existence of bisexuality in men. He comments that even while denying the existence of bisexuality, the study proceeds to describe bisexual men in stereotypical ways. According to Obradors, "we are perceived through those stereotypes even though we are also perceived as nonexisting." Other examples of bisexual erasure are, of course, described in abundance in the previous section of this chapter.

POWERLESSNESS, MARGINALIZATION, AND HETERONOMY

These three faces of oppression (originally separate) complement one another. *Powerlessness*, perhaps better described as *disempowerment*, refers to a situation where people "have little or no work autonomy, exercise little creativity or judgment in their work, have no technical expertise or authority, . . . and do not command respect." *Marginalization* is the process in which

> *persons are excluded from active participation, sometimes throughout the society as a whole. This exclusion makes the marginalized persons unable to interact with others or be acknowledged . . . [M]arginalized persons tend to be condemned to material deprivation . . . because the extreme conditions they are suffering are not even noticed by the broader society.*

Heteronomy is taken from the field of philosophy and means the opposite of autonomy. By this Obradors means that bisexuals are often barred from making autonomous decisions in formal structures.

In his text, Obradors focuses on the *feeling* of powerlessness often experienced by bisexual people, stating that many bisexuals feel disrespected and marginalized within the field of LGBT activism. However, it might also be said that bisexuals not only *feel* these things, but are also materially positioned in these ways within the movement, meaning that they are actively marginalized. Obradors mentions that bisexuals are marginalized in decision-making processes in "LGBT" organizations, as well as in "LGBT" conferences and panels. He also notes the International Day Against Homophobia and Transphobia (IDAHO), which excludes biphobia (as well as lesbophobia) even from its name (not to mention content). Another key example for marginalization in LGBT contexts is organizational leadership: For example, out of fifteen prominent LGBT organizations currently operating in Israel/Occupied Palestine, only one is headed by an out bisexual—the bisexual organization. I've been given to understand that the situation is similar in many other countries, including the United States and the U.K.

In heterosexual contexts, bisexuals are both disempowered and marginalized in many ways, thus preventing them from active participation in a myriad of tangible and intangible ways. As one example (keeping in line with the work-based meaning of the term given it by Young), one might recall work discrimination against bisexuals. U.K. organization Stonewall's report about bisexual people in the workplace indicates that bi people suffer various levels of work discrimination. This includes stigmatization, marginalization, difficulties in coming out as bisexual (some choose to pass as straight, gay, or lesbian for greater acceptance), and prejudice against their abilities as workers. They also report a lack of out bisexual role models in higher management positions, indicating that out bisexual people rarely make it "to the top." Information from the U.S. *Bisexual Invisibility* report reveals that bisexual people both earn less and are more likely to suffer from poverty than heterosexuals, gay men, and lesbians. Combining these together, it isn't too hard to deduce that out bisexuals are most likely relegated to lower positions in workplaces, fitting the descriptions of "powerlessness," "marginalization," and "heteronomy" as defined above. This example might, of course, be expanded to any and all scales of official (and unofficial) hierarchy in the public sphere: Out bisexuals are generally barred from occupying positions of power and are relegated to lower-status positions.

VIOLENCE

Obradors defines violence as "a way of dominating verbally, physically, or symbolically in such a way that causes damage, sometimes irreparable." He continues, "A person who is violent against others is someone who crosses personal boundaries, causing humiliation, degradation, intimidation, pain, or destruction." Obradors also mentions symbolic violence, being the kind of violence

> *that a person unconsciously experiences through norms, customs, symbology and other intangible aspects. Symbolic violence*

*is extremely dangerous because its sources are rarely identified,
whereas it can also lead the victim to depression, lack of self-
esteem, self-destructive thoughts, and the final exertion of them.*

Since the latter kind of violence is only detectable by its consequences, I will describe it more fully later in this chapter, and for the
sake of brevity (and simplification), I'll describe only physical and verbal
forms of violence here.

Obradors mentions that bisexuals often experience verbal violence
within "LGBT" communities when speaking out about bisexuality. For
example, a recent study examining online discussions about bisexuality
in an LGBT environment discovered that 55 percent of the comments
contained some form (or evidence) of biphobia or monosexism, meaning
it is *far likelier* to encounter biphobic comments than to encounter support for bisexual people.

Another form of verbal violence suffered by bisexuals in gay and
lesbian communities is sexual harassment. For example, one female
bisexual activist tells that upon disclosing her bisexuality, the lesbian
woman she was speaking to "proceeded to call [her] 'Germy' for the
rest of the night, with graphic . . . descriptions of how she thought bis
constantly jump from one type of genitalia to the next"; another tells
that a lesbian woman talked about "the cum on [her] breath" in response
to her bisexuality; and one bisexual male blogger shares that he'd been
called a "slut" by pride parade participants.

Sometimes, however, even *physical* violence against bisexuals
might be practiced by "LGBTs": For example, a traumatic moment for
me as an activist was when I, along with several fellow bi activists, got
physically assaulted by the Jerusalem Pride March's security guards *per
the orders of the organizers*, for protesting the exclusion of bisexuals from
the march itself.[21]

On the heterosexual side, bisexuals are subject to biphobic and
LGBT-phobic physical violence, street violence, and bullying. In fact,

two recent studies have found that bisexual teens are at a higher risk for bullying than gay, lesbian, and straight teens. For example, in 1995, seventeen-year-old Bill Clayton committed suicide after having been brutally assaulted by four other teenagers in broad daylight; in 2010, twenty-seven-year-old Aaron Hampton needed twelve stitches after getting bashed by three men on the street; also in 2010, a University of California student was forced to move to a different campus due to the bullying he suffered in his fraternity. (Note that scarcity of news items about this is largely due to erasure of the violence survivors' bisexuality).

Bisexuals (and especially bi women) are also routinely subject to sexual harassment and sexual violence by (mostly straight and cisgender) men. For example, one of the bisexual women in the online research I cited above complains about "men who think all bi women are into threesomes/nonmonogamy, or that if they're dating women who are bi they are *entitled to that*" (emphasis mine); another talks about her husband's response to the fact that she's not attracted to *all* women: "[H]is comment was, 'Maybe you're coming back on this side of the fence. To liking dick, the way that it should be'"; the California university student from the example above also got sexually harassed as part of the bullying. Recent studies in the United States have also found that bisexual women are significantly likelier than both heterosexual and lesbian women to suffer from intimate violence, and that almost *half* of bisexual women experienced rape, and *75 percent* experienced other forms of sexual violence.

In addition, even within the context of direct violence, it would be unfair to ignore the fact that out of heterosexuals, gays, lesbians, and bisexuals, bisexuals have statistically been found to be most likely to experience depression, as well as the most likely to contemplate suicide. This is neither coincidental nor a personal problem, but a phenomenon pointing to a widespread system of indirect, institutional, or symbolic violence. To quote a famous U.S. flier: "There are no queer teen suicides, only queer teen murders."

ALIENATION

Alienation could be also thought of as internalized biphobia/monosexism or "**false consciousness**." Obradors describes it as "a mind-set in which the individual forgets or neglects his or her own needs, desires, and will to overemphasize those of other persons toward whom his or her energy, time, and actions tend to focus."

In "LGBT" settings, Obradors mentions many bisexuals' tendency to neglect bisexual activism while contributing most of their time and energy to the GGGG movement. Indeed, many bisexuals even go as far as denying that a separate bisexual struggle is needed or that unique bisexual issues exist. This tendency is evident, for example, in data recently collected by American researcher Heidi Bruins-Green, according to which only 10 percent of bisexuals are regularly involved with bisexual communities, whereas 30 percent reported on regular involvement with LGBT communities.

> **False consciousness** is a term originally coined by Karl Marx. It denotes a situation in which an oppressed group identifies with the values of its oppressors.

In heterosexual contexts, the same dismissal of bisexuality and its related issues occurs in relation to other topics, as many bisexual activists prefer to contribute their efforts to struggles that are perceived as "more important" than bisexuality on the metaphorical oppression hierarchy. For example, a commentator on one Israeli bisexual mailing list wrote that a bisexual organization focusing solely on bisexual issues (rather than also engaging with Palestine solidarity activism) wasn't worth her time: "An a-political bisexual organization? Well, with all due respect, I have more important things to do . . . " Another commentator in a separate discussion wrote: "What do we actually want? Protection from dismissal? Protection from erasure? Not that this is unimportant, it's just lower on my priorities." Evidence to this might again be found in Green's research, according to which, 57 percent of the bisexuals *who answered the survey* are not connected to bisexual communities at all.

STIGMA

This refers us back to the familiar terrain of biphobic stereotypes. According to Obradors, "a stigma is a mark that symbolizes prejudice or a stereotype and is imposed on an individual by force as an identity feature." Obradors mentions that in many "LGBT" contexts, bisexuals tend to be both stigmatized and treated accordingly. Robyn Ochs also writes about this and mentions some forms of biphobic stigma frequently observed in gay and lesbian communities: that bisexuals are privileged, that bisexuals will ultimately choose heterosexual relationships and life-styles, that bisexual women are reinforcing patriarchy, that bisexuality is not a political identity, that bisexual women carry HIV to lesbian communities, and so on. Biphobic stigma often found in heterosexual contexts, according to Ochs, might be the conflation of bisexuality with nonmonogamy and the perception of bisexual men as carriers of HIV into heterosexual populations.

Obradors's theory provides us with tools to look into the material ramifications of monosexism; however, nearly all of the parameters require much further research in order to become well grounded, exposed, and fully addressed. And so, in order to better base my claim regarding bisexuals' oppression, I would like to look into some statistical findings, which have been gathered into a single report about the state of bisexuals in American society.

BISEXUAL INVISIBILITY REPORT

Published in March 2011, the *Bisexual Invisibility* report (perhaps more aptly called "the bisexual erasure report" or the "monosexism report") is the first report about bisexuality to have been released by a government body in the United States (that being the San Francisco Human Rights Commission). Without a doubt, this is one of the most important texts to have ever been published about bisexuals. Its importance cannot be overstated, as this is one of the only published texts today empirically addressing the material results of monosexism and biphobia on the lives of bisexual people.[22] And just as this report is important, its content is both saddening and infuriating. I've gathered a few of the report's findings, in hopes to shed light on these material effects. This echoes the symbolic and institutional violence that Obradors describes, further stressing that monosexism is a widespread oppressive system influencing bisexual people in many walks of life.

Some facts about bisexual health, as outlined in the *Bisexual Invisibility* report:

- *Bisexual people experience greater health disparities than the broader population, including a greater likelihood of suffering from depression and other mood or anxiety disorders.*
- *Bisexuals report higher rates of hypertension, poor or fair physical health, smoking, and risky drinking than heterosexuals or lesbians/gays.*
- *Many, if not most, bisexual people don't come out to their healthcare providers. This means they are getting incomplete information (for example, about safer sex practices).*
- *Most HIV and STI prevention programs don't . . . address the [specific] health needs of bisexuals, much less those [who have sex with people of more than one gender,] but do not identify as bisexual.*
- *Bisexual women in relationships with monosexual partners have an increased rate of domestic violence compared to women in other demographic categories.*

The report states a wide-scale research performed between the years 2003 and 2007 in which the researchers looked at health disparities between lesbians and bisexual women, and found that:

- *Bisexual women showed significantly higher rates of poor*

general health and frequent mental distress, even after con-
trolling for confounding variables.

• *Bisexual women were more likely to be current smokers and*
acute drinkers.

SOME FACTS ABOUT
BISEXUAL MENTAL HEALTH

The researchers in the above survey also compared the frequency of
mental distress in lesbian and bisexual women in urban and nonurban
environments. They found that while "[i]n nonurban areas, lesbians and
bisexual women experience similar levels of frequent mental distress,
the odds of frequent mental distress *decrease* significantly for lesbians
in urban areas, while [becoming] nearly *double* for bisexual women"
(emphases in original). The researchers theorize that the reason for this
is that gay and lesbian communities are better organized in urban areas,
contributing to the isolation of bisexual people who experience rejection
when seeking support in them.

Another disturbing fact is that bisexuals are far likelier to feel sui-
cidal than heterosexuals, gays, and lesbians. One Canadian study found
that whereas 9.6 percent of straight women and 29.5 percent of lesbian
women reported suicidality, suicidality among bisexual women was as
high as 45.4 percent. As for men, whereas 7.4 percent of straights and
25.2 percent of gays reported suicidality, bisexuals who reported suicidality made up 34.8 percent of the respondents. (Unfortunately, this
research does not differentiate between cisgender and transgender people, and leaves out people of nonbinary genders).

Another study, this time in the U.K., found that young and mid-
dle-aged bisexual adults reported poorer mental health than any other
sexual orientation group examined. The researchers even go as far as saying that "[p]revious studies may have overstated the risk of mental health
problems for homosexuals by grouping them together with bisexuals."

SOME FACTS ABOUT BISEXUAL POVERTY AND ECONOMIC OPPRESSION

The wide-scale health research mentioned above also found some disturbing information about bisexual poverty:

- Bisexual women had significantly lower levels of education, were more likely to be living with income below 200 percent of the federal poverty level, and had more children living in the household.
- Bisexual women were significantly less likely to have health insurance coverage and more likely to experience financial barriers to receiving healthcare services.

Another study, this time in California, found that "while gay men earned 2 to 3 percent less than straight men and lesbians 2.7 percent less, bisexual men earned 10 to 15 percent less and bisexual women nearly 11 percent less."

A 2009 study about poverty analyzed data from three surveys and found that "bisexual women are more than *twice* as likely as lesbians to live in poverty (17.7 percent compared to 7.8 percent), and bisexual men are over 50 percent more likely to live in poverty than gay men (9.7 percent compared to 6.2 percent)" (emphasis in original).

Another form of economic oppression that the report identifies is lack of funding. As mentioned in the previous section, in years 2008 and 2009, out of over 200 million dollars given by U.S. foundations to LGBT organizations as grants, *not a single dollar* went toward funding bisexual-specific organizations or projects. This "LGBT" money did not "trickle down" to bisexuals either: A survey conducted by the editors of the report found that most LGBT organizations in San Francisco (*who were willing to reply to a survey about bisexuality*) do not offer content that is targeted specifically toward bisexuals. While bisexual people make up the single largest group among LGBTs, the report found "only 3 to 20 percent of the people accessing LGBT-focused services are bisexual."

Looking at this data, and considering the theories exposing the oppression behind the numbers, it becomes clear that monosexism is indeed a widespread system broadly influencing the lives of bisexuals. While not intuitively related to sexual orientation, these factors still correlate throughout many parts of bisexuals' lives, and provide a testament to both the existence and depth of this structure.

It might also be said that the very disconnection between popular understandings of biphobia (as personalized and explicit) and of monosexism (as dispersed and invisible) are epistemologically monosexist. The separation between direct explicit mistreatment of bisexuals, and the seemingly unrelated effects of the monosexist structure, forcibly separates between two parts of a whole. This attempt to dismantle bisexual identities and bisexual lives into two separate parts that supposedly have no connection to one another, might be compared to society's attempt to dismantle bisexual identities and meanings into separate and disconnected parts (namely, into heterosexuality and homosexuality).

The lives of bisexual people consist of many parts, all of which are interrelated by the simple fact that a bi person is a whole person. Our bisexual identities are not contained in just one place. We do not stop being bisexual when experiencing emotional distress, we do not stop being bisexual when dealing with the medical institution, and we do not stop being bisexual at work or in our communities. We live our lives as bisexuals—and just as all parts of our lives are relevant to our bisexualities, so are our bisexualities relevant to all parts of our lives.

MONOSEXISM AND MONOSEXUALS

More often than not, when the word "privilege" comes up in relation to bisexuality or bi people, it is coupled with "heterosexual" and with the accusation that bisexuals "enjoy heterosexual privilege" (an issue I will be discussing in the next chapter). On the other hand, the notion that mono-sexuals enjoy privilege is both relatively new and foreign to queer and bisex-ual political thought. I was translating the "Male Privilege Checklist" (by blogger Barry Deutsch) into Hebrew when it occurred to me that I have never seen a monosexual privilege checklist. Indeed, I've never even heard the term spoken or referred to, despite the fact that privilege checklists exist for many groups (especially online). This is why I decided to write one myself.

The significance of such a list, as I see it, is both in highlighting the way that bisexuals experience oppression, as well as exposing the many privileges that monosexual people may take for granted in their lives, and which bisexuals often can't. In this, I once again seek to emphasize that monosexism is a structure and that it operates on a large scale, influ-encing everyone's lives in various ways.

A NOTE ON TERMINOLOGY

I am aware of the problem with using a binary structure such as mono-sexual/bisexual. However, I allow myself to use it strategically, as a political and analytical tool in order to expose unequal power relations in a society that already constructs itself around this binary. Inevitably, privilege checklists are termed in binary language so as to emphasize a structure of oppression working against certain groups. It is no less binary, for example, to speak about cisgender/transgender, male/female, white/black, or straight/queer than is it to speak about mono-sexual/bisexual. The fact that, out of these, the bisexual movement is the one most likely to find itself facing the ubiquitous "binary" accusa-tion (as discussed in chapter 1) is suspicious to say the least.

I use the word "bisexual" as an umbrella term, including anyone attracted to people of more than one gender, who identifies as bisex-ual, pansexual, fluid, queer, heteroflexible, homoflexible, or any other bi-spectrum identity, and who considers herself part of the bisexual movement/community.

I define "monosexual" as any person attracted to people of no more than one gender (including heterosexuals, gays, and lesbians).

I define "privilege" as benefits that society awards some and withholds from others, based on their compliance with social norms.

THE OBLIGATORY DISCLAIMER

By compiling a list of monosexual privilege, I do not mean to suggest that all monosexuals are the same, nor do I mean to suggest that they enjoy nothing but privilege. Specifically, I do not mean to create a false image of equality between heterosexuals and gays and lesbians, or to scapegoat gays and lesbians for the system of monosexism. Power inequalities exist all over the social map, and monosexuals are just as likely as anyone to be on the bad end of one of them—especially if they are gay or lesbian. Many of the points described in the list are obviously shared by people of other marginalized groups—people experience similar forms of privilege or oppression through different identities, and the list isn't meant to be strictly exclusive. Of course, this list would be more accurate the more privileges the person in question enjoys (in particular, male, white, heterosexual, cisgender, and so on). Also, I do not mean to imply that all bisexuals are oppressed and enjoy no privileges at all—many bisexual people belong to other groups that do enjoy privileges. As in any field in life, oppression is complicated and multifaceted. We are all oppressors and we are all oppressed—and we must all deal both with our oppression and our privileges. I hope the readers of this list might take this as an opportunity.

What I do wish to say is that monosexual people are rewarded by society for their monosexuality, and that bisexuals are punished for not complying with this requirement. This means that transgender people, lesbians, gays, asexuals, racialized people, disabled people, and people of many more groups might all be oppressed along any of these axes (transgender/cisgender, gay/straight, etc.), but *on the axis of bisexual/ monosexual*, they are nonetheless recipients of privilege. Feminist researchers have named this *kyriarchy,* meaning intersecting oppressions and privileges. The goal of this list is to acknowledge and expose some of the ways in which privileges take shape in monosexual people's lives.

On a side note, being able to write a list of privileges is not transparent for me: Many privileges benefited me while writing it. As noted in the introduction, I am a Jewish citizen of Israel/Occupied Palestine, and thus have access to many civil rights and privileges denied to many Palestinians; I am an English speaker; I am a university graduate; I have access to academic and political writings about bisexuality and queer theory/politics; I have computer access and the technical skills required to operate a computer; though I am disabled, I am nonetheless able to use my hands for typing and my eyes for reading in a way which complies with how computers are designed; I have free time that I am able to spare for the purposes of writing. All of these are privileges that benefited me—and indeed enabled me—to write this list (and there are probably many more). As you read the list, I urge you to consider your own privileges in light of this paragraph and of the list itself.

MONOSEXUAL PRIVILEGE CHECKLIST

☐ 1. Society assures me that my sexual identity is real and that people like me exist.

☐ 2. When I disclose my sexual identity to others, they believe it without requiring me to prove it (usually by disclosing my sexual and romantic history).

☐ 3. I can feel sure that, upon disclosing my sexual identity, people accept that it's my real/actual sexual identity (rather than assuming that I am lying or simply wrong).

☐ 4. I am never considered closeted when disclosing my sexual identity.

☐ 5. I am considered to have more authority in defining and judging bisexuality than people who identify as bisexual.

☐ 6. Perception/acceptance of my sexual identity is generally independent of my choices of relationships, partners, and lifestyles.

☐ 7. It is unlikely that disclosing my sexual identity in a non-sexual context will be taken as a sign of sexual availability or consent.

☐ 8. I can be confident that people will not rename my sexual identity or use different words to describe my identity than I do.

☐ 9. When seen with a partner I'm dating, I can be certain I will be recognized as a member of my sexual-identity group by members of my community.

☐ 10. I do not have to choose between either invisibility ("passing") or being consistently "othered" and/or tokenized in my community based on my sexual identity.

☐ 11. I am never blamed for upholding heteropatriarchy or cisgender privilege because of the word that I use to identify my sexuality.

☐ 12. I feel welcomed at appropriate services or events that are segregated by sexual identity (for example, straight singles nights, gay community centers, or lesbian-only events).

☐ 13. I can feel sure that if I choose to enter a monogamous relationship, my friends, community, or my partner will continue to accept my sexual identity, without expecting or pressuring me to change it.

☐ 14. I do not need to worry about potential partners shifting instantly from amorous relations to disdain, humiliating treatment, or verbal or sexual violence because of my sexual identity.

☐ 15. I can choose to be in a polyamorous relationship without being accused of reinforcing stereotypes against my sexual-identity group.

☐ 16. I can fairly easily find representations of people of my sexual-identity group and my lifestyle in the media and the arts. I encounter such representations without needing to look hard.

☐ 17. If I encounter a fictional, historical, or famous figure of my sexual identity, I can be reasonably sure that s/he will be named as such in the text or by the media, reviewers, and audience.

☐ 18. I often encounter the word I use to identify myself in the media and the arts. When I hear or read it, I am far less likely to find it in the context of the denial of its existence.

☐ 19. I can find, fairly easily, reading material, institutions, media representations, etc. which give attention specifically to people of my sexual identity.

☐ 20. I can feel certain that normal everyday language will include my sexual identity ("straight and gay alike," "gay and lesbian," etc.).

☐ 21. If I am cisgender, I am far less likely to suffer from intimate and sexual violence.

☐ 22. If I am cisgender, I am less likely to suffer from depression or to contemplate suicide.

☐ 23. If I am cisgender, I am less likely to suffer from poverty.

☐ 24. I am more likely to feel comfortable being open about my sexual identity at work.

☐ 25. I have access to information about the prevalence of STIs in my community as well as prevention methods that are suitable for me. (For example, searching online yields many accurate and accessible results).

☐ 26. Information about the prevalence of STIs in my community as well as prevention methods suitable for me are unlikely to be subsumed under those of any other sexual-identity groups.

☐ 27. If I live in a city, I am more likely to find medical care that will suit my own particular needs.

☐ 28. If I am cisgender, I am less likely to risk my health by avoiding medical treatment.

☐ 29. I have the privilege of not being aware of my privileges.

The idea that monosexuals enjoy privilege on the axis of monosexual/bisexual might help us examine and deconstruct monosexism as it influences people who don't identify as bisexual (or bi-spectrum). However, privilege isn't the only influence of monosexism on monosexuals: Monosexism contains negative influences working on everyone, even as it privileges some. This includes monosexual people.

The first way in which monosexism oppresses monosexual people is by limiting their options. By presenting only two options for people—gay or straight—many people might feel trapped inside their sexual identity or orientation. This applies in particular to heterosexual people, who suffer from the double effect of both heterosexism and monosexism. Very often, acknowledgment of one's same-gender desires also includes dealing with the loss of many privileges only granted in society to heterosexual people. The support that formerly-straight lesbian and gay people receive from lesbian and gay communities somewhat compensates the loss of privileges (as well as often opening up a whole new world of friendship, solidarity, and connection). However, the same support is often denied to people who come out as bisexual, leaving many people with only two viable options: gay or straight. This means that many heterosexual people might fear to acknowledge bisexual desires or to question their heterosexuality, feeling that once they've admitted to same-gender desire, they would "have to choose."

As to gay and lesbian people, acknowledging bisexual desire or questioning their monosexuality might result in rejection from their gay or lesbian communities, meaning the loss of community, support, friendships, and relationships (as has indeed happened to many people who came out as bisexual in gay and lesbian communities). Considering that the community is often the main source of support in lesbians and gays' lives, this kind of loss might be just as painful as, if not worse than, first coming out as lesbian or gay and (often) losing support from their friends and families. In addition and as an extension, many gays and lesbians might be fearful of having to go through a second coming-out process, as the first time was already difficult and painful in an of itself.

In this way, oppression directed against bi people can also be thought of as a warning sign for monosexuals (potential bisexuals) not to stray from the path. People often see the price that bisexuals have to pay for their identity, and, in addition to being a social punishment against bisexuality, this might also serve as deterrent: "Here's what will happen to you if you do not comply."

Monosexism also limits monosexuals' connection with bisexual people. By this I mean that people who are monosexist or biphobic tend to distance themselves from bisexuals (whether or not this is done consciously), preventing the creation of new connections, friendships, and relationships of any kind with an entire population of people. This means that monosexism serves as a separating agent between people, severing connection, communication, and understanding, and promoting alienation and fragmentation. In this way, relationships between monosexual and bisexual people would be stifled in a way that not only harms bisexual people, but also harms monosexuals themselves, by disturbing their connection with others and preventing closeness, intimacy, or collaboration on many levels.

Monosexism also negatively influences monosexuals by pushing them into the role of oppressors of bisexual people (or collaborators with that oppression). Their participation in such a hierarchy, their lack of resistance, and their acceptance thereof creates a notion that such a system of hierarchy and oppression is good, normal, and legitimate, and that it's okay for some people to have more value in society on the backs of others. This, in turn, normalizes the oppression that monosexual people are forced to deal with in other aspects of their lives and identities, and creates a situation in which people are less likely to resist to any kind of hierarchy or to act as allies to others. In this way, too, monosexism serves as a separating factor between different people.

These three factors make it all the more important for monosexuals to acknowledge and confront monosexism, as they are not only recipients of privilege under this system, but also of oppression. Thus, monosexuals who choose to account for and resist monosexism would not only be doing so as bisexual allies (an important goal in and of itself), but also as part of their own liberation. In this way, the bisexual struggle connects not only with bi-specific aspects of fighting biphobia, but also with the broader aspect of resisting and deconstructing monosexism, thus benefiting people of all sexual identities.

CHAPTER 3:

Bisexuality, Privilege, and Passing

As mentioned in the previous chapter, when the words *bisexuality* and *privilege* appear together, it is more often than not in the context of bisexual access to heterosexual privilege. This is often based on bisexual in/visibility inside the **heterosexual matrix**. In this chapter, I will examine and try to redefine the discourse about the relationship between bisexuality, privilege, and passing.

There are three consensus opinions about bisexuality and privilege: First, among monosexual people (and especially lesbians and gay men), the consensus opinion seems to be that bisexuals hold unquestionable access to heterosexual privilege. This relies on the popular idea that "bisexuals can choose" to be straight, meaning that bis are able to make a conscious choice regarding who to date or establish relationships with. It is then assumed that since different-gender (or "straight") relationships are more socially acceptable, bisexuals would inevitably make the "easy" choice, prioritizing privilege, comfort, and pleasure over what is often perceived as a life of discrimination and hardship. This argument, of course, places bisexuals in the role of oppressors, as

The heterosexual matrix is a term coined by Judith Butler. In biology, "matrix" is the material existing between cells, meaning that it is an all-present environment. This term emphasizes how heteronormativity comprises an all-present environment in minority-world cultures.

well as being informed by the stereotype of bisexuals as careless hedonists. On a deeper level, this sort of thinking marks social anxieties about the distribution of privilege and the subversion of hierarchical categories.

Second, within mainstream bisexual movements, bisexual access to heterosexual privilege is considered a stereotype or a "myth," to be rebutted using the familiar mantra of "that's not true"! The way this rebuttal goes, bisexuals have no access at all to heterosexual privilege because they are not heterosexual. However, rather than elaborated, this point is constantly repeated. For example, in the book *Bisexual Politics: Theories, Queries, and Visions*, the term "heterosexual privilege" appears in at least twenty different places, but is only seriously engaged with in two texts. One of the places where this point is repeated is Liz A. Highleyman's essay, "Identity and Ideas: Strategies for Bisexuals," where she writes, "Some gay men and some lesbians see bisexuals as partakers of heterosexual privilege." Later on in the same text, she references the same notion again, writing about "the assumption that bisexuals choose other-sex [sic] partners to gain mainstream acceptance or social privilege." This belief appears isolated from context. Rather than explaining why and how this isn't true, the fact is simply assumed. Even when the question does receive more attention, the explanation often remains incomplete.

The most popular counterargument used by bisexual writers in this context might be exemplified by the essay "If Half of You Dodges a Bullet, All of You Ends Up Dead" by Orna Izakson, which is also one of the two texts to engage with privilege in *Bisexual Politics* in any substantial way. As evident by the title itself, it is claimed that bisexuals are equally vulnerable to homophobia as gays and lesbians by virtue of queer identification and visibility. Izakson writes:

> *Those who would criminalize same-sex [sic] sexual activities don't care how often or exclusively you do it. Bisexual folks suffer from these laws just as surely as the lesbian or gay man who never, ever, has an opposite-sex [sic] partner. Queer-bashers don't care that sometimes bi folks sleep with opposite-sex [sic] partners. In their eyes there is no such thing as half-queer.*

According to this rebuttal, and in the tradition of bisexual discourse on biphobia and oppression, bisexuals are only oppressed inasmuch as their experience resembles that of gays and lesbians. Bisexuals, it appears, suffer only *homophobia* (rather than biphobia or monosexism) by the straight population, and, it is assumed, only suffer *biphobia* at the hands of gay and lesbian communities.

The third consensus opinion around privilege in bisexual discourses is that bisexuals do, indeed, have access to heterosexual privilege, and that as allies to the lesbian and gay movement, we should be accountable and take responsibility for the privileges that we receive. This, too, is mentioned in passing by many writers, presuming the correctness of the fact rather than explaining why it is so. For example, in her essay "Traitors to the Cause? Understanding the Lesbian/Gay 'Bisexuality Debates'" Elizabeth Armstrong mentions that:

> *Some bisexual activists . . . try to emphasize the alignment of bisexuals with gays and lesbians by emphasizing the*

vulnerability of bisexuals to homophobia and gay-bashing from straights, while acknowledging that bisexuals do have access to heterosexual privilege.

In yet another essay from the same book, Brenda Blaisingame writes that she expects "heterosexual-identified bisexuals" to "own their access to power and privilege," but at no point takes the time to tell her readers what "heterosexual-identified bisexuals" exactly are, and what sort of privileges they are presumed to carry.

Two rare texts that do try to engage more deeply with this topic from this third side are to be found online: In a blog entry titled "passing and privileges," blogger Sarah of *Bi Furious!* describes her experience of passing as straight and her participation in "straight privilege," and tries to delineate the mechanisms by which it works. In a blog post titled "Bisexuals and straight privilege," blogger Pepper Mint of *freaksexual* attempts to encourage bisexual "accountability" of alleged access to heterosexual privilege.

All of the texts representing this view, however, seem to stem from the same root as the previous argument: that inasmuch as bisexual experience resembles gay and lesbian experience, bisexuals are oppressed; inasmuch as bisexual experience resembles straight experience, bisexuals have access to privilege. You may notice that both sides of this coin reduce bisexuality to either homosexuality (which results in oppression) or heterosexuality (which results in privilege), repeating the familiar notion that no unique bisexual experience, or oppression, exists. Yet another problem here is that most everyone seem to "know" exactly what they are talking about, dismissing the need to elaborate or prove their point before moving on to discuss something else, or to discuss "what we should do next" (whether that is fighting against biphobia, or taking responsibility for our privileges).[23]

I'd like to take a different route to understanding power and privilege around bisexuality, not by trying to prove or disprove it, nor by running ahead into the proverbial "next point," but by taking a more epistemological approach: examining where the idea of bisexual privilege comes from, why and how it emerges, and what could be done with it.

TAPPING INTO PRIVILEGE

As we might recall from chapter 1, Julia Serano says:

> *For me, the word "reinforcing" is a red flag: Whenever somebody utters it, I stop for a moment to ask myself who is being accused of "reinforcing" and who is not. There is almost always some double standard at work behind the scenes.*

In this case, *reinforcing* can be substituted for *privileged*. When Serano talks about *reinforcing*, she is referring to allegations that certain identities "reinforce" heterosexism or the gender binary. Likewise, allegations of *privilege* place the accused groups as reinforcing—and benefiting from—social hierarchies. These allegations—especially within LGBT communities—often coincide with existing hierarchies, but not the way that you'd expect it: The most marginalized groups are usually the ones most likely to face these allegations.

For example, in the American lesbian movement during the 1970s and 1980s, various groups such as butches, femmes, kinksters, sex workers, polyamorous people, transgender women, transgender men, bisexuals, and many more people, were (and in many cases, still are) considered to be beneficiaries of, or contributers to, heterosexual privilege—therefore unfit traitors to be rejected from community spaces.[24]

In a movement organizing itself around oppression, groups and people perceived as having privilege are also perceived as illegitimate within the movement and often even as a hindrance. In such settings, allegations of privilege, as an idea that carries negative connotations, can often be used as a weapon by the dominant groups against the marginalized ones. This is not to say, of course, that calling people out on their unchecked privileges and oppressive behaviors is always a weapon or should be abandoned as a method. On the contrary, critically looking into power hierarchies and how they influence our behaviors toward one another is one of the most important tools available for creating revolutionary communities. When the privilege discussed is "real," or materially detectable, then being aware of and accountable for our privileges is vital for creating change, both for ourselves and for our movements. However, in many other cases, the "privilege" allegations do not check out (materially) and the underlying power structure needs to be reexamined.

One such case is, of course, that of bisexual access to heterosexual privilege. As we've seen in chapter 2, bisexuals often find themselves on the bad end within many fields of life and society, in a way that proves allegations of privilege to be misdirected at best and suspicious at worst. If the allegations of privilege made against bisexuals were correct, then we could have reasonably expected to find them reflected in the statistics somewhere between gays/lesbians (lowest) and straights (highest).[25] However, looking into the *Bisexual Invisibility* report and other studies, it is clear that this is not the case: Bisexuals are, on average, worse off than both gays and lesbians, and straights.

The trope usually used to justify the "privilege" claim is bisexual *invisibility:* Since being in a different-gender relationship *resembles* heterosexuality, bisexuals have access to heterosexual privilege. Pepper Mint lists three kinds of heterosexual privilege: the privilege of being seen as straight, the privilege of being in a man/woman relationship, and the privilege of knowing oneself to be straight. He then proceeds to claim that bisexuals have access to the first two privileges, since they are sometimes seen as straight, and since they are sometimes in man/woman relationships. I'll go on to deconstruct that in just a minute.

In her article "How to Recognize a Lesbian: The Cultural Politics of Looking Like What You Are," Lisa Walker criticizes the weight given to visibility in queer and lesbian politics. Walker observes that visibility is often thought about as the end-all of oppression, presuming that people who are visible as lesbians or queers are more vulnerable to oppression than people who aren't. In addition to this, it is also presumed that visibility is more politically subversive, since visible queerness is supposedly more challenging to the heteronormative mainstream. This view leaves behind those lesbians who are invisible (and in particular, femme lesbians and lesbians of color), who do not receive acknowledgment both in terms of the oppression that they suffer and in terms of their subversion of heteronormativity and contribution to challenging mainstream society. This, in turn, places butch lesbians and white lesbians both as the most oppressed, and the most subversive of lesbian identities, reinforcing masculinist and racist social hierarchies within lesbian communities.

Walker's critique is particularly useful in regard to bisexuals. In many discourses, bisexuality is depicted as *necessarily and always invisible* whereas homosexuality and lesbianism are dubbed as *necessarily and always visible*. Continuing from this axiom, lesbians and gays are normally considered both more oppressed and more subversive than bisexuals, in ways that rely completely on the visible aspects of bisexual identity and experience, treating the part as if it was whole.

To return to Pepper Mint in light of Walker's theory, his reliance on bisexual in/visibility becomes clear: "Being seen as straight" is quite self-evident; however, I would also like to claim that the category of "being in a man/woman relationship" is also visibility-focused. The term implies a "straight" relationship, echoing Blaisingame's "heterosexual-identified bisexuals." Presuming that a "man/woman relationship" receives heterosexual privilege presents it as heterosexual in practice, regardless of the identities of the people inside it, meaning that if it "looks" straight, then it "must" be so. However, a "man/woman relationship" with a bisexual person in it, is not a "straight" relationship—it is a relationship that *visually resembles* heterosexuality, but might, in fact, be far from it.

The term *man/woman relationship* is also cissexist. It seems to be presumed that the writer means any relationship resembling that of a cisgender man with a cisgender woman. However, many couples exist that may appear to be so but are actually not; namely, relationships with transgender and genderqueer people in them. Pepper Mint also seems to neglect the fact that many genderqueer and nonbinary gender bisexuals will *never actually be* in a man/woman relationship, since they do not identify as men or as women. Even if some of their relationships may visually appear as a "man/woman relationship," they are not in fact so.

Reducing bisexual experience around oppression to the visual aspect only, necessarily means erasing all those other aspects of bisexual oppression that aren't perceived as visible or intuitive. As we've seen in chapter 2, this means most of them. Just to recall: Bisexuals experience oppression through cultural erasure, exploitation, marginalization, verbal, physical, and sexual violence, stereotyping, and internalized biphobia (just to name a few), and in the fields of economics, employment, education, health, mental health, and interpersonal relationships (again, to name a few). Indeed, remembering these multiple faces of monosexism might help us keep in mind that oppression of bisexuals is both widespread and often intangible, and that most of these forms of monosexism work against bisexual people independent of their "visibility" and regardless of their current relationship status. In fact, this reduction to visibility can be thought about as part of the oppression itself, obscuring the effects of monosexism and erasing bisexual experience.

A good analogy to this might be transgender people in mixed-gender relationships. For the sake of the argument, let's imagine a trans woman and a trans man in a relationship together. In terms of visibility, their relationship conforms to the two first kinds of heterosexual privilege listed by Pepper Mint: assuming for a moment that they both pass full time, they are likely to be seen as straight; they are also in a man/woman relationship. However, despite the benefits of access to state-sanctioned marriage and other legal benefits, claiming that these people partake in heterosexual privilege would be inaccurate at best and erasing at worst. Transgender people (including those who pass full time and those in mixed-gender relationships) face a myriad of visible and invisible oppression, including lack of access to medical care and mental health care, unemployment and work discrimination, homelessness and housing discrimination, lack of access to education, police brutality and persecution, physical violence (including several hundred murders per year around the world), sexual violence, harassment, bullying, and many more—all in addition to various effects of internalized transphobia, such as depression, self-harm, and suicide.

Here it might be relevant to remember that transgender people have historically indeed been (and in many cases, still are) accused of pursuing heterosexual privilege, imagined as traitors and closet cases who would rather transition into the "opposite sex" than be out as "gay" or "lesbian."[26] As I hope is obvious to my readers, this view is distorted, being based on the same focus on visibility as the sole indicator of oppression and privilege, just like the allegations of bisexual access to heterosexual privilege. In both these cases, multiple variables of oppression and lived experiences of bisexual and transgender people are erased and denied in light of surface impressions.

These problems demonstrate the limitations of the "heterosexual privilege" discourse in relation to bisexuals and bisexuality. Looking into things from the "privilege" perspective might lend weight to distortion of power relations around bisexuality, and serve as vehicle for monosexist views. Seeing as such, I would like to propose a change in terms around this issue: from privilege into passing. Such a change, I hope, would enrich our understandings of power, hierarchies, and oppression around bisexuality and in bisexual people's lives, allowing us to view the complexities of this issue, as well as its subversive potential.

PASSING UNTO POWER

Passing usually means being perceived by others as a member of the dominant group. This can be any group at all, though the term most often refers to three sites: racial, gender, and sexual groups. The term first gained prominence in nineteenth-century United States, as black people used passing as a method for escaping slavery. Gender passing in the past mostly referred to the phenomenon of women passing as men (especially in contexts of war), and today mostly refers to transgender people passing as cisgender. Sexual passing usually refers to queer people passing as straight. In a bisexual context, the term *passing* is more ambiguous and can be used to describe passing as either straight or lesbian and gay. This is because bisexuals are usually a marginalized/non-default group within *any* sexual setting, placing both groups of straights and lesbians and gays as dominant over bisexuals.[27]

The act of passing can be willing or coercive, by intention or by default. When done willingly, or intentionally, passing is usually done in order to avoid the effects of oppression that come with being part of a marginalized group. Here the original meaning of black people escaping slavery might shed light on other types as well, as any type of passing can be thought of within this framework. People who pass as members of a dominant group are able to achieve access to power and resources that are withheld from them as people of a marginalized group. They are also able to avoid social punishments that they would be subject to by force of belonging to a marginalized group, and thus passing might be thought of as an act of self-protection.

Before I start discussing this in detail, I need to say that although I will be describing bisexual passing in conjunction with other types of passing, it is not my intention to compare between them. Monosexism is not racism, and the oppression of bisexuals pales in comparison with slavery and oppression of black and brown people. Likewise, the oppression of trans and genderqueer people, and of disabled people (also mentioned later on) is very different to that of bis. My intention is not to draw lines of similarity or suggest that these types of oppression are all the same. They are not. Rather, it's my intention to draw meanings and shed light on bisexual passing through other histories and types of passing. By doing so I hope to alert my readers both to the histories and meanings of passing in general, and to the meanings that bisexual passing can lend from them. Later on in the book, I will specifically address connections and intersections between bisexuality and transgender, and between bisexuality and racialization.

INTENTIONAL PASSING

As slaves, black people had to suffer a lifetime of hard labor, torture, humiliation, violence, rape, and many other severe forms of oppression at the hands of white people. As escaping slaves, black people were subject to manhunts and persecution, and, if caught, to heavy lashing, beating, starving, and other forms of severe physical punishment, sometimes even leading to their deaths. Those who managed to escape but remained visibly black still had to deal with intense racism, segregation, poverty, hostility, violence (including institutionalized violence such as prisons and criminalization), and total lack of civil rights (much of which persists to this day). Passing as white has thus allowed those who succeeded both to avoid the penalties of being black in Amerikkka and to gain access to such resources as money, food, housing, clothes, medicine, social status, and, generally, perception as an equal human being—resources which were all but withheld from them as blacks (and in many cases, still are).

With this in mind, we might argue that bisexuals face a myriad of social punishments and sanctions while being denied power and resources. Specifically, bisexuals are subject to the many forms of monosexism and biphobia described earlier, and are withheld from positions of power and resources in contexts of work, community, social status, and many more (as specified in chapter 2). Thus by passing, bisexuals might avoid the social sanctions cast upon those known to be bisexual, and be able to access power and resources otherwise denied them.

However, intentionally passing full time also carries a price:

that of perceiving oneself as other than presented externally. In the case of black people passing for white, this often entails erasure of one's personal history and denial of one's family, at enormous personal cost. It also means living in constant fear of discovery: For example, a famous passage in Reba Lee's autobiographical book, *I Passed for White,* describes how she spent all her months of pregnancy worried that her baby would be born with dark skin. When she had a miscarriage, of a baby boy, she realized that she forgot to wonder whether it was a boy or a girl throughout these months. She then reports of being so relieved that the baby was white that she was able to feel no grief about his death. In addition, passing full time for black people means having to listen to white people speak out their racist opinions without being able to call them out on it, for danger of self-exposure. And finally, it means that if one is discovered to be black, one is stripped of all resources, power, and status that one has gained so far, and is again relegated to one's default oppressed status. Thus the whole apparatus of passing is incredibly fragile, as the benefits gained are dependent solely on one's status as a member of the dominant group.

To draw a parallel, for bisexuals, intentionally passing full time (either as straight or as gay or lesbian) often means not only having to hide one's identity, but also one's past (or present) relationships and one's romantic or sexual desires. It means constantly experiencing the fear of discovery, along with the knowledge that one's treatment as an equal will end upon exposure of one's bisexuality, often to be replaced with rejection and isolation. It also means hiding one's opinions and not being able to call out people's biphobic or LGBT-phobic remarks for fear of discovery. And of course, it means that one is only able to maintain their access to certain power and resources (whether in a heterosexual, or lesbian or gay contexts) just as long as one passes as monosexual.

A classical example of this would be closeted bisexual men married to straight women, one of the LGBT groups most scapegoated for pursuing heterosexual privilege through passing. Passing as straight enables these men to have access to such resources as marriage, children, family support, employment opportunities and promotion at work, or social status. However, passing also entails constant hiding of one's bisexual identity, lack of support for their bisexuality with no ability to talk about it, and the consequent results of depression, denial, and other forms of external and internalized biphobia described in chapter 2. For those who find their outlet in cruising and casual sex, it also means being at risk of contracting HIV and other STIs through unsafe sex, as well as being less likely to know about the importance of safer sex practices, as this group of men is almost never targeted by information programs and brochures. It also means having to deal with straight people's biphobia and LGBT-phobia without being able to call them out on it for fear of exposure. And, most importantly, it means that if they do decide to come out as bisexual (or if they are discovered to be bi), they are likely to face such punishments as divorce, loss of their relationship, loss of their children, loss of family support (including their family of origin), and a general loss of social status and heterosexually dependent benefits and privileges. Thus, these men's access to "heterosexual privilege" is entirely dependent upon their ability to successfully pass as straight, and stops at the moment when their heterosexuality is "proven otherwise." In addition, whereas many gay men in similar circumstance might expect support from the gay community, this kind of support is often withheld from bisexual men. This means that in order for these men to access gay community resources and support, they would be obliged to pass as gay, with many implications similar to those for passing as straight.

COERCIVE PASSING

Passing isn't only intentional, however, and can also be coercive or done by default. What this means is that, unless (and until) proven otherwise, people of any group are most likely to be assumed as members of the dominant group. In a society which constructs itself around a single human default standard (male, white, heterosexual, cisgender, nondisabled, middle class, etc.), all others are marked by deviation from this single standard: The dominant identity is obvious and unmarked, while marginalized identities always require assertion. The "deviation" itself is never assumed as the default: Unless visibly and clearly presenting otherwise, one is never automatically presumed to be racialized, queer, trans, disabled, and so on. Even in regard to cisgenders, research shows that it's "easier" for people to identify male than female features, meaning that the default "visible" person in our culture is male "unless proven otherwise." Concurrently, bisexuality as an identity is never presumed since it is always a deviation and never a default (or even an option).

Coercive passing can be thought of as an alternative term to *invisibility*. Whereas *invisibility* suggests that one is simply "unseen" in their marginalized identity, the concept of coercive passing suggests that one isn't simply invisible but actively perceived as something other than they experience themselves to be (as influenced by social construction and power hierarchies). Thus, being "invisible" in fact means being actively, coercively passed off as a member of the default/hegemonic group, entailing erasure as well as more subtle forms of oppression. This is particularly relevant to the concept of *bisexual invisibility*—taken from this perspective, it's easy to understand that bisexuality and bisexual people are not invisible, but are being actively and coercively erased.

In addition to the difficulties experienced by knowing oneself to be other than what you're presenting, people who pass coercively are forced to deal with the effects of erasure. This means that in addition to being exposed to the dominant group's unchecked oppressive behavior and speech, and to knowing that you're only being treated well because (and only as long as) you're presumed to be something you're not, one is also exposed to other people's doubts, disbelief, questioning, or denial of one's marginalized status, and to the need to "prove" oneself as a "true" member of one's "original" group.

For example, in her article "Passing for White, Passing for Black," American light-skinned mixed-race artist Adrian Piper writes:

For most of my life I did not understand that I needed to iden-
tify my racial identity publicly and that if I did not, I would
be inevitably mistaken for white. I simply didn't think about
it. But since I also made no special effort to hide my racial
identity, I often experienced the shocked and/or hostile reactions
of whites who discovered it after the fact. I always knew when
it had happened, even when the person declined to confront
me directly: the startled look, the searching stare that would fix
itself on my facial features, one by one, looking for the telltale
"negroid" feature, the sudden, sometimes permanent with-
drawal of good feeling or regular contact—all alerted me to
what had transpired. Uh-oh, I would think to myself helplessly,
and watch another blossoming friendship wilt.

In another instance, she writes:

I have sometimes met blacks socially who, as a condition of
social acceptance of me, require me to prove my blackness by
passing the Suffering Test: They recount at length their recent
experiences of racism and then wait expectantly, skeptically,
for me to match theirs with mine. [. . .] I would share some
equally nightmarish experience along similar lines, and would
then have it explained to me why that wasn't really so bad, why
it wasn't the same thing at all, or why I was stupid for allowing
it to happen to me.

This double-edged effect of passing might shed light on many bisexuals' experience, as we often have to deal with other people's doubts and scrutiny about our lives, our choices, and our identification. To pass by default means constantly being presumed and treated as something other than what you are, to always be accepted on the premises that you are *not* bisexual. It means fearing the moment of disclosure, and seeing the spark die in another person's eye as the word "bisexual" hits the surface, to always know to expect rejection. It means being scrutinized and asked to "prove" ourselves: Often we are presented with the demand to provide lists of lovers and sexual affairs in order to prove our bisexual status. In lesbian/gay settings, we are constantly asked to prove the oppression that we suffer, presuming that, because they can't see it, then it doesn't exist at all.

In an essay called "A Hard Look at Invisible Disability," Cal Montgomery suggests an alternative way of thinking about invisible disability (the kind of disability which is not visibly detectable, such as some chronic illnesses, visual and auditory disabilities, mental disabilities, etc.). She writes:

> *In the disability community, we speak as if some kinds of disability were visible, and others weren't. Let me suggest a different approach: Think about the ways different kinds of disability have become more familiar, and more visible, to you as you've gotten to know more disabled people.*

Montgomery continues to say that certain visual signals (or "tools") have become synonymous with disability, such as wheelchairs, white canes, hearing aids, etc.

> *But the tools are only the first step to visibility. The second step is the behavior that is expected, given a particular set of tools. The person who uses a white cane when getting on the bus, but then pulls out a book to read while riding; the person who uses a wheelchair to get into the library stacks but then stands up to reach a book on a high shelf; the person who uses a*

*picture-board to discuss philosophy; the person who challenges
the particular expectations of disability that other people have
is suspect. "I can't see what's wrong with him," people say,
meaning, "He's not acting the way I think he should." "She's
invisibly disabled," they say, meaning, "I can't see what barriers
she faces."*

Montgomery is here drawing attention to passing by default as
informed by social constructions of what it "means" to be disabled.
Cultural knowledge on disability that is solely based on visual signs
misses out on nonvisible disability by default. This means that disabled
and chronically ill people whose disabilities are not visibly detectable are
likely to pass as nondisabled by default. In addition to being a criticism
of society's focus on visibility (much like Lisa Walker's), Montgomery's
text sheds light on the hierarchy of cultural knowledge: It is more difficult for people to understand and detect nonvisible disabilities because
they *know* less about it—and the reason why they know less about it is
that hegemonic knowledge about disability produces visible disabilities
as the only kind of disability that exists. This means that not only is there
a hierarchy of visibility at work here, but also a hierarchy of knowledge.

For nonvisibly disabled and chronically ill people, passing by
default means constantly having one's disability questioned. It means
being told that one doesn't actually have a disability, being presumed
able to perform certain tasks and subsequently perceived as fraudulent,
lazy, stubborn, or selfish when attempting to assert one's boundaries. It
means being less likely to have one's needs accommodated both by other
people and by institutions. It also means being harassed by others for
accommodations that one has managed to achieve. For example, in her
article "My Body, My Closet," Ellen Samuels writes:

*Nonvisibly disabled people who use disabled parking permits
are routinely challenged and harassed by strangers. Recently,*

*a sympathetic nondisabled friend of mine told me that a
colleague of hers had reported triumphantly her detection
of someone using a disabled parking permit illegally. The
colleague's conclusion was based on the fact that the woman she
saw getting out of the car was young and "well-groomed" and
had no sign of a limp. In addition, the colleague continued, she
had followed the woman closely as they entered the building
and had ascertained that she was breathing "normally" and so
could have no respiratory impairments.*

According to Samuels:

*Such constant and invasive surveillance of nonvisibly disabled
bodies is the result of a convergence of complicated cultural discourses regarding independence, fraud, malingering, and enti-
tlement; the form it takes almost always involves a perceived
discontinuity between appearance, behavior, and identity.*

Many things here might shed light on the case of bisexuality, especially as far as it concerns "proving" our bisexuality and our oppression.
Hegemonic discourse about what it means to be queer (and therefore,
oppressed as queer) constructs queerness as a series of visual markers:
certain appearances, certain gender performances, certain clothes, and
above all, the ubiquitous "walking hand in hand on the street" (or simply being in a same-gender relationship). Bisexual people who, for any
reason, do not give out these signs are automatically read as heterosexual by default, because what people "know" about queerness does not
include markers of bisexuality.

A significant difference in this matter between bisexuality and nonvisible disability is the double-edged effect of bisexual passing: While
people with nonvisible disabilities can never seem to automatically pass
as disabled, bisexuals do often pass as queer by default—however, the

same social production of "queer" as this series of visual markers necessarily means that bisexuals who do give out these signals will automatically be read as gay or lesbian by default.

In both cases (unless the bi person in question is carrying a huge sign reading I AM BISEXUAL), it becomes impossible to successfully pass as bi or to assert bisexual identity. Thus bisexuals' visual differences from—or similarities to—homosexuality and lesbianism both hinder "proof" of bisexual identity and of bisexual oppression: Either we pass as heterosexual, and thus are perceived to not be oppressed at all, or we pass as lesbian/gay, and thus are perceived to only be oppressed inasmuch as we resemble them. Since our bisexuality is not "known" to have any visual markers, we are routinely accused of fraudulence, perceived as invisible, and forced to deal with others' doubts regarding our identities and our oppression.

HOW TO RECOGNIZE A BISEXUAL: WHEN BISEXUALS PASS

Despite the above, there still exist several forms of successful passing as bisexual—even without constantly carrying huge BISEXUAL signs. Notably, I can think of two main ways to successfully pass as bisexual: in situations where one is visibly engaged with people of more than one gender, and in situations where bisexual people successfully "recognize" each other.

In her article "What's in a Name? Why Women Embrace or Resist Bisexual Identity," Robyn Ochs says:

> *[B]isexuality only becomes visible as a point of conflict.*
> *Bisexuality becomes visible as bisexuality only in the context*
> *of complicated, uncomfortable situations: A woman leaves her*
> *husband for another woman; a woman leaves a lesbian rela-*
> *tionship for a male lover. (Emphasis in original.)*

To this we can add situations such as three-way relationships, multiple-partner relationships, cheating on a partner of a certain gender with someone of a different gender, walking in the street with two (or more) partners of different genders, being publicly sexual with partners of more than one gender, participating in group sex with people of more than one gender, and so on.

Before I go on to say what this means in practice, I need to say that I absolutely *love* the conflation of bisexuality with "complicated, uncomfortable situations" in Ochs's quote. This oscillation of meanings sets bisexuality as a disruption to order, significantly to monosexual and monogamous couplehood order. That bisexuality is only visible as a point of conflict, and discomfort speaks to its character as a social transgression and thereby a tool for change. It makes way for us to imagine bisexuality as a space for difficulty, discomfort, and disruption—not as simple disturbances, problems to be solved, or barriers to overcome, but as sites of complexity whose very virtues are contradictions, inconsistencies, and incongruities.

To return to Ochs's quote, this kind of passing means that bisexuals are completely dependent upon their (multiple) partners for successful bisexual passing. This also means that only those bisexuals who have multiple partners or who engage in any of the practices listed above are able to visibly communicate their bisexuality—and even this is only possible at specific times. Most significantly, it means that passing in this way can never be done individually, as it necessitates being seen with other people (as "passing accessories"). In addition, there's also something to be said about the very particular type of visibility that this way of passing creates for bisexuals and for bisexuality; one that might create the false impression that bisexuality only exists within these particular "disruptions" but not outside of them. And of course, this type of visibility might also constitute coercive passing for people who give out these "bisexual" visual signs but do not identify as bisexual. Such is the case, for example, for lesbians who sleep with men, for straight-identified

MSM (men who have sex with men), for pansexual or queer people, or anyone at all who experiences desire toward people of more than one gender without identifying as bisexual.

That said, this way of passing can also be an empowering way for bisexuals (who can, and who want) to publicly perform their bisexuality, to make themselves visible, and to challenge monosexist and monogamous social norms. This goes in particular to people in multiple-partner relationships or in other polyamorous and nonmonogamous arrangements. By publicly displaying both bisexuality and nonmonogamy, bisexuals (and their partners) might be able to transform or "taint" spaces otherwise presumed monosexual and monogamous. This sort of display can challenge people's ideas about acceptable types of public displays, forms of desire, and kinds of relationships. It might also create a blatant bisexual presence, using an "in-your-face" type of fabulous, outrageous, bisexual spectacle.

The second way in which bisexuals can pass as bisexual happens when bi people recognize each other. In her article "It Takes One to Know One: Passing and Communities of Common Interest," Amy Robinson suggests that passing is a kind of a three-way theater performance, wherein the person who's passing is performing a "show" to an audience of the dominant group, while the facilitator of the pass, who enables it and contributes to its success, is an "accomplice" in-group member who recognizes the other person for what they are without betraying them to the dominant group.

Now, whereas Robinson is discussing *intentional* passing, her idea of the pass as a dynamic of recognition might nonetheless be useful for looking into this type of passing. She writes:

> *A study of passing thus poses the question of identity as a*
> *matter of competing discourses of recognition. Not only is the*
> *passer's "real" identity a function of the lens through which it is*

*viewed, but it is the spectator who manufactures the symptoms
of a successful pass by engaging in the act of reading that constitutes the performance of the passing subject.*

To simplify: This means that identity is "in the eye of the beholder."
For us as bisexuals, it means that being able to recognize each other is
dependent on our ability to "allow ourselves" to read others. If we use
"the lens" through which we can view bisexuals, then bisexuals will start
appearing there.

This idea can be simply called a bidar (bi + radar)—the bisexual
version of a gaydar. It means that people are able to pick up on the
subtle visual or behavioral cues that others give out and that might indicate their (bi)sexuality. As is the case with the gaydar (or transdar), this
recognition requires two main components: practice, and the constant,
quiet presence of the option. Once one stops presuming that bisexuals are nonexistent, invisible, or undetectable, and starts looking for the
subtle signs of bisexuality, those signs will slowly become apparent. The
more experience one has in recognizing bisexuals, the more sensitive and
skillful one becomes in such identification. Of course, not all bisexuals
are recognizable, and many will easily defy the bidar, whereas others will
appear to be bisexuals without actually identifying as bi. However, many
others can still be identified, and keeping this option in our heads may
well help many of us deal with, and counter, the feeling of isolation and
lack of community that so many of us experience. Instead of advocating
a new bisexual dress code or a standard "bisexual haircut" (as is so often
done), we can just start picking up on the signs of bisexuality—they're
already there.

So how *do* you recognize a bisexual? Intuitively, intangibly. A look in
their eyes, a vibe they give out. Some people look decidedly bi, whereas
others are ambiguous; some people give a "queer" vibe, of liking people of more than one gender but not identifying as bisexual; and some

people give out no vibe at all. One person I once met had the body language of a butch lesbian with the look of a gay man. Others I've met were femme. Still others looked like butch dykes, gay bears, trans boys, and fabulous genderqueers. Not all were recognizable; for some I wouldn't have believed it. For others, I "just knew." With time, I meet and observe more bisexual people and pick up the tools for "knowing" who we are.

Of course, this mechanism of recognition doesn't have to be limited to bisexuals. In-group members don't have to identify in the same way or actually belong to the same identity group. In this way, *in-group* should be taken to mean those "in the know." No one is born with special abilities of identifying bisexuals (or identifying anyone else, for that matter), which means that anyone can learn how to do this. This includes bisexuals as well as monosexuals, asexuals, and any other group of people. The central point is keeping the option of bisexuality in mind, remembering that any person you meet might be bisexual. Once the question "Who is bisexual?" is present in one's mind, the potential of recognition follows. Monosexual and other non-bi people would do well to remember this, as it might help them avoid making presumptions about other people's sexualities.

PASSING IN THEORY
(A BI/EPISTEMOLOGY OF PASSING)

Taken as a symbol or a metaphor, passing carries various subversive meanings in and of itself. As Elaine K. Ginsberg explains in her article "The Politics of Passing," passing is a transgression: a crossing of boundaries. The word itself marks movement from one space into another, as in passing through a gate or "passing the line." The line being crossed here is one of social hierarchy, a socially manufactured line separating the privileged and the disprivileged, using categories whose very purpose is hierarchical distribution of power.

For bisexual people, these lines are multiple: the line of

heterosexuality, the line of homosexuality, the line of lesbianism, the line of queerness (even the lines of transgender and genderqueerness). All of these might be presumed, in different places and times, as the core identity categories to which a bisexual person belongs, according to her visual similarities to what people "know" of these categories. Inasmuch as visual interpretation of identities goes, all of these overshadow and are privileged over bisexuality. However, the privilege doesn't start and end with visual recognition: Visual recognition is only a symptom of the deeper lines of privilege in a monosexist system where bisexuality is produced and located as a disprivileged other, in both heterosexual and queer spaces (as described in chapter 2).

The act of passing exposes these lines and reveals these hierarchies by infiltrating the lines of the social group(s) from which one is banned. The necessity to pass in order to access privilege (in the case of intentional passing), or privilege granted on the premises of *not* belonging to a disprivileged group (in the case of coercive passing) serves as an indicator of the unequal power relations between the different groups. For example, Adrian Piper writes:

> *A benefit and a disadvantage of looking white is that most people treat you as though you were white. And so, because of how you've been treated, you come to expect this sort of treatment, not, perhaps, realizing that you're being treated this way because people think you're white, but falsely supposing, rather, that you're being treated this way because people think you are a valuable person. [. . .] To those who in fact believe . . . that black people are not entitled to this degree of respect, attention, and liberty, the sight of a black person behaving as though she were can, indeed, look very much like arrogance.*

When one stops passing for a member of the dominant group, the privileges that one had enjoyed thus far are revoked. The revoking of the privileges testifies to the existence of the boundary separating privileged and disprivileged groups, making it visible and detectable.

For example, in many bisexuals' lives, these lines are exposed in the context of dating, where an entire bisexual lore exists on whether, when, and how exactly to come out as bisexual to a potential lover. An all-too-common scenario is one where the bisexual person in question goes on a date with another (monosexual) person. The date goes well and everything seems pleasant until the moment when bisexuality is mentioned. The other person responds with shock, feels deceived, proceeds to question the bisexual person about their commitment level, HIV/STI status, or very capability to be honest. In the worst-case scenario, this is where the date ends; in the lesser-case scenario, the date might slowly draw to an end thereafter. In both cases, both parties know that they will not see each other again. Also in both cases, the bisexual person experiences rejection and disappointment on the basis of his bisexuality, on the premises of having been coercively passed off as monosexual. Of course, similar to Piper's anecdote, this scenario is only one small indication of a far broader system of oppression.

Passing also plays out on hegemonic fears of infiltration and invasion, reflecting dominant groups' fear of not being able to distinguish between "us" and "them"—themselves and "the others." This is a direct threat to the distribution of power and privilege in society, since passing, as an act, makes it impossible to differentiate "worthy" benefactors of privilege from "unworthy" targets of marginalization. It breaks down the distinction between hierarchical groups and threatens the privileged groups with loss of relative power.

For example, in her book *Crossing the Line: Racial Passing in Twentieth-Century U.S. Literature and Culture*, Gayle Wald cites a *Saturday Night Live* skit by Eddie Murphy titled "Black Like Me," in which Murphy performs in "white face" (putting on makeup so as to appear white-skinned) and goes out to New York City in order to "actually experience America as a white man." Murphy, in white face, becomes the beneficiary of white privilege, as he receives various humorous favors from his "fellow white men." The skit ends with Murphy's observation that America still has a long way to go before all people can be "truly free." Murphy, however, then goes on to reveal a row of black people disguising themselves in white face as well. "America may not be a land of equal opportunity," Murphy tells his audience, "[but] I've got a lot of friends, and we've got a lot of makeup." This skit's conclusion obviously plays off on white people's fear of not being able to tell themselves apart from black people, since passing disrupts their ability to distribute racial power and privilege hierarchically.

As it comes to bisexuality, we might recall Kenji Yoshino's observation that bisexuality subverts people's ability to distinguish between heterosexuality and homosexuality, and thus disrupts their ability to privilege some people over others. This works in two directions: the heterosexual hegemony, and the GGGG movement. In heterosexual spheres, the idea of bisexuality, and bisexual passing, makes it impossible to ascertain heterosexual (privileged) identity. Since bisexuals may well "appear" to be straight even as they act and perform their bisexuality, it becomes impossible to withhold visibility-based privilege from them on the basis of not "being" straight. What this means is that heterosexual power, status, and resources are being "shared" with an outsider, breaking the rules of the system and "stealing" those resources from their "rightful owners." In addition, this also acts out on many straight people's anxieties that they themselves might be bisexual or gay—for if there's no way to distinguish between a heterosexual and a bisexual person, then perhaps they themselves might be "unwittingly tainted." Such latent bisexuality might indeed be cause for anxiety, as it usually entails loss of privilege and power. This means that the very existence of bisexuality creates a constant anxiety on part of heterosexuals, of losing their privileged social position.

As far as it goes to the GGGG movement, as a movement generally set on catering only to the needs of white cisgender gay men, the ideas of bisexuality and bisexual passing make it impossible to privilege only gays when distributing inner-community power and resources. Simply put, the quicksilver character of bisexual passing subverts the GGGG movement's ability to prioritize the needs of only one group over those of others. In this way, bisexuality might subvert rigid identity-based politics, which only reinscribe the original lines and borders of categorization, and therefore of oppression.

On a side note: It's important to remember again that bisexuals' ability to pass does not equal unequivocal access to privilege. Even those bisexuals who do pass are still oppressed on the axis of bisexuality through a variety of invisible yet highly influential types of oppression, such as those alluded to throughout this chapter and elaborated in chapter 2.

Passing also creates a denaturalizing effect in regard to identity, meaning that it shows how identities, which are usually perceived as natural, are in fact socially constructed. Ginsberg writes that

> *the possibility of passing challenges a number of problematic and even antithetical assumptions about identity, the first of which is that some identity categories are inherent and unalterable essences: presumably one cannot pass for something one is not unless there is some other, prepassing, identity that one is.*

The idea of passing as an act of disguise presumes an essence of identity. Without a "true core," a disguise becomes impossible, for the very meaning of disguise comes from the discrepancy between what one "is" and what one is "seen" and "understood" to be. However, instead of being an essentialist notion, passing can subvert these presumptions by showing, in practice, that appearances—including one's very body—are no guarantee for the "truth" of one's identity. From this point of view, passing becomes particularly useful in demonstrating the way in which *all* identities and appearances are socially constructed, the way identities are written into our very bodies, and the enormous fragility of these constructs themselves.

In the case of bisexuality, we might look at society's insistent attempts to naturalize both homosexuality and heterosexuality, appealing to bodies, genes, hormones, and brains in order to establish that "this" (the sexuality in question) is inborn, natural, and immutable. Under this logic, one is either "born" gay or "born" straight, and thus any performance of their desires is "true to its nature." Being in a same-gender relationship presumes homosexuality, and being in a different-gender relationship presumes heterosexuality, because one's relationship choices are understood to reflect one's inner essence. Bisexuality—and bisexual passing—short-circuits this circular logic by showing that "acting gay" or "acting straight" does not necessarily equate with "*being* gay" or "*being* straight." It allows us to distrust visual presentations and to deconstruct claims of inner essences. In this way, bisexuality may again be one way out of rigid identity constructs, a way of resisting both the lines of separation imposed by them and the hierarchies built upon them.

PASSING/BI

I'd like to suggest that all of these subversive meanings carried by passing are bisexual in character, and that concurrently, bisexuality itself is an act of passing. In thinking how passing can be bisexual, we might recall from chapter 1 the various political meanings of bisexuality and the use of bisexual stereotypes. We might remember that crossing boundaries, exposing hierarchies, invading and tainting social order, and denaturalizing identities are all meanings associated with bisexuality through stereotypes and various discourses.

Such ideas might be found in several bisexual stereotypes. The stereotype of confusion and indecision marks a social anxiety of identity instability, as well as fear of change. This anxiety is reflected by the covert demand put forth in this stereotype, for bisexual people to choose a "stable" identity. We are given to understand that in order to reassure society, bisexuals need to reaffirm binary social order and take on one of two "opposing" identities: either gay or straight. This "refusal to choose" makes bisexuality particularly shifty in the terms of the dominant system of sex, gender, and sexuality under which minority-world cultures operate, making it a destabilizing force on the entire system. This destabilization echoes the effects of passing, which, as explained above, destabilizes identities by making it impossible to distinguish between members of privileged and disprivileged groups.

The stereotype of bisexuals as carriers/vectors of HIV and other STIs "carries" the image of bisexuals as invaders of heterosexual, as well as of lesbian and gay, spaces. This "fear of invasion" clearly echoes anxieties related to crossing of boundaries and subversion of distinctions. As mentioned above, passing is also perceived as a threat to these things, and is imagined as an act of crossing and transgression of boundaries even by its very name.

The stereotype of bisexuals as treacherous or unfaithful recalls the deception, invasion, and exploitation associated with passing. This stereotype presents bisexuals as people who deceive others into believing that they are something other than they "truly" are (for example, "deceive" their monosexual partners into believing that they are trustworthy). This connotation clearly echoes the idea of passing as an act of deception. (For example, Randall Kennedy defines passing as "a deception that enables a person to adopt certain roles or identities from which he would be barred by prevailing social standards in the absence of his misleading conduct").

The stereotype that bisexuals can choose to be gay or straight stands for a denaturalization of sexual-identity categories by disconnecting between sexual identities and the idea that they are inborn. As explained in chapter 1, this stereotype marks a monosexual anxiety that identities are not naturally determined, thus disrupting the connection between identities and biology. Likewise, as mentioned above, passing denaturalizes identities by showing that despite social expectations to the contrary, what one's body looks like (for example, skin tone) cannot testify to any "truth" about one's identity.

Thus, through the parallel meanings of subversion of boundaries, destabilization of categories, and disruption to order, the idea of passing might be thought about as bisexual in character. However, the parallels between bisexuality and passing do not end here: In addition to the closeness and similarities between passing and bisexuality, I'd also like to suggest that bisexuality is close and similar to passing.

The first level in which bisexuality is similar to passing resides in bisexuals' general inability to successfully pass as bi. As discussed earlier in this chapter, bi people are constantly being passed off as anything but bisexual, while only few and relatively rare incidents permit successful bisexual passing. In practice, what this means is that *to be bisexual is to pass*, to be perceived as other than what one understands oneself to be, to be taken as a member of the dominant group. The act of passing is inextricably encapsulated within bisexuality and bisexual experience.

In her essay "Lose Your Face," Mariam Fraser discusses how certain lesbian theorists describe the "bisexual" woman (quotations are in the original) as a trope whose main characteristic is inauthenticity. This inauthenticity, in Fraser's reading, originates from the "bisexual" woman's ability to be seen as something that she is not. Her ability to pass as a lesbian (or to be coercively passed off as one) creates a crisis of meaning that challenges the assumption that what one "looks like" reveals the "truth" about her. Fraser writes:

> Because the . . . "bisexual" fails to pass, the "misfit"—the discrepancy between acting and being, between what we see and what we know—is revealed. And in this misfit, the "bisexual" woman illustrates that acting and being are not after all the same or "naturally" bound.

This crisis of meaning creates further anxiety for the (imaginary) authentic lesbian in the text as she seeks to validate her own lesbian identity using eyesight and her gaze. While expecting to see her lesbianism reflected back to her from others who "look like" her, she is confounded by the "bisexual" woman, whose identity doesn't match her appearance. Thus,

> *by passing through the lesbian community the "bisexual"*
> *woman introduces the possibility that that community, and*
> *the authenticity of lesbian identities, are not after all "ideal,"*
> *that not everyone in the "community" shares the identity and*
> *therefore will not necessarily reflect the authentic lesbian back*
> *to herself . . .*

In the lesbian texts that Fraser writes about, the trope of the "bisexual" is used in order to differentiate "true lesbians" from "bisexual" pretenders, who pass as "true" lesbians, but in fact exploit lesbian women's conditioning to "service and nurturance." This differentiation brings to light two points: First, it emphasizes exactly the kind of anxiety described above. Because of the "bisexual" woman's ability to destabilize lesbian identities (by refusing to reassure their authenticity), the "authentic" lesbian (in this case, the theorist) is required to redraw the lines so as to shut out the bisexual. In other words, the theorist needs to redefine what it means to be a lesbian in order to defend herself from the confusion brought about by bi women. In this way, the entire theoretical argument in these texts rests within the anxieties raised by bisexual women regarding lesbian authenticity.

Second, the word *bisexual* seems to be enough for these theorists in order to convey inauthenticity, meaning that bisexuality "passes" this meaning without the need for an accompanying clarification. We don't need to be told that bisexuality is inauthentic, because "it just is." Thus again we can see that to *be* bisexual *is* to pass. The "bisexual" woman who passes through the lesbian community need *do* nothing in particular

in order to pass–and confound–the "authentic" lesbian's identity—
she only needs to be bisexual and to be in a lesbian community. Her
presence, as a bisexual woman, is enough to raise anxieties and destabilize identities. In this, we might see yet again that bisexuality and passing are one and the same, encapsulating one another, carrying mutual
meanings and creating similar effects.

Another level in which bisexuality encapsulates passing is in what
Clare Hemmings terms *bisexual partiality* in her article "A Feminist
Methodology of the Personal: Bisexual Experience and Feminist Post-
structuralist Epistemology." What this term refers to is a state in which
bisexuals' identities and experiences are always formed and articulated
in relation to "communities that do not recognize bisexuality as discrete (or viable), and filtered through competing discourses of identity."
Since in most locations in the world, no (explicitly) bisexual community
exists—and even if it does, it does not connect with a broader bisexual
culture—bisexuals find themselves coming to terms with our identities
in, and through, communities where we are strangers. As suggested
above, these communities almost always presume that their membership
is homogeneous, presuming bisexual identities and bisexual people out
of (imagined) existence. Simply put, in most communities, bisexuals are
never thought of, acknowledged, or accepted as bisexuals, but always as
something else. For example, in L, G, and T communities, bisexuals are
accepted only inasmuch as we "are" (or are perceived to be) lesbian, gay,
or transgender (respectively). In other communities, the parameters of
acceptance might be any descriptive factor of the community (for example, being a feminist, a geek, an anarchist, vegan, etc.); however, in none
of these spaces are we accepted on the basis of being *bisexual*.

This constant presumption that we are other than we understand
ourselves to be makes our bisexual identities particularly contested,
making us always partial to our environments, no matter what spaces
we inhabit. Hemmings writes:

Precisely because of bisexuality's production as "inauthentic,"
and the lack of separate bisexual spaces, passing as lesbian, gay,
or straight (whether intentionally or not) is inevitably a forma-
tive part of what it means to become bisexual.

To return to the meanings of passing—this bisexual experience of
partiality echoes experiences of passing in which the passer is alienated both
from their current communities and their communities of origin, never fully
part of anything, but fluent in all dialects. Here again we may see that it's
impossible to be bisexual without having the experience of passing.

In another essay called "Resituating the Bisexual Body: From
Identity to Difference," Hemmings envisions the bisexual body as a
"double agent," moving between and against multiple spaces, but never
being a part of them. Here bisexual passing might be thought of not
only as an act of *passing for* (or being *passed off as*) but also as *passing
between*. This passing between might echo the experience of people who,
following the process of passing, continue to move between different
identities and spaces linked to their current and past lives (for example,
white and black). Bisexuality in particular seems very flexible in this
regard, as it often represents not a linear journey with a beginning and
an end (as passing narratives are often imagined to be), but a complex
formation of movements in multiple, often contradicting, dimensions.
In this way, as Hemmings claims, bisexual partiality becomes "a sign of
[bisexuality's] transitivity and [its continual] reformation."

Another aspect of *passing between* is the elusiveness of bisexuality
as an identity "core," even as one is enacting their bisexuality honestly
and straightforwardly. In her article "Invisible Sissy: The Politics of
Masculinity in African American Bisexual Narrative," Traci Caroll writes:

An identity that defines itself not as subject position but as a
movement between positions suggests that what one appears to
be is always a sincere expression of one's sexual identity; there is

no true, essential, or repressed identity to be exposed
or contradicted.

Not only does this type of coercive passing imply that appearances can be deceiving (subverting people's presumptions about the relationship between appearance and identity), but it also means that since many bisexuals' behavior and performance are indeed sincere, there is no "secret identity" to expose, even when people presume that there is.

Here it's also worth mentioning that in minority-world societies, secrets are often perceived to hold an essential truth about oneself. In her blog post "10 Things We Didn't Know About Yossef/a Mekyton," Israeli blogger Yosef/a Mekyton writes:

> *In our psychologistic society, the things that are most hidden*
> *are considered most real. If someone is hiding some secret, that*
> *secret is considered more real than what is openly known about*
> *them. Thus the gay and lesbian coming-out model, for example,*
> *presumes that the most real identity is the closeted one, the one*
> *which was secret.*

The act of *passing between* eliminates the "secret," along with the perceived "gap" between appearance and identity, and thus has the potential to subvert the notion of a "true" identity.

You might have noticed that all of these meanings of bisexual passing come together to create a very particular vision of bisexuality: one associated with inauthenticity, partiality, illusion/illusiveness, hybridity, and danger. While perhaps unpalatable at first sight, these meanings can serve as one wonderful basis for bisexual politics.

* * *

TOWARD A BI POLITICS
OF INAUTHENTICITY

As we've seen, bisexual passing might cause all sorts of anxieties regarding
the stability and naturalness of monosexual identities. It might denatu-
ralize monosexual identities, since appearing monosexual is no guarantee for monosexual identity; it might disrupt the presumed uniformity
of communities and monosexual spaces, and thus also trigger anxieties
of deception and treason "from within"; according to Hemmings, the
bisexual person's partiality and her cultural production as inauthentic
are the very things that enable her to move through and between various
spaces and to be "fluent" in different subcultures; according to Caroll,
one effect of this fluidity is subversion of presumed "natural truths"
about identity.

It is impossible to be bisexual without also passing. This is because,
as bisexuals, we are constantly being coercively passed off as monosexual,
or pushed into stealth modes about our bisexual identities as a means of
gaining safety from monosexism and biphobia. Passing is also an inseparable part of bisexuality because very few distinct and named bisexual
spaces exist, and therefore as bisexuals, we find ourselves articulating
our identities always in relation to subcultures that do not recognize
bisexuality as an identity or us as bi people.

All put together, we might be able to say that to be bisexual is not
only to pass, but also to be *inauthentic*. It is to be partial, to be hybrid,
to be the metaphorical axis of deceptiveness, treason, and danger. As
I hope I've shown so far, these things are inseparable parts of bisexual
experience and of bisexual existence.

But why is this a good thing? Because all of these qualities are signs
of subversive power.

In his essay "Activating Bisexual Theory," U.K. researcher Jo Eadie
proposes the ideas of pollution and hybridity as bases for bisexual politics. Eadie invokes American anthropologist Mary Douglas's theory about

purity and danger, in which she explores the idea of pollution and dirt
in the context of society and social norms. According to Douglas, dirt is
"matter out of place"—something that is not where it's supposed to be.
Food on your plate, for example, is fine, but if it falls onto the kitchen
floor, it immediately turns into dirt and requires cleaning; a hair on your
head is a part of your body, but if it should fall it would end up in the trash.

Douglas uses the concept of "dirt" in order to question the way
that certain groups in society are considered a "dangerous pollution"
to an otherwise "pure" state. To take a common example, in minority-
world countries, asylum seekers are people in the wrong place, at the
wrong time, and often with the wrong skin color, who are therefore perceived to be infiltrating and polluting the purity of the white race and
the nation to which they migrated.[28]

With regards to bisexuality, we can very easily find this idea
reflected in many of the aspects related to passing, and in particular
within the stereotype of bisexuals as transmitters of HIV into heterosexual and lesbian populations. According to Douglas's analysis, one might
say that bisexuals represent dirt and pollution since they are *always* out
of place. The fact that the overwhelming majority of cultural spaces are
defined as either straight or gay means that bisexuals will always dirty
the purity of this presumed monosexuality.

Douglas concludes that "dirt is the by-product of a systemic
ordering and classification" and argues that the will to eliminate dirt
represents a social attempt to control and organize the environment.
This means that the cultural concept of dirt and pollution has very
little to do with "real" (life-threatening) danger, and much more to do
with social categorization and order. This is why Douglas supports the
idea of pollution as conducive to social change, writing that "purity
is the enemy of change, of ambiguity and compromise." According
to her (and as Eadie puts it), the best way of dealing with such dirty
"category violations" is to "find some way of acknowledging them, in
order to disrupt existing limited patterns." "Pursuing this last option,"

he continues, "requires models of a non-devouring relationship to difference, which operate by miscegenation and hybridity, in celebration
of boundaries transgressed and never simply unified."

One of these models suggested by Eadie is that of the cyborg—a
political manifesto put together by American feminist theorist Donna
Haraway. In her article "A Manifesto for Cyborgs: Science, Technology,
and Socialist-Feminism in the Late 20th Century," Haraway presents
a political mythology of cyborgs as a metaphor for the transgression of
binaries. The cyborg—cybernetic organism—is a patchwork of identities, combining multiple components into a single body. A hybrid combination of organism and machine, the cyborg represents a whole made
out of parts, and stands for "transgressed boundaries, potent fusions,
and dangerous possibilities." Echoing Douglas, Haraway writes, "cyborg
politics also insist on noise and advocate *pollution*, rejoicing in . . . illegitimate fusions" (emphasis mine); echoing Hemmings, the cyborg represents "*partiality*, irony, intimacy, and perversity" (emphasis mine).

According to Haraway's parable, the cyborg takes pleasure "in the
confusion of boundaries" and "responsibility in their construction." It is
not a creature of unity and wholeness—the cyborg "would not recognize
the Garden of Eden." Instead, the cyborg is about resistance, about "oth-
erness, difference, and specificity," a "many-headed monster" who is not
afraid of "partial identities and contradictory standpoints."

Why the cyborg might be considered bisexual may very well be
obvious by now, as it shares so many of the same qualities we've seen
attached to bisexuality. Like the cyborg, bisexuality is made up of multiple, sometimes contradicting components. Bisexuality is a patchwork
identity, always partial in the sense that we articulate our identities based
on the leftovers that we scavenge from other spaces, communities, and
identities. Confusion, infiltration, and pollution of boundaries is one
more quality associated with bisexuality that is shared with the cyborg.

For Haraway, the cyborg is a way of approaching politics without trying to unify various standpoints, a way of recognizing multiplicity and difference within any group and society as a whole. It's also about learning to identify and resist dominant power structures. While the cyborg might often be an "illegitimate offspring" of these very structures, it does not follow in their footsteps, and instead uses its mixed heritage to "seize the tools" of power and to "subvert command and control." According to Haraway, "cyborg imagery can suggest a way out of the maze of dualisms" constructed around us by society. "It means both building and destroying machines, identities, categories, relationships, spaces, stories." She concludes: "I would rather be a cyborg than a goddess."

Another model that I'd like to suggest is that of the *mestiza,* the mixed-race Chicana. Articulated by Chicana feminist Gloria Anzaldúa in her book *Borderlands/La Frontera: The New Mestiza,* the mestiza is a hybrid identity made up of multiple races, locations, and cultures, containing contradictions and complexities within a single whole.

The mestiza might perhaps be best introduced through this (rather bisexual) quote by Anzaldúa from her essay "La Prieta":

> *I am a wind-swayed bridge, a crossroads inhabited by whirl-*
> *winds. . . You say my name is ambivalence? Think of me*
> *as Shiva, a many-armed and -legged body with one foot on*
> *brown soil, one on white, one in straight society, one in the gay*
> *world, the man's world, the women's, one limb in the literary*
> *world, another in the working class, the socialist, and the occult*
> *worlds. A sort of spider woman hanging by one thin strand of*
> *web. Who, me confused? Ambivalent? Not so. Only your labels*
> *split me.*

The mestiza might be thought of in conjunction with Haraway's cyborg. Like the cyborg, she lives between and on the borders of Western binary constructions. A "hybrid," "mutable," "malleable species with a rich gene pool," the mestiza "is a product of crossbreeding" who speaks "half and half" and both straddles and transcends such dualities as subject/object, white/of color, male/female, and straight/gay. Her ambiguity and plurality mean that "she can't hold concepts or ideas in rigid boundaries," a quality with which she copes by "developing a tolerance for contradictions" as well as for ambiguities. Anzaldúa writes:

> As a mestiza I have no country, my homeland cast me out; yet all countries are mine because I am every woman's sister or potential lover. (As a lesbian I have no race; my own people disclaim me; but I am all races because there is the queer of me in all races.) I am cultureless because, as a feminist, I challenge the collective cultural/religious male-derived beliefs of Hispanics and Anglos; yet I am cultured because I am participating in the creation of yet another culture, a new story to explain the world and our participation in it, a new value system with images and symbols that connect us to each other and to the planet. Soy un amasamiento, I am an act of kneading, of uniting, and joining that not only has produced both a creature of darkness and a creature of light, but also a creature that questions the definitions of light and dark and gives them new meanings.

Similar to the mestiza, bisexuality is a hybrid identity, mutable and malleable in that it's often given to change. Bisexuality is made up of the cultural bits and pieces that we, bisexuals, scavenged, and our fluency in multiple subcultures could certainly be seen as speaking "half and half." Like the mestiza, bisexuals are homeless; our communities have cast us out, yet all communities are ours because every person is our sibling or potential lover. Out of our homelessness, we might create another culture, new stories, and new questions.

The mestiza stands in contrast to racial purity and to essential/inner core identities. Her ambiguity and complexity mean, in Douglas's language, that the mestiza is a form of social pollution, a way of challenging social categories and subverting social order. The mestiza might offer us a way of both transgressing and transcending boundaries, creating, in Haraway's words, a "'bastard' race of the new world." Thus the mestiza marks yet another way of using such qualities as partiality, hybridity, pollution, and danger in order to affect social change.

What all of this means for bisexual politics is that we should double-check our positions. As we've seen in the discussion about stereotypes in chapter 1, when encountering biphobia, bisexual activists usually respond by insisting that bisexuality is *very* authentic, *very* stable, and *very* coherent. Viewed through Douglas's theory, these notions may very well seem like an attempt to reassure hegemonic order and to "clean bisexuality up" from the dirt and pollution that it represents. But instead of stressing what Douglas and Anzaldua might call the "purity," and what Haraway might call "organic wholeness," of bisexuality, we should try utilizing the force that bisexuality holds as an impure, inauthentic, and hybrid identity.

What I mean is that we work *through* pollution, *through* invasion, and *through* danger to social order, that we fuck things up and then build anew. This means giving up on the notion that we need to redeem bisexuality by being "better than good" or "purer than pure," and taking up the subversive options held in a bisexuality that is disturbing, inconsistent, incoherent, contradictory, and multiple. Instead of trying to prove ourselves as worthy of mainstream recognition, a radical bisexual politics would adopt the idea of bisexual inauthenticity and use it as a tool for breaking down the rules of identity politics and sexual categorization. Instead of trying to unify differences, we need to celebrate them. What we need is to take up pollution and hybridity as metaphors through which to disrupt hegemonic order and create social change.

At this point, it needs to be stressed that in this I do not mean unification of sexual and social categories, as is sometimes attempted in certain bi discourses. Claiming that "everyone is bisexual really," that "we are all simply queer," or that "we're all just people" erases differences. Rather than celebrating difference, this creates, as in Tolkien's *Lord of the Rings,* "one category to rule them all." Instead of subverting social categorization, we end up preserving it.

I'm stressing this not only as a way of avoiding one certain hole that bisexuals seem very good at digging ourselves into, but also because I need to be accountable to my sources. In the cyborg manifesto, Donna Haraway writes that the cyborg "has no truck with bisexuality, pre-Oedipal symbiosis," or "other seductions to organic wholeness through a final appropriation of all the powers of the parts into a higher unity." Haraway connects bisexuality with exactly this kind of unifying or utopian discourse that stands in contrast to cyborg, mestiza, and pollution metaphors. She makes this connection because at the time of her writing, bisexuality was indeed propagated in academic writing as a sort of "origin and utopian promised land" (as described by Michael Du Plessis in his essay "Blatantly Bisexual; or: Unthinking Queer Theory"). We still need to be wary of falling into those patterns, as the notion of bisexual utopianism still carries much currency in popular views on bisexuality.

In addition, neither does all this mean giving up on bisexual identity, as so many people would have us do (especially upon hearing such arguments as the ones above). The power of bisexuality as a hybrid identity can only work if bisexuality as a word is maintained, since it is this identity, in particular, that provides us with this particular option in this particular way. Disseminating bisexuality, then, would be counterproductive to the political pursuits I describe above, since my intention is for them to be specifically *bisexual.*

What I mean, however, is for bisexual politics to stop working though methods of assimilationism and normativity and to start working through methods of danger and deconstruction. It means refusing the social appeal for bisexuality as a reassuring and docile identity, and beginning to utilize the discomforting, dangerous aspects of it. It means shifting our points of view in questions of normativity, acceptability, or palatability, starting to question the power hierarchies underlining these stances and to oppose them. It means refusing to reassure hegemonic order that we are not a threat to it, and instead reclaiming these threatening powers for ourselves and using them to overthrow social order.

To conclude, the ideas of privilege and passing attach to bisexuality various meanings that represent social anxiety of the breaking of order. The fact that bisexuals are always presumed to be other than we are creates a threat to the homogeneity and purity of monosexist society. Bisexual passing also exposes the often-invisible structure of monosexism, since by crossing the monosexist line, we show that it exists. Our passing also threatens people's own "pure" identities, because despite the fact that we may look or act like them, we are not in fact like them. This means that we represent their anxiety of being "polluted,"—that is, that they are like us.

These meanings all place bisexuality at the unique vantage point of an identity that is always partial, always impure, always inauthentic and hybrid. Using these meanings as methods of disruption and subversion of social order might enable bisexual politics to step outside of the system and to work toward radical social change, and subversion of binaries and hierarchies, building and destroying new categories and creating a complex, multiple, radical world.

CHAPTER 4:

Bisexuality, Feminism, and Women

The connection between bisexuality and feminism might not be intuitive for everyone. Many people might view feminism as a "sectarian" movement, only concerned with cisgender and white women's issues; others might feel identified with feminism as a movement but see no connection between feminist issues and bisexual issues; and still others might feel that making any connection between two forms of struggle against oppression only hinders both movements. In this chapter as well as the next, I would like to draw a few connections between feminism and bisexuality, and to advocate for a bifeminist politics that would benefit both movements and contribute to our understandings of both bisexuality and gender-specific oppression.

It is my opinion that no analysis of bisexual people, their oppression, or their lives could ever be complete without also looking into specifically gendered oppression (oppression working against women as women, or men as men), as similar kinds of oppression take shape quite differently in the lives of bisexual women and bisexual men. For example, the perception of bisexuals as hypersexualized (promiscuous/ will fuck anything that moves) often leads to sexual violence against bisexual women, whereas in regard to men it often leads to rejection by biphobic potential partners and thus to isolation. In many other cases, bisexual men and bisexual women suffer from completely different forms of oppression. For example, male bisexuality is often presumed to be nonexistent ("there's no such thing as bisexuality"), whereas female bisexuality is often considered to be widespread or even default ("everyone is bisexual really"). Thus, ignoring gender differences between bisexual people might impede our understandings of how oppression works around different groups of bisexuals.

Feminism is also a useful tool for bisexual politics because even within the bisexual community itself, gender hierarchies continue to exist. Regardless of the relatively low number of men in bisexual movements, it must still be acknowledged that men—and cisgender men in particular—are recipients of privilege in society, and thus carry this privilege wherever they go—including the bisexual movement. Acknowledging the importance of feminism for bisexual politics might help us work to end sexism not only "out there" in the "outside" world, but also on a "domestic," inner-community level.

At this point, you might have already noted the fact that I'm speaking only about two gender groups: women and men, an act which might appear to be perpetuating gender binarism (the presumption that only two genders exist). The reason why I allow myself to do this, for the next two chapters only, is the fact that minority-world society is gender-binary, one that actively genders each and every one of us as either "man" or "woman" whether or not we want to be, and that treats us according to that category.[29] In speaking, temporarily, in the binary terms of the system, I do not mean to agree with it or perpetuate it; on the contrary, my ultimate goal is to dismantle it. However, in order to dismantle it, we first need to look into what it does to the people it genders as "women" or "men," so that we might strike at it accurately and incisively.

QUICK INTRODUCTION: WHAT IS FEMINISM?

I take after American black feminist bell hooks, who defined feminism as "a movement to end sexism, sexist exploitation, and oppression," and define feminism as a movement to end patriarchy, all forms of patriarchal oppression, and all forms of oppression as a whole. This is the most basic ideology of most forms of feminism, and while many differ in their understandings of patriarchy, sexism, and how exactly to end them, this is the basic motivation that most of us share. (While I acknowledge that some may not, I must also acknowledge that their feminism might be a bit awry.)

I define patriarchy as a social structure in which men are the dominant group and are beneficiaries of many privileges in all fields of life by sole virtue of being gendered as men. Literally, "patriarchy" means "male rule"; it reflects a social structure in which men have both material and symbolic control over every sphere in life. Patriarchy means over-representation of men in governments and parliaments (in relation to their portion in the population); patriarchy means over-representation of men in management positions or in workplaces; patriarchy means men getting paid more for equal work; patriarchy means men holding most of the world's resources but women performing most of the labor; patriarchy means men controlling and benefiting from women's labor both outside and inside the home; patriarchy means men controlling women and their bodies via street harassment, sexual harassment, intimate violence, sexual violence, and rape; patriarchy means men controlling women's reproduction capacities through permitting or denying them birth control and/or access to abortion; patriarchy means that men and masculine behavior are appreciated and validated by society while women and feminine behavior are derided and dismissed; patriarchy means that masculine language is the rule and feminine language the exception ("mankind," "he," etc.); patriarchy means that men are encouraged to express themselves while women are encouraged to be silent; patriarchy means male control and validation above all else, at the direct expense and on the backs of women, in all of these ways, and in many others.

Here we must also remember that in minority-world cultures, patriarchy specifically refers to control held and wielded by a very particular group of men over all others. This particular group consists of white, native/citizen, college/university-educated, cisgender, heterosexual, monogamous, middle- and upper-class, nondisabled men of ages usually ranging between thirty and fifty. This particular group of men holds power above all other social groups along any and all of the axes described, and enjoys multiple forms of privilege as social rewards for belonging to the dominant group.

When I say this, it's important to remember that I am not counting separate groups of men here, but a single standard that is always invisible because it's considered "the norm." In a culture where this is the one standard, only *deviation* from these characteristics is considered an identity. Society only marks and names those characteristics that are incompatible with the single standard—this is why "women" are considered a "minority" group but men are not, and this is why "people of color" are considered as such while "white" people aren't ("white" being marked as a noncolor, in contrast with the "color" of "those other people"). Even though both these groups are the majority in the world, they are imagined as minorities because of their deviation from the standard. This is also why "transgender" is marked as an "identity group," but "cisgender" is not; why "queer" is likewise marked, but "straight" is not; and of course why "bisexual" is marked, but "monosexual" is silent.

It's important to note that in contrast to bisexual erasure (or erasure of any other group), the reason that these identities are never named and spoken is that they are considered the rule. People are considered a part of them unless and until proven otherwise, and the entire cultural production, material and symbolic alike, is set to accommodate them, their identities, and their needs. There is no need to state them because they are the *default*.

If you want an example for this, try watching some TV, reading some papers, or looking at the government (all forms of mass control and cultural production), and count how many people you see who match the single standard and how many don't. You'll find that even when some people deviate from the standard, the target audience remains the single-standard group and its tastes. You'll also find that people from marginalized groups represented in these cases will mostly be represented negatively or stereotypically. You might also find that these people will mostly only deviate from the single standard by one characteristic only (except where there's connection between characteristics, for example: Many people of color are also working class).

This also gives us a peek into how privilege works within marginalized groups and in particular in social justice and political movements (especially mainstream ones): The way that privilege is distributed in society means that in most cases, those dominating the group or the movement would only be removed from the single standard by one degree. For example, the mainstream women's movement would be mostly dominated by white, native/citizen, college/university-educated, cisgender, heterosexual, monogamous, middle- and upper-class, non-disabled *women*; the mainstream people of color movement would be mostly dominated by native/citizen, college/university-educated, cisgender, heterosexual, monogamous, middle- and upper-class, nondisabled men *of color*; the mainstream LGBT movement would be mostly dominated by white, native/citizen, college/university-educated, cisgender, monogamous, middle- and upper-class, nondisabled *gay* men; etc. In feminist terminology, this is also sometimes called *kyriarchy*, referring to the complex and intersectional character of oppression wherein a person who is oppressed in one context might be privileged in another.

It's worth noting that the mainstream bisexual movement in minority-world countries is mostly removed not by one but by two (and sometimes three) degrees from the single standard, being mostly dominated by white, native/citizen, college/university-educated, cisgender, monogamous, middle- and upper-class, nondisabled *bisexual women* (sometimes also *polyamorous*). I consider this a positive fact, but certainly not enough. Among other things, this is part of why it's important to examine issues relating to bisexual women and men separately, so as not to unify them into the single *bisexual* standard that ignores differences.

All this is to say that *patriarchy* is a term referring to the single-standard group, focusing on the gendered dominance of men and masculinity but not ending there. For me, feminism is about opposing all forms of oppression relating to patriarchy as I defined it above, including every link on the chain of privilege held by the single standard. This is why feminism, taken to this extent, is an inclusive movement for ending patriarchal oppression in the broadest sense possible. That feminist movements themselves do not always adhere to this rule is, in my opinion, less a failure of feminism as an idea and more a result of patriarchal oppression to be opposed through feminist tools.

In this chapter and the next, I use feminism as a tool for examining specifically gendered patriarchal forms of oppression against bisexual women (including transgender women) and bisexual men (including transgender men): How are bisexual women specifically oppressed as bi women? How are bisexual men specifically oppressed as bi men?

BISEXUALITY AND WOMEN

[Trigger warning: Among other things, this chapter discusses sexual violence and includes explicit descriptions of sexual harassment, sexual assault, and mainstream hardcore pornography. More warnings will be given in specific places.] There seems to be a consensus opinion among the bisexual community and the general population that female bisexuality is more socially acceptable than male bisexuality.[30] This is considered such "common knowledge" that usually no elaboration is given to this claim, and many times a step is being skipped when people simply ask each other "Why is female bisexuality more acceptable?" instead of questioning if this is really so. In fact, if you run an online search for this phrase, you'll encounter many pages asking this very question, but not even one explaining how and where exactly this is so.

A rare, but (ironically) typical paragraph can be found in British journalist Mark Simpson's blog under a post called "Curious and Curiouser" discussing biphobia against bisexual men. "It's unquestionable," Simpson writes, "that female bisexuality is today much more socially acceptable than male bisexuality, and in fact frequently positively encouraged, both by many voyeuristic men and an equally voyeuristic pop culture." "What's more," he continues, "female homosex has never been legally or socially stigmatized to anything like the same degree as male homosex." It may be difficult for those angry feminists to grasp, he says, "but 'patriarchy' was always much more concerned about where men's penises went than women's tongues." He finishes his argument by stating that "straight women" have "something to gain and little to lose by admitting an interest in other women. Rather than exile them to the acrylic mines of Planet Lesbo, it makes them more interesting, more adventurous, more modern . . . just more."

Typical, as Simpson seems to be tapping "straight" into the undercurrent of these social presumptions and explaining exactly the kind of (false) notions they're based on. Simpson bases his argument on three points: First, female bisexuality is considered "hot" and "sexy" by men and by pop culture; second, society has historically been more preoccupied with male sexuality than female; and third, "straight women" benefit from "going bi."

I'd like to treat these three points as themes for this chapter while refuting the notion of higher acceptability of female bisexuality. First, female bisexuality is appropriated and co-opted by the cisgender and heterosexual **male gaze**; second, social preoccupation with and prioritizing of male sexuality is the cause of this appropriation of female bisexuality;

and third, these two things combined constitute and generate sexual violence against bisexual women, and against all women in general.

The root reason for this lies in the threat that female bisexuality poses to patriarchy. As we've seen in chapter 2, the threat that bisexuality poses to the structures of heterosexuality

> **The male gaze** is a term coined by Laura Mulvey. It describes any form of media which puts the viewers into the presumed perspective of a heterosexual cisgender man. Following this, the male gaze is also voyeuristic and objectifying towards women.

and homosexuality can be considered the cause for bisexual erasure. This particular case operates in a similar yet different way: Instead of erasing female bisexuality per se (avoiding mentioning or naming it), media representations—and society in general—neutralize the "sting" that it carries by appropriating it into the heterosexual cis male gaze. From being a potential threat, female bisexuality is converted and rewritten into something else, something that's both palatable and convenient to patriarchy and the hetero cis male gaze, and which caters to its needs.

One can think about this in conjunction with the American "sexual revolution" of the 1960s. Until then, female sexuality was both unheard of and denied through and through. To have a sexuality, sexual needs, or sexual pleasure as a woman was not only discouraged and denied by society, but also seen as a problem in and of itself. For example, according to Freud, women who experienced clitoral orgasms were considered childish and immature, and their clitoral pleasure was considered a symptom of deeper emotional problems.

[Trigger warning: discussion of sexual violence and mainstream pornography]

During the 1960s, female sexuality began to be publicly acknowledged (though hardly accepted as legitimate even to this day); however, this acknowledgment only existed inasmuch as it pertained to cis male (hetero)sexuality. Instead of promoting women's pleasure and women-centered understandings of sex and sexuality, this new acknowledgment was only used in order to increase women's sexual availability to straight men. Women were expected to actively desire sex with men (rather than just serve as receptacles), and were often characterized as "frigid," "boring," or "prudish" if they dared to refuse sex or constitute their sexual boundaries. This, in turn, created a new type of sexual violence, as women were increasingly coerced to sexual activity using this type of argument and urging them to "loosen up," to act "liberated," or to stop being a "control freak." These attitudes, of course, survive and are widespread to this day.

A good example of this shift is the 1972 porn movie *Deep Throat*, the first pornographic film to have received wide public success in the United States. Filmed shortly following the height of the "sexual revolution" of the 60s, the film depicted the story of a young woman in search of sexual pleasure. The storyline is obviously a product of its time, as a movie revolving around a woman heroine, who is leading the plot and is seeking a way of fulfilling her independent sexuality. Quite feminist, huh? However, as we soon discover in the movie, the reason why our heroine has never experienced an orgasm is that her clitoris is located at the bottom of her throat, a plot trick providing the movie's sexual theme— the act of deep-throating. During the movie, the heroine searches for a man with a penis big enough to reach the clit at the bottom of her throat, and subsequently deep-throats a long cast of male characters.

As is clear to see, despite the *appearance* of acknowledgment and exploration of female sexuality and sexual pleasure, the movie makes use of these themes only inasmuch as they are convenient and palatable to cis male sexual needs and the heterosexual cis male gaze, pretending as if "it just so happens" that the heroine' sexual needs completely mirror this particular penis-centered act. This is an excellent example of how the concept of female sexuality is negated and neutralized by co-opting it into the male gaze and reproducing it on the exclusive terms of heteropatriarchy.

It's also worth mentioning that later on, the movie's lead actress,

Linda Boreman, admitted that her performance in the movie was entirely imposed on her by her partner at the time (who also received the payment for her acting). Famously, she said: "Every time someone watches that movie, they're watching me being raped." Thus again, we see the idea of female sexual pleasure and sexual independence being forcibly appropriated by the hetero cis male gaze, this time physically, and directly causing sexual violence against women in the name of female sexual liberation.

In light of all this, it is of little surprise that female bisexuality has received a similar treatment (as we will also see later), nor is it surprising that it similarly produces sexual coercion and violence against bisexual women (and all women in general). First, however, I would like to take a step back and explore how it is that female bisexuality poses a threat to patriarchy.

[End of trigger]

THREAT

In researching this section, I was struck by the fact that no one else has ever written about this topic before. Despite the existence of a respectable volume of feminist bisexual writings, no one seems to have taken the time to explore this basic point of how bisexuality might be threatening to patriarchy or conducive to feminism. What this means for me is that I've had to distill this theory by myself, using the few available hints from bisexual writings themselves (and many more hints from lesbian writers). That no bisexual writers have ever engaged with this topic raises a lot of questions about the way that we, as a movement, are used to thinking or talking about bisexuality. Why did no previous bifeminist writers see the need to explore these themes? This is certainly a topic for further research.

Despite this near-silence, bisexuality holds an enormous potential for subversion and disruption of the patriarchy. Out of the multiple ways in which bisexuality, women, and feminism connect together and pose a threat to patriarchy, I chose to write about three ways which I think are the most powerful and influential: First, bisexuality poses a threat to patriarchy by constituting a subversion of gender and a disruption of the continuity of sex, gender, and sexuality; second, it poses a threat through the idea of bisexual choice, which empowers bi women to engage with men only on their own terms; and third, bisexuality generates accompanied meanings of multiplicity and plurality that stand in contrast to patriarchal values of unity and singularity.

At this point, it's important to note that I am here talking only about ideas and metaphors, rather than about actual people's lives or bisexual identities. I emphasize that simply identifying as bi is not necessarily feminist or subversive in and of itself, and is certainly not enough to smash patriarchy. In order for bisexual identity to have these effects, we need to actively work on it through politics and activism.

GENDER SUBVERSION

First and foremost, bisexuality—and female bisexuality in particular—subverts the gender binary. In a presentation named "The Best of Both Worlds?" given at a recent gender studies conference in Tel Aviv University, Israeli researcher Alon Zivony claimed that the base form of monosexism is sexism. The social structure of sexism (and cissexism) sets up an oppositional model of only two sexes and genders, enforcing a strict order in which people who are **assigned a male sex at birth** are also assigned a masculine gender and a heterosexual sexuality, whereas people assigned female at birth are assigned a feminine gender and a heterosexual sexuality. These two binary sexes/genders are perceived as oppositional and mutually exclusive, dictating an oppositional structure of desire in which attraction to each gender is again considered oppositional and mutually exclusive, because of this imagined difference between men and women. According to Zivony, such a binary structure makes bisexuality unintelligble by its very nature. Men and women are perceived as so completely and irreconcilably different that the option of desiring more than one gender (within or outside the binary) seems unimaginable. The idea that an individual might desire people of more than one gender creates "a crack" in the wall of the

The sex/gender assigned at birth is the sex/gender attributed to a person at the time of birth based on the appearance of their genitals.

binary, a wall that is meant to be impenetrable. It also forces the binary open to additional options of sex, gender, and desire.

American theorist Judith Butler talks about this sequence of sex, gender, and sexuality as a continuity that is required by society in order to maintain and enforce gender and sexual order. According to Butler, "intelligible genders are those which in some sense institute and maintain relations of coherence and continuity among sex, gender, sexual practice, and desire." What this means is that in order to be understood by society, one needs to embody a "coherent" continuity of sex (male or female), gender (man or woman), and sexuality (heterosexual). For example, for a woman to be culturally understood as a woman, she needs to have been assigned a female sex at birth, to perform a feminine gender, and to be heterosexual. Having a binary-sexes body (that is, being either male or female, rather than intersex), being cisgender, and being heterosexual are the three conditions required in order to make a person intelligible in this sense. Deviation at any of these points leads to what Butler terms "gender trouble," making this person into a "disturbance" for the order of sex, gender, and sexuality, and making their gender unintelligible to the social order. Further, Butler states that the order of sex, gender, and sexuality is dependent upon the elimination of identities that threaten it, meaning that any combination of sex, gender, and sexuality that is incoherent by this single standard simply cannot exist.

American theorist April S. Callis adds that, while homosexuality and lesbianism do produce this kind of gender trouble, they are nonetheless popularly heterosexualized by imagining gay men as effeminate and lesbian women as masculinized. Their genders are imagined as complementary to their sexualities within the continuity. According to Callis, this keeps "the 'correct' gender and sexuality matched up, and [minimizes] the challenges to the gender system."

"Bisexuality, on the other hand, cannot be so easily matched, because it does not allow gender to be wholly tied with sex object choice." For example,

> A woman who sleeps with men and women cannot be read as either feminine or masculine without causing gender trouble. Either her gender is constantly changing (with her partner), or her gender does not match her sexuality. Further, by desiring men and women she has really removed herself from either gender category, as "men and women" is not an option in either masculinity or femininity.

One thing that neither Callis nor Butler emphasize is that this continuity of sex, gender, and sexuality is patriarchal, and is instrumental in upholding the patriarchal structure in minority-world (and other) societies. This is because the binaries of the continuity are arranged in order to create a hierarchy of value and domination in each category: male-assigned bodies over female-assigned bodies; cisgenderism over gender nonconformity; heterosexuality over queer sexualities, and monosexuality over bisexuality. As we saw in the introduction, the single standard of patriarchy requires a cisgender heterosexual masculinity. In order to comply with the standard, one needs to be assigned male at birth, to perform a masculine gender, and to be heterosexual. These conditions of domination both result from and uphold the system of sex, gender, and sexuality described by Butler.

French theorist Monique Wittig has written about lesbianism as a type of resistance to patriarchy that is based on gender, in a way that might be helpful for understanding bisexuality. According to Wittig in her essay

"One Is Not Born a Woman," "men" and "women" are political classes rather than natural categories, and what causes women to be socially recognized as women (in terms of gender) is their subordination to men. Lesbians' independence of men in terms of relationships (as well as in other ways) makes them, socially, into nonwomen while still remaining outside the category of men, thus transgressing social gender categories.

Wittig writes, "The refusal to become (or to remain) heterosexual always meant to refuse to become a man or a woman. For a lesbian this goes further than the refusal of the *role* 'woman.' It is the refusal of the economic, ideological, and political power of man." Later she writes, "Lesbian is the only concept I know of which is beyond the categories of sex (woman and man)." In this way, lesbian subversion of sexuality can also be seen as subversion in terms of gender categories; in turn, this subversion of gender categories creates a subversion of patriarchy. This might also apply to bisexuality.

Another model for subversion of patriarchy through sexuality is offered by American poet and theorist Adrienne Rich in her seminal article "Compulsory Heterosexuality and Lesbian Existence." Rich describes the structure of compulsory heterosexuality, a social structure whose purpose is to ensure male control of—and access to—women in various ways, through the promotion of heterosexuality as the one appropriate choice for women. According to Rich, women who feel identified with other women and prefer them as partners (in various ways and contexts) create a form of resistance to patriarchy since they disobey the structure of compulsory heterosexuality, which states that their primary identification must be with men.

While both these theories leave little room for bisexuality (and indeed, both explicitly reject it as a viable option), they might still be of use to us in acknowledging that certain types of sexuality can function as forms of resistance to patriarchy. Both Wittig and Rich show that deviating from heterosexuality comprises an act of resistance and subversion of patriarchal power structures, not only in terms of sexuality itself but also in terms of gender. By analogy, this might help us understand how bisexual subversion of gender (as described above) can also be viewed as a subversion of patriarchy. This again helps us understand how bisexuality poses a threat to patriarchy.

While this point relates to bisexuality as a whole rather than to bisexual women in particular, it's easy to think about the particular context of *female* disobedience to patriarchy as posing a unique threat to it, separate from that of other genders. This is because, as we've seen in the works of Wittig and Rich, social rules of gender and sexuality are meant to secure male dominance over women. In this way, the bisexual woman who deviates from the rules of gender creates a form of resistance to patriarchy—once because of her disobedience to those rules, and again because men's access to her is not secure.

This point is particularly relevant to bisexual transgender women, as they already break one rule of gender: that of cisgenderism. As we recall, the sex, gender, and sexuality continuity requires that a person not only be heterosexual but also cisgender: For a woman to be accepted as a woman, she needs to have also been assigned a female sex at birth. The fact that transgender women have been assigned a male (or intersex) sex at birth creates the kind of gender trouble that Butler discusses, since it disrupts the continuity. In this way, bisexual transgender women subvert gender (and thus pose a threat to patriarchy) on two points: first, by disrupting the coherence between sex and gender (by being trans), and second, by disrupting the coherence between gender and sexuality (by being bisexual).

THE POWER OF CHOICE

The second major way in which female bisexuality poses a threat to patriarchy is by symbolizing sexual choice. As we've already seen in chapter 1, bisexuality in general is already associated with the ability to choose between heterosexuality and homosexuality. In this context, the choice associated with female bisexuality poses a threat to patriarchy because bisexual women are thought to embody the choice of whether or not to have relationships with men.

One quote from Adrienne Rich might be telling here: "It seems more probable," Rich writes, "that men really fear, not that they will have women's sexual appetites forced on them, or that women want to smother and devour them, but that women could be indifferent to them altogether, that men could be allowed sexual and emotional—therefore economic—access to women *only* on women's terms, otherwise being left on the periphery of the matrix" (emphasis in original). I'd like to argue that this is the axis on which this second threat lies, and that female bisexuality in fact means a realization of this very threat.

In her article "Pleasure Under Patriarchy," American theorist Catharine MacKinnon claims that under patriarchy, women's pleasure is socially designed in accordance with men's pleasure and needs, meaning that whatever is deemed pleasurable for men is socially imposed on women and presented as something that women actually want. Taken in conjunction with the idea of compulsory heterosexuality, it is easy to see that women are not supposed to want anything related to their own pleasure, and are not even meant to be able to articulate their own will in any way that goes outside the patriarchal framework of society. Under these conditions, being able to step aside (or even outside) is subversive of the system. If women are only supposed to want what men want *of* them, then choosing something else is an act of resistance.

It's worth mentioning here that MacKinnon herself would probably say that female bisexuality (as well as any other form of female sexuality) fails to challenge patriarchy since it's constantly co-opted and reproduced by men on men's terms. I will go back to that later and claim that this appropriation comes as a backlash response to the threat posed by female bisexuality to patriarchy, that is: It's the effect, rather than the cause.

As explained above, bisexual women sidestep the patriarchal system of pleasure and compulsory heterosexuality, a sidestep that means an ability to choose. This choice of whether or not to have relationships with men enables bi women a vantage point: Much like the lesbian in Wittig's theory, they are independent of men in that they do not *require* them for relationships. What this means is that relationships and various connections with men are only *optional* for bisexual women, that they can choose whether or not to interact socially or romantically with men. This choice, in turn, empowers them to choose interactions with men on their own terms and to negotiate power and hierarchy within those interactions from a starting point of power.

One might say that this type of choice is not unique to bisexual women and that women of all orientations are just as able to make that choice. However, I would argue that as opposed to heterosexual and lesbian women, bisexuals are situated at a vantage point for this type of choice. This is not because bisexual women are inherently more likely to make that choice, but because social discourses around bisexuality mark the concept of choice as connected to it—and to female bisexuality in particular.

A useful case in point is the recurring film character of the bisexual femme fatale. This trope character is a bisexual woman, highly seductive and very dangerous, who is also often the source of trouble or conflict in the plot of the film. Her dangerousness is in particular connected to her (bi)sexuality in that she is often perceived as a sexual threat. Such characters as Catherine Trammel of *Basic Instinct*, Violet of *Bound*, or Laure of *Femme Fatale* are all (behaviorally) bisexual, and each of them is the axis of either trouble, danger, or both within their respective plots.

In an article about the bisexual femme fatale called "Stay Still So We Can See Who You Are," U.K. researcher Katherine Farrimond writes about these characters. She argues that one of the reasons they are perceived as so dangerous is that we don't know where their loyalties lie. The plots revolving around them become elongated quests for "solving the riddle" or "cracking the mystery," where both the other characters and the viewers try to comprehend whose side the bi femme fatale is on. Here we will notice that these characters' duplicity and unclear loyalties clearly reflect stereotypes about bisexual people—and bisexual women—meaning that their bisexuality comprises a significant part of the threat that they pose.

This danger that the bi femme fatale represents also stems directly from the concept of bisexual choice. The fact that these bi characters are presumed to have a choice between men and women (bisexuality in films is always shown only in terms of the gender binary) provides the basis for their duplicitousness as well as the suspicion and anxieties that they stir in other characters. Their plots invariably situate them where they must make a choice between a man and a woman in a way that creates the conflicts, mysteries, and riddles on which these plots are based. The bi characters' choice is both detrimental to the plot and is the source of the threat that she poses.

Here it's also worth noting that the threat that these characters pose is mostly a threat to patriarchy: male characters and their domination (and always a threat to monosexism and the movies' monosexual characters, in movies where no men are around). An excellent example of this is the character of Catherine Trammel in *Basic Instinct*, who might or might not be a killer of men, and who provides in herself the dangerous riddle that Nick, the male detective, must "solve." According to Israeli researcher Ronnie Halpern, the movie itself might be thought of as Nick's journey to neutralize the danger that Catherine poses to him and to other men—a straight man's journey to neutralize the danger posed to him by a bisexual woman.

The fact that the bi femme fatale is a riddle is also worth noting: A riddle indicates missing information or knowledge; in order to solve the riddle one must first possess the full knowledge of it. The bi femme fatale is a riddle because she carries knowledge that neither the characters nor (presumably) the viewers possess. Her full knowledge of "both worlds" indicates missing knowledge on part of the other (monosexual) characters. This is knowledge that only she has access to and that is ultimately the key for solving her riddle. Thus the fact that this character has a choice also indicates that she has more knowledge—knowledge that is again perceived as a threat in light of her duplicitousness and unclear loyalties.

The case of the bisexual femme fatale sheds light on how and why female bisexuality might pose a threat to patriarchy, since these movies present female bisexual characters who represent this very threat. What it tells us is that this is an existing anxiety under patriarchy, and therefore a potential power to the benefit of bisexual women for threatening patriarchal structures. The concept of choice is connected to knowledge, duplicitousness, and unclear loyalties: It is unclear whether the bisexual woman is loyal to patriarchy or not. This very lack of clarity poses the danger that she represents to patriarchy and to men. As in Rich's quote, the bi femme fatale has connections with men only on her own terms, and her power of choice is the basis for that threat.

As with gender subversion, here too trans bi women embody two types of subversion related to choice. In addition to the choice associated with bisexuality of whether to be *with* men or women, trans bi women are also perceived to have a choice between *being* men or women. As opposed to bisexuality, however, (most) trans women *have* made a choice to live their lives as women (and only women). As Julia Serano explains in her book *Whipping Girl,* trans women subvert patriarchy by having chosen the choice that is opposite to patriarchal and masculinist values—femininity over masculinity, womanhood over manhood, and so on. Thus, the concept of choice reflects on transgender bi women in two ways: first, the threat encapsulated in the bisexual potential to choose whether or not, and on what terms to be with men; and second, the choice to live as women, which undermines masculinist values.

MULTIPLICITY
The third major way in which bisexuality threatens patriarchy is more epistemological or symbolic. As we've already established in the previous

chapters, bisexuality often represents multiplicity in the face of a culture demanding unity or "oneness." However, one piece that has been (partially) missing from this point is that singularity or unity is a patriarchal value connected to dominant masculinity, whereas multiplicity is a value connected to femininity. I want to argue that this multiplicity comprises a threat to patriarchy.

The way in which singularity is connected to masculinity and patriarchy could be seen by looking at the patriarchal single standard that I discussed in the beginning of this chapter. As already mentioned, the single standard consists of a long chain of mandatory characteristics that together are considered both the one standard for society and as no characteristics at all. A person characterized by all the mandatory chain links (male, white, cisgender, heterosexual, etc.) would simply be called "man," whereas any person deviating from any link of the chain would be named according to their deviation ("woman," "black man," "trans man," etc.). Here we can see that in order to qualify into the single standard, one also has to be describable only by that one word.

In addition, being described by anything other than the singular "man" not only disqualifies a person from the single standard but also reduces their perceived masculinity as well as their social value. This is because the single standard is what also defines "normal" or dominant masculinity. Thus racialized men, trans men, disabled men, bisexual men, and many more are perceived as having defective masculinities.

Here we might remember that monosexuality is one such singular value: not only because it is one of the requirements for the single standard, but also because singularity is central to its character. Monosexuality represents attraction to no more than one sex or gender, meaning that it carries "oneness" as an inherent part of itself.

[Trigger warning: explicit discussion of male and female genitals]

Femininity, on the other hand, has been culturally connected with multiplicity. In a seminal article called "This Sex Which Is Not One," French theorist Luce Irigaray takes cissexual male and female genitals as a metaphor for social meanings of male and female genders. She suggests that the cis male phallus is a symbol of patriarchal singularity whereas cis female genitals, which are comprised of lips, a clitoris, and a vagina, create a potential subversion of this singularity. She writes: "*She* [the woman] *is neither one nor two*"; "She resists all adequate definition. Further, she has no 'proper' name. And her sexual organ, which is not *one* organ, is counted as *none*." (All emphases in original).

[End of trigger]

There's much to be said about this quote in terms of bisexuality. Just as femininity in relation to dominant masculinity is "neither one nor two," so is bisexuality in relation to monosexuality. It's especially important to remember that bisexuality also constantly goes through attempts to reduce it to either oneness ("Bisexuals are actually gay" or are "actually straight" or "will choose in the end," etc.) or twoness ("Bisexuality is binary," "bisexuality means attraction to cisgender men and women only," etc.). Like Irigaray's woman, bisexuality also "resists all adequate definition," since no definition of bisexuality can ever be either inclusive enough or specific enough. Bisexuality also "has no proper name," as we might see by looking at the bisexual umbrella, and at the general discomfort surrounding bisexuality as a word even by those who identify by it. And of course, since bisexuality is an identity marking attraction to *more than one* gender, it is generally counted by society as *none*.

From this we can see that in many ways, bisexuality is symbolically aligned with femininity and femaleness, and works in contrast to monosexuality, which is symbolically aligned with dominant masculinity and patriarchy. Like Irigaray's woman, bisexuality defies patriarchal definitions and singular logic. It subverts patriarchal order by representing a different value, and through it a subversion of the system that depends on singularity for its existence.

French theorist Hélène Cixous has also made this connection between bisexuality, femininity, and multiplicity; and monosexuality, dominant masculinity, and singularity. In her article "The Laugh of the

Medusa," Cixous argues that "in a certain way, 'woman is bisexual.'"
Man, on the other hand, is "being poised to keep glorious phallic monosexuality in view." The bisexuality that Cixous is referring to here is a
symbol for a state of things in which no gender takes precedence over the
other, thus undermining patriarchal logic in which men and dominant
masculinity are considered superior. According to Cixous, bisexuality
has the potential to subvert the singularity/monosexuality of patriarchy,
since, as opposed to the latter, it "doesn't annul differences but stirs them
up, pursues them, [and] increases their number."

Another way in which bisexuality is connected to femininity and
multiplicity is by biphobic stereotypes and their accompanied meanings.
Instability, confusion, inability to make decisions, and fickleness are all
characteristics that are often stereotypically connected to bisexuality,
and that also have been long assigned to women and femininity (just
ask Freud). They also all suggest a multiplicity of positions, viewpoints,
emotions, and opinions.

Here we can also see that bisexuality is symbolically connected not
only with multiplicity, but also directly with women and femininity. In
addition to the feminization of bisexuality described above, women as a
gender have also been bisexualized, as bisexuality or "sexual fluidity" has
been thought of as inherent or "natural" to women. According to Alon
Zivony, this has also been justified using a concept of female multiplicity, since women are considered inherently capable of emotional fluidity and flexibility, occupying various imagined roles at different times
(being supportive, being seductive, being motherly, etc.).

These connections, it should be noted, are mostly based on misogyny (especially the stereotypes). Since society views femininity as inherently inferior, feminizing people or ideas is considered humiliating and
is thus used as a weapon against marginalized groups, describing them
as feminine in order to degrade them. However, as we've also seen, these
ideas often testify to the threat that the group in question holds over
dominant order. Thus my intention here is to extract this threat out of

the fears of the dominant culture and to use them in order to subvert it. The symbolic connection made in minority-world culture between bisexuality and women/femininity testifies to the anxieties that these two ideas stir in society when seen in conjunction, and might help us reclaim the subversive power that female bisexuality can hold.

Trans women, too, have often been imagined as multiple—having more than one gender or being a "combination" of maleness and femaleness. It's important to note that these beliefs are transphobic, as they fetishize trans women's bodies and often contradict their actual identities. However, as we will see later on in this chapter, the thought of trans women as having multiple genders has been threatening enough for the patriarchy to want to appropriate them through mainstream porn and hypersexualization, in the same way that it has cis female bisexuality. Since trans women are imagined as "both man and woman" in one, they, too, are perceived as threats to the unity and singularity of dominant masculinity. Thus bisexual trans women symbolize a double threat to the unity and singularity values of patriarchy, by being both bisexual and transgender.

To conclude, female bisexuality has subversive potential against patriarchy, comprising a threat against it. This threat, in turn, creates an anxiety within patriarchal culture that expresses itself through the social treatment of female bisexuality as an idea and bisexual women as people.

HOT, SEXY BI BABES

We started out with a quote from Mark Simpson, who wrote, "Female bisexuality is today much more socially acceptable than male bisexuality, and in fact frequently positively encouraged, both by many voyeuristic men and an equally voyeuristic pop culture." I would now like to look a bit deeper into this "encouragement" and to question whether it's really so positive.

Simpson, of course, is right. Female bisexuality truly is encouraged by voyeuristic men, as well as by voyeuristic (male-dominated) media. Spelling out media presumptions, Simpson writes that as opposed to male bisexuality, female bisexuality is considered "almost universal. It's as natural and as true as it is wonderful and real and . . . hot!" And indeed, it seems that the main context in which female bisexuality appears in mainstream media is that of "hotness."

Rather than looking at the superficial level of "acceptance," I'd like to look at media representations of female bisexuality in attempt to show the ways in which it is depicted, and the terms under which it is allowed to appear in mainstream culture. Rather than accepted, female bisexuality is "encouraged" on the sole grounds that it be palatable to straight men. Bisexual women are presented in hypersexualized contexts, as sexual objects for the hegemonic cis straight male gaze, while directly or covertly appealing to a quasi-pornographic fantasy of a (two females and one male) threesome, and while also reassuring us that these women are not *really* bisexual, but are simply behaving so for the satisfaction of the presumed male spectator. Note that I only discuss cis female bisexuality in this section because I could find no examples of trans female bisexuality in the mainstream media. That said, bi trans women will be given attention in all other parts of this chapter.

Now, before I go on to talking about all these things, I need to say something about sexuality and context: My arguments about hypersexualization and sexual objectification might sometimes be read as implying that there's something wrong about female bisexuality, female sexuality, or sex in general, in and of themselves. This is not so. The reason I think that these depictions are negative is not that they are sexual, period. Rather, it is because they reflect a form of imposed sexualization that centers around the presumed needs of the cis straight male viewer—above, beyond, and instead of those of the women themselves. Therefore, my goal here is to expose how patriarchal and phallocentric understandings of bisexuality are projected onto bisexual women for the purpose of satisfying the presumed male viewer.

MEDIA

Running an online search for "bisexual celebrities" yields several lists such as "11 Famous Bisexual Babes," "The 30 Sexiest Bisexual Celebrities [PHOTOS]" or "Hollywood's Bisexual Leading Ladies [PHOTOS]" right on the first page. As the titles seem to suggest, these magazine items contain lists of female bisexual celebrities alongside pictures containing varying degrees of revealing clothes and sexual postures. The texts, in the same vein, present these bisexual women as delectable objects for the cis straight male gaze and sexual appetites, often under a thin guise of "supporting" bisexuality, and always while reassuring us that these women are not *actually* bisexual.

COED Magazine, in what seems to be stroke of grim irony, has assembled its list of "The 30 Sexiest Bisexual Celebrities [PHOTOS]" in honor of the international Bi Visibility Day. Eschewing any political meanings attached to this day, the only bi visibility that counts here is that catering to the eye of their cis straight male reader. The list contains thirty pictures of bisexual celebrities who all appear in a sexualized context, shown in seductive or sexual positions, beckoning to the viewer or looking invitingly. In fact, in only six of the thirty pictures, the women in question can be said to be fully clothed. One particularly telling picture shows American TV personalities twins Erica and Victoria Mongeon photographed together, hugging each other and looking at the camera, in a way suspiciously echoing the accompanying text of the item: "To quote Andy Samberg and Justin Timberlake, 'it's okay to put us in a three-way' with any of these ladies." Another telling sentence appears before this one, stating that the writer has "argued ad nauseum with many friends about whether or not someone can be a 'true' bisexual." How reassuring for the straight readers, who mustn't feel threatened, but rather aroused, by these women's bisexuality.

Likewise, *The Frisky*'s "11 Famous Bisexual Babes" contains eleven photos of famous bisexual women in revealing photos. The text follows suit, using such terms as "the occasional girl-on-girl action," "lady-loving," "a lover of lady parts," and of course, "bisexual babes." In addition, and just like at *COED*, the text at the same time reassures us that bisexuality doesn't really exist and that these women are only out as bisexual to satisfy the cis straight male viewers' tastes. A telling example: "Tila Tequila has spent her career trying really hard to make us believe she is, in fact, bisexual. [. . .] Whatever, Tequila."

In general, it seems as though various publications use female bisexuality as a really great excuse for posting pictures of "hot" women, in a way equating female bisexuality with hypersexualization. News of female celebrities coming out as bisexual are often treated in similar ways.

The Sun, in an item about Gillian Anderson's coming out as bi, sees fit to mention that Anderson was "voted the sexiest woman in the world in 1996." At the same time, it also reassures us that she couldn't *really* be bisexual by writing that she "started *experimenting* with girls after moving to the United States from London as a *teenager*" (emphasis mine), and that "despite [her] enjoying many lesbian flings they were 'the exception, not the rule.'" Of course, in a "traditional" vein, the item is accompanied by photos of Anderson in revealing dress and suggestive postures.

One *Star Plus* headline screams "Sofia Vergara & Sharon Stone to Get Hot and Heavy as Bisexual Lovers." The item is accompanied by— you guessed it—a revealing photo of actress Sofia Vergara. The text of the item also follows the same route, stating that "*Sexy* Colombian actress Sofia Vergara and Sharon Stone are set to *heat up* the big screen as bisexual *lovers* in a new comedy." It also includes a source quote, according to which "Sharon thinks it's going to be a lot of fun playing the *lover* of one of the *hottest* actresses out there. The scenes will be *steamy*!" (all emphases mine). As per usual, the text also reassures us that the women in question aren't *really* bisexual, since they're only acting in a ("sexy!") movie.

As we can see, bisexual women are only allowed to appear in mainstream media when they follow certain conditions:

- They must be considered conventionally "sexy."
- They must appear in a sexualized context, including suggestive texts and photos.
- They mustn't be thought to be "true" bisexuals, but presented as women who perform bisexuality for men.

Female bisexuality is thus co-opted into the hegemonic male gaze, which in turn produces female bisexuality on its own (patriarchal, phallocentric) terms.

The fact that these women are bisexual, and that some of them have spoken in ways that suggest a fondness of threesomes or casual sex, is only used here to exacerbate these effects of the male gaze. In "Pleasure Under Patriarchy," MacKinnon argues that, in the hegemonic male imagination, women are allowed to want sex—as long as what they want reflects men's wishes: "[T]he object is allowed to desire, if she desires to be an object." Further, she argues, "Anything women have claimed as their own—motherhood, athletics, traditional men's jobs, lesbianism, feminism—is made specifically sexy, dangerous, provocative, punished, made men's in pornography."

What this means for bisexual women is that their desires are appropriated and transformed by the mainstream media, into the cis straight male gaze. In this case, it doesn't really matter what a bisexual woman wants herself, as long as what she wants can be taken to comply with straight men's presumed desires. What she truly wants doesn't matter at all, since she is only there to be sexualized and objectified.

MAINSTREAM PORN

[Trigger warning: general discussion of sex and filmed mainstream pornography]
As you've probably already gathered, mainstream media depictions of bisexuality appeal to a deeper or greater genre of mainstream pornography. They can only hint (in various levels of subtlety) at explicit sexual acts, but never actually show them. The use of such words as "hot,"

"steamy," "sexy," and even "threesome," and the sexualization of these bisexual women, all point this way.

Now before I begin my commentary about pornography, I must once again make a disclaimer: In many cases, feminist criticisms of pornography suggest or presume that porn, in and of itself, is the source and cause of sexual violence against women, or that it always and in all cases constitutes sexual violence in and of itself. In my critique of mainstream porn below, I do not mean to suggest that all porn is inherently the end-all of violence against women, or against bisexual women in particular. I therefore take care to only criticize *mainstream* pornography (as separate from gay, queer, and feminist porn). I also acknowledge that sexual violence against women existed long before the emergence of pornography as a popular genre, and that therefore mainstream porn is not so much the cause of sexual violence as it is a reflection of a sexually violent society.

Notwithstanding, I have not been able to find evidence that this type of objectification of bisexual women existed before mainstream pornography. In addition, bisexual women have been a trope in pornography (written, drawn, photographed, or filmed) from the eighteenth century to the current day. I therefore tentatively conclude that mainstream porn does provide the ground logic for modern hypersexualization, objectification, and sexual violence against bisexual women.

The first thing to remember about mainstream porn is that this is a capitalist industry revolving around heterosexual men. What this means is that the fundamental purpose of porn is to make money, and that the target audience for this purpose is constructed as cis male and heterosexual. Pornographic films are manufactured by and for straight cis men, while the women appearing in those films only serve as conductors for straight male desire and for appeasing the cis straight male fantasy and gaze.

This logic also defines porn genres and types, which are defined by and through the male gaze and by male sexual actions. For example, the porn website *YouPorn.com* contains three search categories: *straight,*

164 BI: Notes for a Bisexual Revolution

gay, and *cocks*. A search for the word *lesbian* under the category *gay* only yields gay male videos. The "lesbian" videos, as it turns out, are categorized under *straight*. As we can see, the pornographic category isn't defined by the sexuality of the women appearing therein, but by the sexual tastes of the straight male target audience—since the audience is presumed to be comprised of straight men, the "lesbian" videos have been categorized under *straight*.

Likewise, what determines the definitions for pornographic genres or acts is the presence, or sexual activity, of a man in the scene (epitomized by the erect penis). When the word *lesbian* shows in titles of porn movies, it is not meant to define the sexuality of the women, but to answer the question of whether or not a penis is present/active in the scene. The women's sexuality is irrelevant since the definitions are not about them but about the men fucking or watching them.

I say all this to explain why bisexual women or bisexual acts in porn are never named as bisexual. Scenes in which women are shown having sex with women (exclusively or in addition to men) are named *lesbian* rather than *bisexual* because what defines them is not the women's sexuality, but the men's. This also explains why the term *bisexual porn*, which does exist, in fact refers specifically to *cis male* bisexual porn—a genre that shows cis men having threesomes with cisgeder men and women, and is again defined by cis male sexuality and the presence/activity of erect penises. It is also defined *bisexual* according to the sexuality of the target audience, which is presumed to be comprised of bisexual men.

Following all of this, I think it would be more accurate to discuss "lesbian" porn in terms of bisexuality. If we follow from the sexual acts performed by the women appearing in these types of scenes, it would be very hard not to notice that bisexuality is here at work. The women in scenes titled *lesbian* have sex with each other, as well as with men. Even in scenes where no man is present at all, the logic behind the activity is still bisexual, since the women are perceived to be performing for a cis straight male audience.

These representations of bisexuality, in turn, contribute to the cultural construction of female bisexuality as we've seen it in the media depictions above. The media take up on the pornographic logic of bisexuality and send the same messages, but in covert ways. Thus, looking into pornographic representations of bisexual women might help us shed light on social and cultural treatment of female bisexuality in general.

Here it's important to note that, true to the straight-cis sensibilities of pornography, all the women represented in these kinds of scenes are cisgender. This is because mainstream pornography fetishizes particular types of women according to their deviation from the single standard (of whiteness, heterosexuality, cisgenderism, thinness, nondisability, etc.), separating them into different genres. Thus, trans women (including bi trans women) only appear in movies and videos categorized as "tranny" or "shemale" porn (these will be discussed later).

Performance and pleasure

For cisgender women, female bisexuality in mainstream porn is presented as a sort of "foreplay," something that women only do when there's no penis around, to prepare each other for the "real thing" or to arouse the cis male spectators watching them. Instead of a sexuality in its own right, bisexuality in these films is perceived as a derivative of straight cis male sexuality. The women in these movies don't "do" the bisexual acts for themselves or their own pleasure, but rather as a conduit for the satisfaction of men—both those active in the scenes, and the viewers who are watching.

In addition, and true to the logic we've seen in media representations, the bisexual cis women in the films are marked as "actually straight." This is done by several means. First, visually: The women have a "straight look," wearing long hair, makeup, jewelry, long fingernails, and nail polish, as well as having no visible body hair and other such visual cues. Second, sexually: The sexual acts that these women perform with each other are generally acts that are socially perceived as "foreplay," such as kissing, petting, oral sex, and manual sex (though many times no penetration takes place, even using fingers). Vaginal penetration is only performed by a penis following the "foreplay" between the two women. Finally, the sexual acts performed by the women are also constructed under a straight logic—any non-intercourse activity is viewed as foreplay, and the only act considered "real sex" is penis-vagina intercourse.

[Trigger warning: explicit descriptions of sex and filmed pornography]
Possibly the best example for cis female bisexuality in filmed pornography is a genre named "FFM" (standing for "Female, Female, Male"), a genre showing two cisgender women having a threesome with one cisgender man. The two women in these films usually focus their attention on the one man. They perform "lesbian" acts for his visual pleasure, as well as for arousing each other prior to (or during) vaginal intercourse. The man, and his penile penetration of the women, constitutes both the center of attention and the center of pleasure in the scenes. The bisexual acts performed by the two women with each other are often done at the man's encouragement and even instruction. As mentioned above, the women in this genre are also marked as "actually straight" both by their gender presentation and by the sexual acts they perform with each other. I'd like to look into two such videos as examples.

Case in Point:
"Lesbian Action before Having a Real Cock in Their Pussy"
This online porn video begins by showing two cis women, a blond and a brunette (both white), making out on a sofa. A while later the camera reveals a man (also white) who seems to be sitting adjacent from them, masturbating to what he sees. The camera then returns to the women while the blond one goes down on the brunette. At the same time, the man joins into the frame and takes the underwear that the blond woman had just removed. The camera focuses on him as he sniffs the underwear

and then returns to focus on the oral sex between the two women. At the same time, however, the man's hand is seen touching the brunette woman, until finally he kisses her. At this point, the brunette stops going down on the blond woman and instead starts going down on the man. From here, the camera cuts to showing the man penetrating the brunette woman, while the blond one touches her various body parts. Later, with encouragement by the man, the two women lean on the sofa with their legs pulled up, and the camera focuses on him as he goes down on each of them while touching the other with his hands (the women don't touch each other). After that, the camera cuts to the man as he is penetrating the brunette woman again while the blond one touches her, and afterward they both go down on him. The video ends as the two women kiss while the man masturbates over them and cums into their mouths.

As we can see, this video includes all of the elements mentioned above. For starters, simply reading the title of the video already shows the attitude at play here. A title such as *Lesbian Action before Having a Real Cock in Their Pussy* marks the sexual acts between the women as foreplay and focuses sexuality around penile penetration. In addition, the words "lesbian action" define woman-woman sexual acts by the absence of a penis rather than by the sexuality exhibited by the women themselves (which is bisexual).

The visual cues in this video mark the women as "actually straight": long hair, makeup, long fingernails, etc. In addition, their sexual performance is slightly awkward, as they look very tentative about touching each other. No passion is visible, nor any focus on each other, but rather a very clear awareness of the performativity of their actions. After a few seconds, we see the man masturbating and realize who this show is going on for and who's the real center of the action. All this means that even at this point, before there's any physical touch between the women and the man, it is already obvious that they are performing for him, for the purpose of providing him with visual satisfaction and to arouse him toward vaginal penetration.

As the man starts touching them, he becomes the center of attention for both the women and the camera, dominating both the picture frame and the women. From the moment that his hand enters the frame, he is marked as the center of attention, both by the brunette woman and by the camera. The woman is looking at him rather than at the other woman (who is going down on her!), while the camera places his hand at the center of the frame.

From that moment on, he also dominates the action physically: As he's penetrating the brunette woman, the blond's role is to assist. She touches the brunette, adds lubrication, and generally aids the act of vaginal intercourse taking place between him and the other woman. Later on, the man also physically directs the women's bodies, positioning them on the sofa. He determines what will happen, while they only comply.

True to mainstream porn conventions, the peak of the scene is the male orgasm (also known as "the money shot"); the man cums while the kiss between the two women serves both for his arousal and as a receptacle for his ejaculate. This shot, of course, emphasizes the fact that the man is the center of pleasure in this video, and the treatment of the bisexual women therein as no more than props for attaining this pleasure.

Throughout the video, the women's bisexuality is presented as subordinate to the man's gaze and his sexuality. The bisexual acts taking place between them are performed for his pleasure. The man is constructed as the center of pleasure, sexual action, and the gaze. In this way, the video presents the women as "actually straight" and female bisexuality as performance for male pleasure.

"FFM Threesome with Two Hot Girls in Stockings Masturbating and Fucking"

This video starts by showing a cis man penetrating a cis woman on the floor, while an additional cis woman sits by them touching herself. After this, the man backs away from the woman whom he was penetrating and beckons for the other woman to come over. He directs her to the other woman's genitals and instructs her to go down on her. He starts penetrating the same woman from behind, while she goes down on the other woman and fingers her. This scene continues until the end of the video, while the shot angle and the sexual acts change from time to time. Sometimes the women touch each other and sometimes one of them is distracted by the man. The video also includes several point-of-view (POV) shots—camera shots taken from the man's point of view, showing him penetrating the woman. The video ends with no orgasms, with the last shot being a POV shot as described above.

Here, too, the women are marked as "actually straight," using their clothes, their long hair, their makeup, and jewelry. The fact that the video opens with a shot of the man penetrating one of the women while the other one waits testifies to the perception of penile penetration as the center of the scene. Later the man moves the woman's head in order for her to go down on the other one—this shows us that he is in charge of both the scene and the women's bodies. He also determines the position of the woman's body in order for him to penetrate her, and he is the one initiating the intercourse with her.

In addition, it's clear from the video that the oral sex that he orders the woman to perform on the other one is meant for his visual arousal, in order to intensify his pleasure in penetrating her. The woman he is penetrating is often distracted by him and seems as though she's touching the other woman not out of passion or desire, but in order to please him. This is particularly visible in a part of the scene where she is distracted, and he, in response, pushes her head back onto the other woman. In addition, the two women often look at the man, but never at each other—this element also emphasizes the man's centrality in this scene.

A particularly interesting element in this video is the use of the POV shot several times. According to American film researcher Laura Mulvey, POV shots in classic Hollywood film are often used in order to mediate between the viewer's male gaze and the point of view of the male character while observing the body of a woman. Using this technique in that way renders both the woman and her body as objects for the male gaze, giving agency, subjectivity, and visual pleasure only to the male character/viewer.

In this video, the POV technique works in a similar (though more extreme) way: The man's point of view enables the viewer to see his erect penis penetrating the woman, almost as a conduit for the viewer's desire to penetrate the woman himself. Thus, this technique constructs the man both as the beholder and as the active agent controlling the scene and performing the actions. It also emphasizes the perception of straight sexuality that produces vaginal intercourse as the center of sexual action. Similar to Hollywood film, here, too, the women are denied a POV of their own, and remain positioned as objects for the male gaze.

In this video, too, the bisexual acts between the women are only performed as a means for ensuring the man's satisfaction. The acts between the women are performed according to his instructions, in order to provide him with visual pleasure while he penetrates one of them. The camera work in the video constructs the man as the active agent and owner of the gaze, while leaving the women as objects for both his gaze and sexual pleasure. Thus here too cis female bisexuality is presented as a performance held for the straight cis man's pleasure only.

In addition, we might also note that these pornographic representations of cisgender female bisexuality also comply with the three conditions for the appearance of bisexual women in the media; namely:

- They must be considered conventionally "sexy."
- They must appear in a sexualized context.
- They mustn't be thought to be "true" bisexuals, but presented as women who perform bisexuality for men.

[End of trigger]

Bi trans/sexual performance

[Trigger warning: discussion of sex and mainstream pornography]

Surprisingly enough, the rules for bisexual trans women in porn are very different from those concerning cis women. Whereas cis women in porn are presumed to be performing their bisexuality for the satisfaction of cisgender men, transgender women in porn are perceived as inherently and naturally bisexual. This notion seems to be based on the transphobic belief that transgender women are "both man and woman in one." Combined with the heterosexist logic of porn—and of society in general—we are to presume that the "female" part of a trans woman desires cis men, whereas her "male" part desires cis women. In addition to being heterosexist, this notion is also transphobic since it suggests that trans women are not real women but a kind of "third gender."

True to this heterosexist logic, trans women are also presented as always desiring each other. This echoes a notion of narcissism: The trans woman, who is fetishized as a particularly exotic sex object in mainstream porn, also fetishizes other trans women just as she is fetishized by her audience. In her book *Whipping Girl*, Serano explains that many psychological theories presume that trans women want to transition as part of a sexual fetish. In particular, J. Michael Bailey (yes, the same researcher who denied the existence of male bisexuality) identifies some trans women as *autogynephilic*, "essentially men who are attracted to women and who seek sex reassignment because they are turned on by the idea of having female bodies themselves." This notion is yet again echoed in this genre, first by hypersexualizing and objectifying trans women, and second by presuming that trans women will always and necessarily be narcissistically attracted to one another.

In terms of genre, "tranny" or "shemale" porn (especially that involving threesomes) includes elements from both genres of "bisexual porn" and "FFM." As we recall, bisexual porn is a genre showing a cis man in a threesome with a cis man and a cis woman; FFM is a genre showing a threesome comprised of two cis women and one cis man.

What is interesting here is that these two genre influences are both bisexual, making "tranny porn" a genre combination of cis male and cis female bisexuality. Apart from situating trans women as inherently bisexual, this is another way in which trans women in porn are presented as "both men and women": They perform sexual acts associated in porn with those two genders, as in the following two examples.

"1 Man + 1 Woman + 1 Shemale = Lots Of Fun"

This online video seemingly starts as an ordinary FFM video: showing two women making out with each other on a bed, while a cis man is sitting opposite them on a chair, watching. Before long, however, we discover that one of the women is trans, as the other woman pulls out her penis from under her panties and starts masturbating her. At the same time, the man watching pulls out his own penis and starts masturbating himself. This continues for a while as the cis woman goes down on the trans woman, and as they later switch to a 69 position going down on each other. The camera then cuts to showing the man naked on the bed after having joined the two women. This is followed by various shots depicting different sexual acts in the threesome: The trans woman goes down on the man while the cis woman goes down on her, the cis woman goes down on the man while the trans woman rims him, and so on. The video ends with a male orgasm, given to him by the cis woman while he is kissing the trans woman.

As we can see, this video situates the trans woman both as "man and woman in one" and as naturally bisexual. She performs sexual acts associated in porn both with cis women and with cis men, namely and especially: She both penetrates and is penetrated using a penis (note that this is an element shared both by this genre and cis male bisexual porn). Further, similar to bi cis women in porn, she is represented as an object for the male gaze while "performing" bisexuality with the cis woman—an element that genders her as a woman. However, at the same time, she is also also gendered as a man through the sexual focus on—and fetishization of—her penis. In addition to this, she is specifically sexualized and fetishized as a trans woman, particularly through her representation as "a chick with a dick."

Her gendered representation as "both man and woman" through these elements also constructs her as "naturally" bisexual in the video: She performs sexual acts both with the man and the other woman. There seems to be no "performance" in her bisexuality such as is usually depicted in cis FFM porn. Rather, it seems almost "natural and normal" that she should be bisexual—in the same way that it appears "natural and normal" that she should appeal to both the cis man and the cis woman. The trans woman, we are set to understand, has "something for everyone."

"2 Shemales and 1 Guy"

This video also opens in the tradition of the FFM genre, with two trans women on a bed (one brown and one black), telling the viewers that they're waiting for "a hot friend" who's "running a little late." "We'll see him soon enough," says the brown one, "but right now we're gonna play a little." As suggested, in order to "pass the time" before the cis man arrives, the two women make out with each other, kissing and licking each other's nipples. The camera then cuts to a moment where the man "has finally made it." He is naked on the bed with the two women, and the three start having oral sex together in different combinations. The video ends without orgasms, as the two women go down on the man together.

In this video, too, the trans women are presented as "both man and woman": They are gendered as women through their feminine appearance, and as men through their penises (being the fetishized focus of the oral sex). In addition, they're gendered as women through their bisexuality, which echoes cis femininity as represented in the FFM porn genre. At the same time, they are also particularly fetishized as trans women through their representation as "chicks with dicks" and through the sexual action's focus on their penises.

Here, too, the trans women's gendered representation as "both man and woman" constructs them as "naturally" bisexual, being attracted to

both each other and the cis man. In addition, they're presented in the tradition of the FFM genre, as performing bisexuality with each other only as a pastime or preparation for the man, marking them again as bisexual in traditional pornographic terms. As opposed to the previous example, here we can also see the element of narcissism associated with trans women, since they are shown fetishizing each other. In particular, they both focus on each other's breasts and penises, thus echoing the terms under which trans women are fetishized by porn ("chicks with dicks").
[End of trigger]

To conclude, mainstream pornography produces distorted representations of female bisexuality. In order to alleviate the patriarchal anxiety caused by the threatening potential of female bisexuality, mainstream porn co-opts it and reproduces it on patriarchal terms. Cis female bisexuality is presented as mere performance for the satisfaction of straight men, whereas trans female bisexuality is presented as inherent and natural, as part of the fetishization of trans women and their depiction as "both men and women." In all of these depictions, bisexual women in general are hypersexualized, objectified, and are depicted as instruments for hetero cis male pleasure.

This appropriation of bisexuality into patriarchy, however, does not end here on the symbolic level, but is also carried into reality. The ways in which female bisexuality is represented in mainstream porn, as well as in the mainstream media, provides the basic logic upon which sexual violence is directed against bisexual women.

SEXUAL VIOLENCE

[Trigger warning: general discussion of biphobic sexual violence]
A recent study, performed by the U.S. government's Department of Health and published in January of 2013, discovered that *almost half* of all bisexual cis women were raped at least once in their lifetime, and that

75 percent have experienced other forms of sexual violence.[31] Bisexual women routinely suffer from sexual harassment and other forms of sexual violence directed at them because of their bisexuality. This type of harassment is well known as the "Can I watch?" syndrome—when, upon realizing that a woman is bisexual, straight men ask to watch her having sex with another woman, or to join a threesome. In addition, the man in question would normally presume that the woman is also sexually available to him regardless, and would consider himself invited to be sexual with her simply by the fact of her bisexuality.

Oddly enough, these incidents are almost never named as sexual violence by mainstream bisexual movements. Instead, they are spoken of in terms of stereotypes, and especially the one about bisexuals being promiscuous. According to those discourses, bisexual women get this type of "offer" because men assume that they're promiscuous. The "solution" to this problem is to fight the stereotype and prove that bisexual women aren't really so.

This is problematic because it misses the point of opposing sexual violence, taking the blame off of patriarchy, rape culture, and sexually violent men. Instead of placing the blame where it belongs, this type of thinking moves the blame onto "promiscuous" (sexually independent) bisexual women, normalizing the notion that it's bad for a woman to be sexual (or to be thought of as sexual). I will pay more attention to the second part later on in this section. For now, however, I would like to try and shift the terms of the discussion: from those of "stereotypes" and "false presumptions" into those of sexual violence. What I hope this contributes is an understanding of the sexist and misogynist context of biphobic sexual violence, an option to name the source of this violence, and hopefully also to combat it more accurately and efficiently.

That biphobic sexual violence seems to be directed by the logic of mainstream porn and media representations of female bisexuality is almost too obvious. We have already seen how both mainstream porn and the media depict female bisexuality as performance that women do in order to satisfy straight men, situating bisexual women as objects for the cis straight male gaze and sexual pleasure. Here these notions are carried out into reality, as cis straight men treat bisexual women as objects for their sexual fulfillment.

[Trigger warning: explicit descriptions of biphobic sexual harassment]

In "Compulsory Bisexuality? The Challenges of Modern Sexual Fluidity," (an article otherwise highly problematic for its treatment of bisexuality), American researcher Breanna Fahs quotes bisexual and monosexual women who were, in Fahs's words, "asked to perform bisexuality." What this phrase means is that these women were pressured by straight men to make out with other women in front of them ("Can I watch?") or to join threesomes ("Can I join?").

For example, one interviewee says:

> I get [asked to perform as bisexual] a lot because when people hear that you're bisexual, they automatically assume. Some people automatically assume that you do it for men's pleasure . . . .
> I've definitely felt pressure to indulge in fantasies about men watching women together.

Another one says:

> Well, like I have these guys, these neighbors down the hall that, like, the other night they kind of know that me and my roommate are more than just friends. They keep saying to us, "Come on, make out," like that kind of thing.

These are just two examples of incidents of this type. For bisexual women, these incidents are incredibly frequent, to the extent that this topic is one of the most often discussed issues between women when talking about biphobia. For bisexual women in various communities, this is part of day-to-day experience, making it near-impossible to be out as bisexual in most environments without experiencing this type of sexual harassment.

In her (otherwise problematic) book *Look Both Ways: Bisexual Politics*, Jennifer Baumgardner evocatively describes such a situation:

> *One night Anastasia and I found ourselves in a straight bar . . . drunk and with me practically sitting on her lap. [. . .] It was 2:00 AM. "Me and Bobby McGee" was on the jukebox and I was singing my best Janis Joplin into her ear . . . when I kissed her.*
>
> *The entire noisy, grotesque, jabbering bar receded and all I could hear was her skin. Or maybe I was smelling it. [. . .] I do recall that my hand went directly to her breasts. [. . .] I could feel her downy mustache, which she bleaches, feathery against my upper lip.*
>
> *I felt a tap on my shoulder, and a woman said, "I don't think this is the safest situation for you." She gestured at the semicircle of guys around us making no effort to conceal that this was a show for them.*

As we can see from Baumgarder's quote, as well as from Fahs's interviewees, bisexual women often cannot express their sexuality safely in public without fear of sexual harassment or other forms of sexual violence. Here it's worth mentioning that in addition to staring and pressuring women to "perform" for them, men also often feel entitled to join in without asking. For example, it happened to me several times during parties that while kissing a girl, a man tried to join in by touching us both, nonconsensually and without asking first.

Sexual violence toward bisexual women doesn't end here, but also goes into the realm of sexual coercion and exploitation. Many bisexual women are coerced by men to participate in threesomes or to have sex with other women, even when they're not interested in doing so. For example, one of Fahs's interviewees says:

> [T]here've been times where I have engaged in sexual situations with another woman where the husband has been there. It was more like an ego thing for him, or a notch on his belt or whatever. It didn't feel like I was being honored as a person.

As we can see, this interviewee felt objectified by the man who was present and felt that the situation existed for his pleasure rather than hers or the other woman's. Another interviewee says:

> [T]his one guy asked me to join [him] and his girlfriend and it ended the relationship. . . I think that is again for the man's benefit and it is not necessarily for the women's benefit. It is coercion. They basically want it for their own pleasure. [. . .] I felt pressured and embarrassed because we did not talk about it. That was not something that was agreed upon. I was afraid that I would go to his house and he would have someone there waiting for me, and I would have to figure out how to get out of that situation because I'm not going to do that and it's not what I want. (Emphasis mine).

This interviewee felt that the situation was being imposed on her and was afraid of being coerced into doing things that she wasn't interested it. Meaning, she feared sexual violence.

[Trigger warning: general discussion of rape and sexual violence against bisexual women]

This, of course, is only the tip of the iceberg, as the recent statistics I mentioned above indicate. The lack of discussion about sexual violence in bisexual communities, in addition to society's general silence around the topic (and especially the silencing of survivors), means that much more is happening than is actually reported and talked about. From these descriptions, though, we might be able to understand the type of circumstances that produce this frighteningly high number of rapes and sexual violence directed at bi women. Specifically, we might be able to name them as a result of biphobic misogyny.

The rate of bisexual women who were raped or experienced sexual violence is so high because in a culture where we can be harassed so frequently and easily, there's simply no way that this violence could only stay at this "low" level. The biphobic and misogynist behaviors and perceptions aimed against bisexual women create a public atmosphere that produces sexual violence against them on all levels. A man who touches bisexual women in public nonconsensually might also be the kind of man who forces his girlfriend into a threesome she's uninterested in. A man who thinks that a woman's bisexuality equals consent might also be the kind of man who forces himself sexually on that woman. This means that biphobia and misogyny not only give men a license to objectify and harass bisexual women, but also gives them a license to rape.

Of course, men are not the only perpetrators of sexual violence against bisexual women.[32] Sexual violence might be directed at women by people of any other gender, including other women. It's important to say that I do not note this to alleviate men's responsibility, nor to create a false image of equality. Rather, I raise this because the topic of sexual violence of women against women is one of the most silenced issues in public discourse, including within LGBTQ communities.

Just as men might presume that women's bisexuality equals automatic consent, so might other women. Bisexual or monosexual women presume that because a certain woman is bisexual, then it must be okay to touch her or engage with her sexually without prior consent. They might also presume that bisexual women would automatically want to participate in a threesome with them, to the extent of initiating and imposing contact without discussion or prior consent. This is especially true in cases where there are unequal power dynamics at work between the two women in question (such as race, age, ability, or class). This means that in addition to being at a heightened risk for sexual violence by men, bi women are also at risk of sexual violence by other women.

[Trigger warning: general discussion of sexual violence against bi transgender women]

As to bisexual trans women, in addition to all of the above, they are also subject to a whole other set of sexual harassment and violence as a result of transphobia and **transmisogyny** (this goes especially for trans women of color). For example, once a woman is recognized as trans on the street, she might be automatically presumed to be a sex worker, and as such receive the kind of street harassment directed at sex workers: Offers of sex for money ("$50!"), whorephobic catcalls, and attempts of sexual assault. Indeed, even if they aren't presumed as such, trans women are still subject to this same type of street harassment; and of course, trans women who *are* sex workers are in much more danger in this aspect.

Transmisogyny is hatred of transgender women.

[Trigger warning: explicit descriptions of transphobic murder and violence]

In dating and sexual settings, trans women are in grave danger of rape, violence, and even murder, especially if dating straight cisgender men. If a trans woman has been presumed by her partner(s) as cisgender, and then later "discovered" to be trans, she would often be in danger of all the above. For example, in 2002, Gwen Araujo, an American trans woman of color, was brutally beaten, tortured, and murdered after having been "discovered" by her sexual partners to be trans at a party. Before they killed her, these men forcefully undressed her so as to expose her genitals. In 2009, a trans woman was raped and attacked by a local man in Trinidad, Colorado, while staying there waiting for consultation on gender reassignment surgery. After having raped her, the man proceeded to try and kill her, but failed. He warned her not to come back, however, since "her kind" were not wanted there.

Violence and sexual violence against trans women are incredibly widespread. Murder cases of trans women amount to several hundred each year worldwide, with the most violent areas in the world being the United States and Latin America. Other cases of violence, including sexual violence, are frequent, multiple, and underreported, meaning that cases of "less severe" violence such as street harassment, sexual harassment, and rape are likely to be silenced and hidden from public attention. All of this means that in addition to being subject to *biphobic* sexual violence, bisexual trans women are also in danger of *transphobic* sexual violence. In this case, being bisexual might even be a risk-reducing factor in the lives of bi trans women, as their contact with straight cis men might be reduced.

[Trigger warning: general discussion of biphobic sexual harassment]

At this point, some of you might be wondering why I consider these types of violence against bisexual women as biphobic rather than lesbophobic, since lesbians are often harassed in very similar ways to the ones I described. This is biphobia, however, rather than lesbophobia because this type of harassment is based on biphobic beliefs and perceptions even when they are aimed against lesbians. As explained throughout this chapter, the logic of this type of sexual violence is that bisexual women are "actually straight," or only performing their bisexuality for male pleasure. When lesbians are harassed in the same way, they are first presumed to be bisexual, and then attached with the same biphobic notions used against bi women. What happens here is a combination of lesbophobia and biphobia: Lesbians first have their lesbian identity erased, and then are presumed to be "actually straight" as a result of being presumed as bisexual. Thus, biphobia constitutes the center here, and remains biphobia even when it is aimed at lesbians.

What we can see here is that this type of biphobia not only harms bisexual women, but also monosexual women, as it is also aimed against them. As explained above, lesbians often receive the same type of harassment as bisexual women when being affectionate or sexual in public. Heterosexual women are often also subject to pressure by straight men to perform bisexuality (privately or publicly) for their pleasure. In many communities (especially ones that consider themselves "alternative," "open," or "liberal"), performative bisexuality might be a standard that all women must meet. This means that in those communities, women are expected and pressured into being sexual with other women for the satisfaction of straight men. Although this mostly harms *bisexual* women (who are presumed to want this simply because they identify as bisexual), it also works against *monosexual* women.

What all of this means is that biphobia against women is not only the concern of bisexual women, but of all women regardless of their sexual identity. This goes back to the notion expressed in chapter 2 that biphobia harms everyone rather than just bi-identified people. This is yet another reason why monosexuals should also be concerned about biphobia—they also have a stake in the matter.

[End of trigger]

To conclude, following depictions of bi women in mainstream media and porn as objects for the male gaze, these attitudes are then carried into reality and used against bisexual women. Bi women then become objects of sexual harassment and sexual violence, as (mostly) straight cisgender men pressure and coerce them into performative bisexuality. Transgender bi women are doubly endangered as they are already in risk of transphobic sexual (and other) violence. The same sexual violence directed against bi women is then also displaced unto monosexual women: Lesbians are presumed to be "actually bisexual" and thus willing sexual objects, while heterosexual women are pressured into performing bisexuality for male pleasure.

Surprisingly enough, however, instead of naming this sexual violence for what it is, most bisexual movements have responded to this by backlashing against bi women who choose to be publicly sexual. In a classical move of victim blaming and slut shaming, these women have been framed as the ones guilty of biphobic sexual harassment.

BACKLASH

[Trigger warning: explicit descriptions of slut shaming]

"I don't know about you," says Cass King of the Canadian bisexual cabaret duo The Wet Spots, "I get a little sick and tired of the bi-curious. I mean, it's okay if you're bi-curious, you know, it's fine. I just don't think you should get to be bi-curious for *very long*." This funny little quote is part of The Wet Spots' performance of "sophisticated sex comedy." In an otherwise delightfully sex-positive show, this tiny slip reveals more than meets the eye.

This negative sentiment against bi-curious women is not only limited to one comedy act, but also has a significant presence within many bisexual communities. According to this sentiment, bi-curious women, "barsexuals," or "party bisexuals" are to blame for the existence of biphobic sexual harassment. This is because, according to many people, these women "reinforce" the negative stereotype of bisexuals as promoted by the mainstream media and pornography. According to this logic, had these women not been "compliant" with it, then the stereotypes would all disappear and sexual violence against bi women would be forever ended.

In his book *Bi America: Myths, Truths, and Struggles of an Invisible Community*, William E. Burleson quotes bisexual women in an online support group talking about the topic of bi-curious women. "The term 'bi-curious' makes me very angry," writes one woman. "As one of the first bi women I talked to told me, 'Either you like girls, or you don't. There is no maybe.' You don't have to 'try it out' to see if you are bi! I mean, you should know if you like members of the same sex! [sic]." "I hate it too," replies another. "It can also mean 'I'm a straight girl who wants to sound hip' or 'My boyfriend gets a hard-on from thinking about me with another woman.'" Yet another adds: "I hate the 'bi-curious' term because it gives the impression one can change one's mind and orientation at will, instead of coming to terms with the fact you're attracted to members of the same sex [sic]."

This attitude isn't only reserved to women who identify as bi-curious. In her article "Ambiguous Identity in an Unambiguous Sex/Gender Structure: The Case of Bisexual Women," Amber Ault quotes a bisexual woman talking derogatorily about bisexuals who are "promiscuous" or "unpoliticized":

> There is a bi community in this city, but I don't participate in it anymore. I used to go to the events and it felt very sleazy. There were a lot of people there who were totally obsessed with sex, some who were very promiscuous and held group sex parties, and others who had chosen to make their livings in sex-related ways, ranging from sex therapists to porno-telephone-call women. People like me, who just wanted to organize mainstream bis into a community, got disgusted and left.
>
> On a local [computer] bulletin board, we created gay rooms and almost all of the women in them identified as bi. These women were extremely irritating in that the fact that they found men attractive was exceedingly important to their sexual identity and they made sure to differentiate themselves from lesbians. Many of them were in het relationship [sic] and had never had a gay affair [sic], simply had found women attractive in the past, had maybe kissed a woman once. To me, these women were hets who simply were able to acknowledge that all of us are bi in some respect. However, when one said, "I am attracted to women but I could never fall in love with one," most of my gay male friends and I were disgusted that this person chose to label herself bi.

One American blogger seems to have taken this sentiment to, perhaps, its bitter end, writing that the behavior of bi-curious women or "barsexuals" "creates a hostile and unsafe environment for bi/queer women not only around lesbian circles, but straight guys as well." Later she adds, "[C]onsidering that the behavior in question is often used as a means for male attention, I would say yes [they are to blame for sexual harassment of bi women]. [. . .] I find it disturbing that they feel that female sexuality is solely used as a means of male entertainment and attention."

[Trigger warning: general discussion of slut shaming]
What we have here is a convergence of several biphobic stereotypes, ones usually used against bisexual-identified women: promiscuity, indecisiveness, being "actually straight," only doing it for male attention, political cowardice, inability to commit to a "stable" identity, and lack of commitment to the gay/lesbian movement. However, this time, instead of being used against bisexual women by monosexual people, these very same biphobic notions are displaced and used by bisexuals in order to denigrate bi-curious (and other) women. To call this irony would not even begin to cover it.

To put it clearly, this is internalized biphobia, meaning that biphobia is being used as a weapon by bisexuals against other bisexuals (or behaviorally bisexual women). This stance in practice divides the lines between "good bisexuals" and "bad bisexuals," constructing two mirror images of female bisexuality while absolving one and condemning the other. As Amber Ault writes in her article:

> [B]i women deploy the terms of the dominant system to construct a deviant bisexual other. The outlines of the dominant cultural code and its lesbian interpretations in these interviews are evident: honesty, fidelity, sexual responsibility, and commitments to the unitary and empirically demonstrable sexual

*subject; even so-called traditional conservative values emerge as
constitutive features of the true, proper, really real bisexual.
Bi women do not unequivocally deny the veracity of negative
stereotypes of themselves. Instead, they legitimate the stereotypes
by delimiting a subgroup of bisexuals about whom these beliefs
are accepted as true.*

What this means is that instead of naming the problem for what
it is—sexual violence against bisexual women—bi communities choose
to respond by placing the blame on the women who are in most danger by this system. Instead of working against men who sexually harass
and assault bisexual (and behaviorally bi) women, bisexual communities
choose to work against these women themselves. It seems that in order to
receive mainstream approval and acceptance, bi communities adopt and
repeat the same mainstream values that are normally used against them.

In addition, what we have here is slut shaming. According to the blog
Finally, A Feminism 101 Blog, slut shaming is

> *the idea of shaming and/or attacking a woman or a girl for
> being sexual, having one or more sexual partners, acknowl-
> edging sexual feelings, and/or acting on sexual feelings.
> Furthermore, it's "about the implication that if a woman has
> sex that traditional society disapproves of, she should feel guilty
> and inferior" (Alon Levy, "Slut Shaming"). It is damaging not
> only to the girls and women targeted, but to women in general
> and society as a whole.*

What it means in this case in that bi-curious women are shamed
and attacked for being publicly sexual and for behaving in a way that
society deems sexually deviant. In addition, this might also be thought
about as a form of "bi shaming," meaning that these women are shamed

and attacked specifically for publicly displaying bisexuality. Moreover, not only are these women shamed for being sexual and behaving bisexually, but they are also considered guilty of the sexual violence directed toward "real" or "good" bisexual women.

But, as Irish blogger Aoife O'Riordan writes in her blog post "In Defense of Barsexuals and Faux-Mos," biphobia and objectification of women "are things that have been around a long time. They were there long before Katy Perry, before Madonna kissed Britney, before t.A.T.u. . . . They've been around since before the ice melted in the world's first mojito, and nothing the drinker of that mojito did afterward is to blame for their existence."

As we've seen in this chapter, the sources for the fetishization of bisexual women as objects for the cis straight male gaze stem from mainstream media and pornographic depictions of bisexual women and female bisexuality. Likewise, biphobic sexual violence is informed by these depictions and enacted mostly by straight men. Bi-curious women, or "barsexuals," have not invented these stereotypes, and they are not the ones to enact the violence.

In addition, as pointed out by American blogger Kaley Perceful in her post "In Defense of 'Party Bisexuals,'" many of these women actually do identify as bisexual. This means that calling them anything else—including "bi-curious," "barsexual," or "party bisexual"—erases the existence and legitimacy of their bisexual identity. If someone identifies as bisexual, then her identity should be accepted and respected without the need to pass a "true bisexuality" test or to get an official "seal of approval."

Moreover, for many bi-identified women, this type of situation was the starting point and one of the only possible gateways for exploration of their bisexuality. Perceful writes:

> [L]iking members of the same sex [sic] is really difficult for a lot of people to admit to themselves as well as others. It can also be really difficult to act on. [. . .] With all of the shame and

insecurity that can come with being attracted to members of the same sex [sic], is it really so surprising that it takes a few drinks before some girls are able to act on their attraction to women?

And again:

Coming to terms with your bisexuality can be really fucking difficult. Sometimes it takes a really long time. I used to only make out with girls when I was drunk, and I still probably couldn't act on my attraction toward a woman without a little bit of liquid courage.

This means that this kind of discourse delegitimizes bisexual women's right to be sexual or to explore their sexuality. This not only limits the options for women who like to be sexual in public, but also for everyone else. Separating between "good" bisexuals, who are only "properly" sexual, and "bad" bisexuals, who are "improperly" sexual, means that being sexual is less legitimate for everyone.

However, whether or not these women are bisexual is hardly the point. Women are (and should be) entitled to be consensually sexual in whatever way they like, wherever they like, and whenever they like, without having to fear sexual violence, harassment, or shaming. By being sexual in public, they are not encouraging violence against bi women, but creating legitimacy (however narrow and constricted by the male gaze) for women to be visibly sexual and explore their bisexuality.

Instead of policing bi (and behaviorally bi) women, bisexual movements need to start taking a clear stand against sexual violence against bi women. Instead of following the path of misogyny and biphobia, bisexual women can reclaim our sexualities as our own, and reaffirm our right to be sexual without being objectified or becoming the target of sexual violence. We need to start addressing the problem for what it is, while creating tools for subverting the male gaze and for representing our sexualities on our terms rather than those of hegemonic cis straight men. Instead of rejecting our (bi)sexualities or attempting to desexualize ourselves, we can reclaim bisexuality and bi ways of being sexual, and call out biphobic sexual violence while still affirming women's bisexual choices.

In order for this to happen, we, as a movement and as bisexual women, first need to assert two basic understandings: first, that women have the right *to be sexual* whenever and however they wish; and second, that women have the right *not be sexual* whenever and however they wish.

YES MEANS YES; NO MEANS NO

Bisexual women become the target of sexual violence and slut shaming as a result of popular cultural imagination that sexualizes them and then punishes them for either consenting (slut shaming) or refusing (sexual violence). But what if we can reclaim our "Yes"? Reclaim our "No"? Create a world where anyone is free to say either without fearing violence?

The very fact that female bisexuality is hypersexualized opens a window, however narrow, for women to explore their sexuality and their bisexuality. It creates a certain space for women to question and experiment, making bisexuality an option for women to consider. An environment that encourages women to be bisexual may very well be coercive, objectifying, and sexually violent; but at the same time it might also open up a "crack" in the system for many women—a crack at which we can begin to break down the system.

One of the things that we, as bisexual women, can do is to reclaim our right to be sexual in any we way like while still opposing objectification and sexual violence. This means acknowledging that there's nothing wrong with female bisexuality in any and all of its forms. Whether bi women choose to make out in public, be sexual in private, have threesomes, have twosomes, have orgies, want other women only for sex, want all genders equally, be polyamorous, be monogamous, be a sex worker, be a kinkster or anything else—all of these choices should be equally legitimate, and none should be used as an excuse for justifying sexual violence against them.

Reclaiming our "Yes" means that we start looking at bisexuality on the terms of bisexuality rather than on the terms of the patriarchal and monosexist system that leaves bi women with only two options: prude or slut. Instead of judging bisexual women according to their compatibility with sexist and biphobic images of female bisexuality, we can start validating and appreciating their expressions of bisexuality. We can create our own wide and enabling standard of female bisexuality instead of the constrictive one imposed on us by heteropatriarchy.

Reclaiming "Yes" means that bisexual women would not need to fear saying "Yes" to something that they're interested in for fear of judgment by bisexual communities or fear of reinforcing biphobic stereotypes. It means that women are allowed to say "Yes," knowing that their consent is going to be respected, creating a safe space for them to be sexual.

Reclaiming our "Yes" also means the ability to express ourselves, our wishes, and our bisexualities. It means being able to speak our bisexualities through our own experiences and from our own perspectives— write our own stories, create our own images—ones that deviate from the ways we've been defined by patriarchy, and that subvert the current biphobic images of female bisexuality.

A good example of how to do this is in the sex-positive feminist movement (a movement that is in many ways also bisexual). Queer feminist writers and filmmakers create and redefine erotics and pornography that validate and celebrate female and queer sexuality in all forms, in a language that isn't based on, nor appeals to, heteronormative logic. The same can be done for female bisexuality, discussing and redefining its terms in a language that accommodates us rather than the straight cis male gaze.

Alongside reclaiming our "Yes" and our bi sexualities, we can also reclaim our "No"—our right not to be sexual if and when we're not interested in being so. Bisexual women are constantly and coercively hypersexualized, always imagined as sexually available, even when we're uninterested. Reclaiming "No" first and foremost means acknowledging the fact that not *all* bisexual women are *always* interested in being sexual. It means acknowledging the fact that anyone's lack of sexual interests is legitimate, that we all have a right to refuse to be sexual regardless of the situation we're in.

Reclaiming our right to "No" also means that we understand that "No" needs to be respected regardless of who says it, and when and how it's said. Whether a woman is at a bar or party, in the street, or at her house. While making no contact at all, while flirting with someone, in the middle of sex, or any other state. No matter what this woman did first, how she behaves, how out she is as bisexual, or what people think about her. "No" must always be taken at its word and must always be taken seriously.

Reclaiming "No" means we understand that sexual violence is not the fault of the woman whose boundaries were crossed. It is not the fault of other bi women who choose to be sexual publicly. It is not the fault of the out bi celebrities or bi women who are sex workers or porn stars. It is not the fault of anyone except our patriarchal rape culture, and of the people who disrespect the boundaries of bisexual women.

Reclaiming "No" means acknowledging the fact that many of us, bisexual women, are survivors of biphobic sexual violence. It means making space within bisexual communities to speak about biphobic sexual violence and to listen to others' experiences. It means believing survivors and their stories, without trying to judge them or blame them. It means creating tools, in our communities, for dealing with trauma and for supporting survivors. It also means raising awareness and promoting education about biphobic sexual violence in attempt to prevent it.

Reclaiming "No" also means acknowledging the fact that women can also be the perpetrators and breaking the silence around the issue of women's violence against women. It means giving women tools for recognizing and addressing sexual violence directed at them by other women. It means giving them words and legitimacy to express their trauma. It means believing the women who choose to speak and holding the perpetrators accountable for their actions.

Reclaiming our "No" also means acknowledging the fact that without the option to say "No," there's no real meaning to "Yes." Knowing that even if you say "No" it will not be respected means that you really only have one option. Reclaiming "No" means acknowledging that only when we are completely free to say it, can our "Yes" be real and significant.

Instead of responding to biphobic sexual violence by shaming bisexual (or behaviorally bi) women, we can change the terms of the discussion. Start talking about sexual violence and reclaim bi women's right to say "Yes" or to say "No" to whatever they like. Bi communities should promote a culture of consent; they should create and maintain sexually safe environments and spaces. Reclaiming "Yes" as well as "No" might serve as an antidote or a counterculture to the dominant culture of rape, slut shaming, and victim blaming. Using these attitudes means that bisexual spaces and movements can participate in the creation of a radical social change and can be subversive, empowering, and feminist.

CHAPTER 5:

Bisexuality, Feminism, and Men

Feminism doesn't start and end with women alone, but also concerns people of all genders—including men. This is because feminism is about taking down patriarchy, a structure that, although it is focused on domination and oppression of women, also hurts everyone else. Men have a stake in feminism because patriarchy hurts them too. In this chapter I'd like to look into the oppression working specifically against bisexual men and then link it back to patriarchy and feminism.

FEMINISM AND MEN

Before we look at oppression specifically against bisexual men, I'd first like to look into the difficulties experienced by men in general under patriarchy. Patriarchy hurts men by pushing them into the role of the oppressor. This means that men occupy a complex position within the patriarchal power structure, since they both benefit and get hurt by it. Acknowledging male privilege, then, is the first step in understanding how men are hurt by patriarchy.

Men enjoy many privileges and benefits under patriarchy in all walks of life—especially if they fit into the single standard, but also otherwise. On average, men make more money than women, they own more property, and they are likely to be employed in higher positions. Men are far likelier to have access to power—they receive more respect and acknowledgment for their achievements and garner far more symbolic capital than women, including within their own race and class. They are more likely to reach positions of wide social influence, such as the government and media. When they speak, they are listened to and are far less likely to be interrupted midspeech than women. They also receive more opportunities to speak or voice their opinions, and, unlike those of women, these views are considered socially valuable. Men are taught a sense of personal safety—unlike women, they might feel safe walking alone on the street (at any time of the day or night), or being alone with another person. Men are taught to believe in their own intelligence, strength, and independence—they are more likely to have high self-esteem and are far less likely to suffer from depression or suicidality. Men are also taught to consider their own experience as the default and therefore only rarely notice or acknowledge their many privileges.

In an online article named "Why I Am A Black Male Feminist," American activist and filmmaker Byron Hurt tells about the first time he realized his privilege as a man. While attending a workshop about preventing gender violence, the facilitator asked the men in the room "[W]hat things do you do to protect yourself from being raped or sexually assaulted?" Byron writes:

> *Not one man, including myself, could quickly answer the question. Finally, one man raised his hand and said, "Nothing."*

*Then [the facilitator] asked the women, "What things do you
do to protect yourself from being raped or sexually assaulted?"
Nearly all of the women in the room raised their hand. One by
one, each woman testified:*

*"I don't make eye contact with men when I walk down the
street," said one. "I don't put my drink down at parties," said
another. "I use the buddy system when I go to parties." "I cross
the street when I see a group of guys walking in my direction."
"I use my keys as a potential weapon." "I carry mace or pepper
spray." "I watch what I wear."*

*The women went on for several minutes, until their side of
the blackboard was completely filled with responses. The men's
side of the blackboard was blank. I was stunned. I had never
heard a group of women say these things before. I thought
about all of the women in my life—including my mother,
sister, and girlfriend—and realized that I had a lot to learn
about gender.*

As a way of explaining male privilege to men (and specifically,
straight white male privilege), American blogger and writer John Scalzi
suggests imagining life as a role-playing game called "The Real World."
In his blog post, "Straight White Male: The Lowest Difficulty Setting
There Is," he describes this type of privilege as (you guessed it) the lowest
difficulty setting to "The Real World" role-playing game. The people
who play at this setting face far fewer barriers when it comes to suc-
ceeding in the game, and in addition receive several bonuses that other
players do not. He continues:

*As the game progresses, your goal is to gain points, apportion
them wisely, and level up. If you start with fewer points . . .
or choose poorly regarding the skills you decide to level up on,
then the game will still be difficult for you. But because you're*

> *playing on the "Straight White Male" setting, gaining points*
> *and leveling up will still by default be easier . . .*
>
> *Likewise, it's certainly possible someone playing at a higher*
> *difficulty setting is progressing more quickly than you are,*
> *because they had more points initially given to them by the*
> *computer . . . and/or simply because they play the game better*
> *than you do. It doesn't change the fact you are still playing on*
> *the lowest difficulty setting.*
>
> *You can lose playing on the lowest difficulty setting. The*
> *lowest difficulty setting is still the easiest setting to win on.*
> *The player who plays on the "Gay Minority Female" setting?*
> Hardcore. *(Emphasis in original).*

It's important to say that if a certain man is neither straight nor white, this still doesn't cancel out his male privilege. Obviously, the more someone fits into the single standard of patriarchy, the "lower" his "difficulty setting" becomes. However, while misfitting some links on the chain might make it harder for him in some ways, as far as it goes to *male* privilege, he still benefits from it. This means he also needs to acknowledge and address it.

Although it might seem so, I am not only talking about cisgender men. While transgender men cannot simplistically be called "privileged," they still enjoy certain benefits that have to do with being perceived as male or masculine. This means that although they do not enjoy structural privileges (such as bigger salaries or more access to power), they still enjoy benefits having to do with interaction with other people. I've had trans male friends tell me that once they were perceived as cis men on the street, they stopped receiving street harassment. They also felt that people gave them more respect, listened to them more, and interrupted them less. Within some queer and trans communities, trans men might be considered more attractive than anyone else, or have their issues considered more important than other groups' (for example, trans women). For these reasons, while their privilege certainly doesn't compare to that of cis men, trans men should still acknowledge and address their benefits as men.

The topic of privilege leads us to the way in which men get hurt by patriarchy. According to Canadian writer Michael Kaufman, this is intimately connected with men's privileges. In his article "Men, Feminism, and Men's Contradictory Experiences of Power," he argues that men internalize patriarchal values and learn to view their own power as power to dominate others. He writes:

> *My masculinity is a bond, a glue, to the patriarchal world. It is the thing which makes that world mine, which makes it more or less comfortable to live in. Through the incorporation of a dominant form of masculinity particular to my class, race, nationality, era, sexual orientation, and religion, I gained real benefits and an individual sense of self-worth.*

Having internalized these patriarchal values, men learn to see themselves in terms of control, power, and domination. However, herein lies the sting: Since men are forced into the role of oppressor, they are expected to constantly be in control of both themselves and their environments. Kaufman writes: "We have to perform and stay in control. We're supposed to conquer, be on top of things, and call the shots. We have to tough it out, provide, and achieve." "Paradoxically, men are wounded by the very way we have learned to embody and exercise our power."

Men are expected to express their domination in various ways that end up hurting them. They are expected to be physically capable, strong, and able-bodied. Since early childhood, they are encouraged to engage in sports, be able to fight, be able to lift heavy objects, or otherwise physically manipulate their environments (build things, fix things, etc.).

In certain cultures and groups, as they grow up they are also encouraged (or indeed, obligated by law) to become soldiers and to physically "fight for their country,"[33] even to the death. By doing all of these things, men exhibit their ability to dominate their environments by exerting physical control. This expectation hurts the men who do not, or for any reason cannot, par with the standard. They get perceived as weak, or as having deficient masculinities, and therefore as lesser human beings (remember that fitting into the single standard of patriarchy is also the condition for being considered a valuable human). It also hurts the men who do engage in these activities, as the pressure and the intensity required of them often leads to physical injuries, permanent damage, or even death.

Men are expected to be able to provide for the physical needs of their (presumably heteronormative) families, to be the "breadwinner" or the one "putting the food on the table." They are expected to do this by working hard, making money, and deciding what to do with it. By doing this, men prove their ability, status, and their domination of their families (women and children). They also earn respect for their work, and they control the money and its expenditure. This again hurts men who cannot fit into this standard, as they are perceived as lazy or incapable. The men who do perform this expectation get hurt because it means reducing their lives to working under capitalism, meaning that in most cases they feel alienated from their work and from other people (since they're left with very little time for their personal lives).

Despite the fact that men are encouraged to provide for the physical needs of women and children, they are also expected to be emotionally distant from them, and from other people in general. As a general rule, men are expected never to act in ways that are nurturing, caring, or tender toward others. In fact, they are expected to never feel these things, want them, or admit to them. Their emotional distance is supposed to back up their controlling status over their families by showing that they are impartial and that emotional needs are insignificant in relation to the material needs that the man is obliged to provide. This hurts the men who do provide emotional support to their families by painting them as overcaring, overemotional, or even as being "pussywhipped" by their wives. It also hurts the men who do embody this expectation because it denies them of emotional intimacy and closeness to other people.

In addition to maintaining emotional distance, men are supposed to be emotionally invulnerable and never to feel hurt, scared, or sad. Even if they do feel any of these things, they are expected to internalize them and never to speak of them or express them otherwise ("boys don't cry," as the popular saying goes). This expectation is supposed to be an expression of a man's eternal and enduring strength, his ability to "take anything" without getting hurt or breaking down. Men who do express their emotions or indeed cry are often mocked or ridiculed. They're considered to have deficient masculinities, or not to be "manly enough." They are consequently derogated through comparisons to women, using nicknames such as "sissy," "pussy," etc. The men who do perform this expectation are hurt by it because they are forced into emotional numbness at best and into internalized negative feelings at worst. These internalized feelings might often lead men to self-destructive behaviors, hurting themselves as well as others since they can find no socially acceptable way to admit and express their emotions.

On par with the perception of men as "purely physical" beings, they are also expected to always want and be ready for sex. In fact, they are taught that not only does their masculinity depend upon it, but also their value as human beings. Sex is also supposed to be the only legitimate way for men to receive intimacy (since emotional intimacy is forbidden to them). The expression of sexual prowess is supposed to support the image of men as those who conquer and dominate women. Popular imagination compares men's sexual encounters with women to imaginary notches on the belts of their masculinity. Men who do not fulfill this expectation are seen as losers or (god forbid!) as gay. Men who do internalize it learn to view women as objects rather than people, a distancing and alienating notion that might hurt their ability to create emotional intimacy.

[Trigger warning: general discussion of sexual assault and trauma]

In addition, and importantly, this hurts men who have been sexually assaulted or raped. They sometime presume that, because they were hurt, then they were somehow "asking for it" or actually "wanting it." It also leads society to question them and deny their trauma, because, as popular "wisdom" goes, "you can't rape the willing" (presuming that men must always be willing).

[End of trigger]

Men are also expected never to do anything perceived as feminine. This applies to everything from clothing through body language to behavior, preferences, and beyond. A good example is external appearance: While women have fought—and still are fighting—for their right to wear pants, to not be required to wear makeup or shave their entire bodies, men are still strictly forbidden to wear skirts, jewelry, or makeup, to shave their body hair, or to otherwise "feminize" their appearance. Hell, even men who wear masculine clothes with colors that are too bright, or with the appearance of putting too much effort into it, are policed for their deviation. The complete ban on anything perceived as feminine is meant to secure masculinity's status as superior and femininity's status as inferior. (Famously, Iggy Pop said, "I'm not ashamed to dress like a woman because I don't think it's shameful to be a woman.") Men who behave in ways that are perceived as feminine are regarded as "sissies," "queers," or "homos," and undergo various forms of social policing and violence for their gender deviance. Men who act according to this expectation are denied a full spectrum of options for self-expression, creativity, and play, and are forced to limit themselves to a narrow standard of acceptable behavior.

Men are expected to be strictly and always heterosexual. As alluded to above, being gay is one of the most dreaded things that a man might be suspected of, and is often used as a derogatory term for policing men who have deviated from the sacred lines of manhood. That said, as American writer Greta Christina mentions in her blog post "Five Stupid,

Unfair and Sexist Things Expected of Men," once a man actually comes out as gay, this message of "[D]on't be even a little bit gay" is replaced with "Well . . . okay." More than anything, this tells us that men are allowed to be monosexual (however begrudgingly in the case of gay men), but are strictly forbidden from being bisexual. Heterosexuality for men enforces their compliance with dominant masculinity as well as their value as human beings. Monosexuality for gay men secures their masculinity by exhibiting perceived decisiveness and stability. Bisexuality, however, does not fit together with this framework because its perceived instability, confusion, and indecisiveness clash with those values expected of men.

It is of little surprise, then, that male bisexuality is constantly erased and denied. As mentioned in the previous chapter, while the popular "wisdom" regarding bi women says that "everyone is bisexual, really," popular "wisdom" about bi men says that "bisexuals don't exist." I'd like to look into the ways in which male bisexuality is erased and into what this erasure means about social treatment of male bisexuality.

ERASURE OF MALE BISEXUALITY: THE BAILEY STUDY

Bisexual men and male bisexuality are routinely erased and denied out of existence, making bi men one of the most closeted populations among LGBT communities. When it *is* discussed, male bisexuality usually appears in only three contexts: medical, sexual, and denial (the latter usually coupled with one of the former or both). This tells us that male bisexuality is only perceived as relevant in discussions about medical health and sex, while the full context often serves as a conduit to prove that bisexual men either do not really exist or are dangerous to society.

For example, searching online for the term "bisexual men" only brings up "relevant" results (that is, those related to bi community, identity, or politics) on the first page. Starting from the second page and thereon, the results show an increasing number of either dating-, porn-, or AIDS-related links. From page four onward, the links increasingly clump bisexual men in with gay men, meaning that they are not discussed specifically. Among all of these pages, various links lead to discussions of the question of whether or not male bisexuality really exists (with various answers).

Looking at online academic search engines, the situation is much worse, as literally *all links* on the first few pages lead to articles about HIV/AIDS while also conflating male bisexuality with homosexuality. The academic *Journal of Bisexuality* doesn't fare much better: Many of the articles in the journal discussing male bisexuality relate to HIV/AIDS and sexual health. In addition, most of the articles published there on the topic of male bisexuality are social science studies, discussing male bisexuality in "scientific" or "medical" terms. Very few theoretical or cultural perspectives on the topic exist, even within this bi-specific journal. This means that even within the field of bisexual studies, male bisexuality is still discussed mostly in sexual and medical terms.

Perhaps the epitome of everything that's bad about public attitudes regarding male bisexuality is American researcher J. Michael Bailey's study, "Sexual Arousal Patterns of Bisexual Men," or as it's more famously known: "Straight, Gay, or Lying?" In this study, Bailey and his team sought to scientifically disprove the existence of male bisexuality by reducing male bisexual identity to patterns of sexual arousal.

The experiment was performed thus: Thirty straight, thirty-three bisexual, and thirty-eight gay cisgender men were recruited through newspaper ads. Upon making contact, they were asked to fill out a form regarding their sexual identity and their sexual desires. After being categorized according to his sexual orientation, each man in question was taken to a private room and shown eleven minutes of three filmed stimuli: The first was "neutral," containing images of natural landscapes; the second contained mainstream girl-on-girl porn (of the type discussed in the previous chapter); and the third contained mainstream gay porn. A penile gauge was put on the participants' penises in order to measure erections. In addition, the participants could move a lever forward or backward in order to indicate their subjective arousal.

According to Bailey's reported results, most bisexual men responded (that is, received erections) in the same way as gay men. Some responded the same way as straight men, and still others responded like, well, bisexual men. Pretty straightforward, no? No. Here are some problems with the study.

First of all, as pointed out by U.K. writer Sue George on her blog post "Why Michael Bailey is still so very wrong," the methods used in this study were shady at best. The overall number of participants analyzed in his sample was only sixty-eight. Out of the thirty-three bisexual men initially recruited, only twenty-two had "sufficient genital arousal for analyses," meaning that the others were discounted. In addition, it seems as if the researchers didn't work according to people's self-identification at all. "Instead," says George, "the researchers rated men as gay, straight, or bi according to answers they gave to questions about their sexual desires." Yet another problem is the question of whether arousal by mainstream porn in a lab setting can at all be considered an accurate measure of sexual identity. And still another issue is that, according to Bailey's numbers (rather than reported results), nearly all the men who responded sexually were aroused by *all* the sexual images, male *and* female.

Yet other problems emerge once you look into the context and history of this researcher. As alluded to in the previous chapter, J. Michael Bailey is also the author of a highly transphobic book called *The Man Who Would Be Queen*. The book describes transgender women in the most pathological of terms, as either "homosexual men" who transitioned in order to have more sex with men, or as "autogynephiliacs," who transitioned out of a sexual fetish for having a female body. In addition, at least some of the women "studied" in the book were included without their consent. Indeed, some never even knew they were participating in a study. One of the women also claimed that Bailey slept with her. This breach of ethics cost Bailey his position as chair of the psychology department in Northwestern University, where he is still employed.

And as if that wasn't enough, Bailey is also known to have spoken several times against gay people, for example saying that "Evolutionarily, homosexuality is a big mistake." He also coauthored an article defending heterosexual eugenics, or parents' "right" to abort gay fetuses (if it were possible to predict). Famously, he wrote that such abortions would be "morally neutral" and that doing so is "unlikely to cause significant harm."

In addition, even before his controversial study about bisexual men, Bailey had made several remarks to the extent that no bisexual men exist and that all women are actually bisexual. He even used the expression "Gay, straight, or lying" several times. For example, in *The Man Who Would Be Queen*, he writes:

Although there are clearly men who call themselves "bisexual" and who have sex with both men and women, both scientists and laypeople have long been skeptical that men with bisexual arousal patterns exist. . . . They have a saying: "You're either gay, straight, or lying." In contrast, many women are bisexual, at least in their sexual arousal patterns.

And again:

If bisexuality—meaning indifference to the choice between male and female sex partners—were in them, then it should have been easy for them to conform to the heterosexual norm. But it wasn't.

Recall gay men's skepticism about men who claim to be bisexual. ("You're either gay, straight, or lying.")

To conclude thus far, Bailey as a researcher has a problematic background to say the least, one that should encourage more scrutiny regarding his study and its results. Very obviously being homophobic, transphobic, and biphobic even before the publication of the "Straight, Gay, or Lying?" study means that the man has an agenda, and that agenda is not in our favor.

That said, the major problems with this study are not so much in the details as they are in the general scheme. Even if Bailey were an impeccable researcher and his methods sound, this study still would have been problematic. This is because it perpetuates the three trends I described above about social treatment of male bisexuality: Medicalization, sexualization, and denial.

MEDICALIZATION

According to Wikipedia, "medicalization is the process by which human conditions and problems come to be defined and treated as medical conditions, and thus become the subject of medical study, diagnosis, prevention, or treatment." Historically, the medicalization of male bisexuality started with nineteenth- and early-twentieth-century minority-world sexologists such as Henry Havelock Ellis, Magnus Hirschfeld, and Sigmnund Freud. These people observed the human behavior of desiring more than one gender, named it "bisexuality," and studied it in medical terms. Bisexuality became a subject of medical study. As with all other medicalized behaviors, the notion behind the research was the presumption that bisexuality is a problem in and of itself, needing to be poked and prodded in order to be "understood"—and sometimes treated.

Bailey's study about bisexual men was conducted using medical techniques (physical erection measures, Kinsey-scale sexual assessments, etc.). It also discussed bisexuality in "scientific" terms, using charts and numbers. In addition, it quite obviously viewed bisexuality as a "problem" to be studied and "understood." This can be seen in sentences such as, "Although bisexual behavior is not uncommon in men, there has long been skepticism that it is motivated by strong sexual arousal and attraction to both sexes," or, "Skepticism about male bisexuality must . . . concern claims about bisexual feelings, that is, strong sexual attraction and arousal to both sexes."

In his article "The Discovery of Hyperkinesis: Notes on the Medicalization of Deviant Behavior," American sociologist Peter Conrad identifies four main problems with medicalization: expert control, medical social control, individualization of social problems, and the depoliticization of deviant behavior. All of these problems exist in Bailey's study of male bisexuality.

Expert control means that the medical institution not only gets to decide whether or not being like us is wrong, but also gets to define us—and our identities—for us. They get to decide the terms of the discussion, the working definitions, and the conclusions about any behavior that happens to be under their scrutiny. Bailey's study of male bisexuality decides the terms of the discussion because it defines male bisexuality in a very particular way: "sufficient" genital arousal to both girl-on-girl and mainstream gay male porn. Deciding what male bisexuality is and how it should be measured gives the researcher complete control to decide who can qualify as bisexual and who cannot. This makes for a very convenient path to the denial of the existence of male bisexuality as a whole.

Medical social control refers to "the ways in which medicine functions (wittingly or unwittingly) to secure adherence to social norms; specifically, by using medical means to minimize, eliminate, or normalize deviant behavior." This means that the medical institution is also a normalizing agent, deciding which behavior is "normal" and which should be "corrected." Bailey's study suggests that male bisexuality is abnormal, and strongly insinuates that bi men lie about their identity. The article even goes as far as comparing male bisexuality with pedophilia, writing that "when self-report is suspect, genital arousal may provide a more valid measure. For example, genital arousal to stimuli depicting children is an effective method of assessing pedophilia, even among men who deny attraction to children."

Individualization of social problems means "seeing the causes of the problem in individuals rather than in the society where they live." This means that instead of addressing existing social problems, the medical institution turns its attention to the individuals who are hurt by the problem at hand. Instead of addressing the social problem of monosexism, which in all ways discourages men from being bisexual, Bailey's study turns its accusation against bisexual men themselves, and blames them for being rendered invisible.

Depoliticization of deviant behavior means that the behavior is taken outside of its social context. It is the result of the individualization of social problems, and its function is to neutralize the political deviance of the behavior in question. By reducing male bisexual identity to bodily functions, Bailey's study extracts bisexuality of its wide political context. Instead of viewing it in light of its political deviance, the study depoliticized male bisexuality.

SEXUALIZATION

Sexualization means viewing someone or something solely as sexual. As we've seen in the previous chapter, this is a biphobic notion that also works against bisexual women, turning them into sexual objects for the pleasure of straight cis men. Working against bisexual men, the same notion rises again but in a different form: reducing male bisexuality to nothing but sex as a method for eliminating (rather than exploiting) male bisexual desire and identity.

Sexualization of male bisexuality happens when the topic of bisexual men is only discussed in relation to sex—for example, as mentioned above, when online searches only yield results related to either porn or sexual behavior (usually in conjunction with HIV/AIDS). In general, it seems that male bisexuality is only relevant or acknowledged where sex or health are discussed. However, the very same notion serves many people in their attempt to erase bisexuality, using the sexualization of male bisexuality as proof of the fact that it's nothing more than sexual behavior.

Bailey's study does exactly this: It uses a purely sexual or physical definition of male bisexuality in order to prove that it doesn't exist. Though he acknowledges bisexual behavior, he repeats several times in the article that even though there's no doubt that men who identify and behave as bisexuals exist, it is doubtful whether male bisexual arousal patterns do.

This not only means that male bisexual identity is being reduced to a narrow definition, but also that it ignores the wide social context of bisexuality. As we recall from chapter 1, bisexuality can be defined through many aspects, including politics, community, culture, and desire (which, as opposed to pure physical responses, is multiple and complex). Reducing the definition to this level necessarily means erasure of most aspects of bisexual identities.

Another reduction caused by this sexualization is the erasure of bisexual transgender men and intersex men. By only examining cisgender men, the study confines masculinity to bodies assigned male at birth. This kind of definition is cissexist because it assumes that people's genitals define what gender they are (male or female), and presumes that there are only two binary sexes. Furthermore, men who didn't have "sufficient" sexual response were excluded from the results. To judge by the study, "man" means a person with a functioning penis capable of erection. In this way, the study erases not only trans and intersex bi men, but also asexual bi men who do not experience erections.[34] All these groups of bi men are erased by the study twice: first by excluding them from the study itself, and second by denying that male bisexuality exists.

The study also reduces male bisexuality to attraction to cisgender men and women only, again maintaining a cissexist definition. By doing so, it again erases trans men and women, as well as the many genders that do not fit into a binary definition (for example, genderqueer, bigender, agender, pangender, etc.). The binary division between "biological" females and males also erases the existence of intersex people. This means that the study—and perhaps the researchers themselves—cannot even conceive of a type of desire that includes more than two genders or sexes. All the rest of us, the study implies, can neither desire nor be desired.

This sexualization is part of the medical control practiced here on male bisexuality. It is the tool through which this control is performed on all of its levels: The level of expert control is performed through determining the definition of male bisexuality as purely sexual; the level of medical social control tries to "correct" male bisexual identities by suggesting that bisexuality doesn't exist on a sexual level; the last two levels (individualization of social problems, and depoliticization of deviant behavior) work by looking solely at bi male bodily functions, isolated and detached from their context.

DENIAL

Denial of male bisexuality is both an inseparable part and the ultimate goal of this type of medicalization and sexualization. In Bailey's study, all three are entangled and work to reinforce one another. Denial of male bisexuality is both the motive behind and the goal of the study. Medicalization and sexualization are both the tools and the path leading between the motive and the goal. In order to produce a result that denies the existence of male bisexuality, Bailey's study uses a purely sexual definition and discusses it in medical terms. The definition and the medical terms then become the way in which he "proves" that male bisexuality does not exist.

From a broader perspective, male bisexuality is routinely erased because it stands as a direct threat to dominant perceptions of masculinity. As we've seen in the previous chapter, bisexuality as an idea is associated with characteristics that are perceived as feminine, such as instability, indecisiveness, and confusion. In addition, bisexuality threatens patriarchal values by being associated with multiplicity rather than singularity or "oneness." This means that bisexuality in men fractures their compliance with the demands of dominant masculinity, creating "gender trouble" (per Judith Butler), and therefore must be eliminated. This threat to dominant masculinity posed by male bisexuality also directly relates to male bisexuality's feminist potential. I will return to this later on in this chapter.

SCIENCE AND PATRIARCHY

Through the example of Bailey's "Gay, Straight, or Lying?" study, we've seen how the medicalization of male bisexuality (performed through sexualization and for the purpose of denial) is harmful to bisexual men. I would now like to show how the very outset of scientifically "studying" bisexual men is a result of patriarchal thought. In doing so, I'm hoping to show that bisexual men have a stake in feminism, since patriarchy directly harms them.

Science is generally used to indicate methodical and systematic learning and observation regarding material phenomena in the world. Its values are rationality, objectivity, logic, and universality. Those are considered both the tools of science and the characteristics of science itself. "Good science" is achieved by being rational, logical, methodical, and objective, and by aspiring to universality (meaning that the results or conclusions are always true regardless of circumstance). Science in general and by itself is also considered to stand for the same values. These characteristics provide both the method and the goal of science and scientific thought.

Historically and currently, all of those characteristics have been imagined in minority-world cultures as the sole domain of men. Even though the standard for the "man of reason" or "man of science" has often been described as "universal" and as applying to all people regardless of gender, looking more deeply into the context of this notion shows us otherwise. In her article "The Man of Reason," Genevieve Llyod describes how seventeenth-century philosophy (which gave rise to the creation and perception of modern science) defined rationality and logic as belonging solely to men. In those same discourses, women were describes as inherently irrational, illogical, and emotional, and vice versa—irrationality, illogic, and emotionality were described as inherently feminine or "womanish."

This also contributed to and reinforced the view of women as inherently inferior to men: The fact that positive value was attributed solely to "masculine" traits while negative value was attributed to "feminine" traits meant that women were necessarily perceived as inferior. The ideal of the scientific thinker was imagined specifically as a man, barring women from the impossible standard that it set for them.

In addition to creating a problem concerning the values of the system, it also created and maintained a situation in which women were materially barred from being scientists. In a circular logic, since women were presumed to be incapable of rational thought, they were also barred from training in sciences and philosophy. Instead, they were taught life skills meant to help them in their futures as wives caring for their husbands and children. This created a situation in which materially, only men could become philosophers and scientists.

Though perhaps more subtle, these notions remain relevant today. Values associated with masculinity are still given more importance, while values associated with femininity are either dismissed or treated as inferior. By the same token, men and boys are still considered far more capable of rational thought and are much more encouraged than women and girls to take interest in science. In light of all this, it is of little surprise that, for example, the main image on the Wikipedia entry on "Science," showing a collage of influential scientists, only includes two women out of thirty people (most of whom are also white).

To expand on this notion a little bit further, the values of science have not only been associated with men and masculinity, but also with every link on the chain of the single standard of patriarchy. In particular, they have been associated with whiteness, viewing white minority culture men in the same way (as rational, logical, objective), while

viewing majority-world people and people of color as inherently irrational, illogical, and so on. Specifically regarding the matter at hand,
these "positive" values have also been associated with heterosexuality
and monosexuality, while rendering queer sexualities and bisexuality as
respectively "inferior."

Rendering certain social groups as mentally "inferior" is not the
only problem with science, however. Yet another problem rises from
those same patriarchal notions: the idea of the (white, heterosexual,
male) scientist as an objective, impartial observer. Following this
notion, the topic or person studied becomes an object of study and
research—actively objectified by the scientist. This means that the scientist is the one whose opinion matters above all, above and beyond
that of the people discussed. The person "studied" becomes the "raw
material" that must be analyzed by the researcher. This person's interpretation of *herself* is considered irrelevant or even impossible, since it's
presumed that the scientist "always knows best" and that the person
studied is somehow "biased."

Unsurprisingly, then, we might often find that human "objects"
of scientific or medical investigation are ones who "fail" on one or more
of the chain links of the single standard. For example, women have historically been and currently are used as the objects of research. Male
scientists are considered objective and therefore the highest authority on
many matters relating to women (for example, women's health, wom-
en's psychology, or women's life circumstances). Women, on the other
hand, are not to be trusted since they are allegedly emotional, irrational,
and subjective (rather than rational, logical, and objective). Likewise,
white researchers studying majority-world cultures often see themselves
as objective observers who know better than "the natives," judging their
cultures according to white standards while dismissing the views of the
people studied. In the same way, monosexuals—and especially heterosexuals—are often considered as the authority on matters relating to
bisexuality. In Bailey's study, the role of the scientist is to question and

doubt male bisexuality, while presuming that he possesses an objective and impartial point of view. This objectifies bisexual men by using them as the "raw material" for him to interpret, instead of considering their own opinions and interpretations of their bi identities.

This relation of "objective scientist" versus objectified "raw material" creates a hierarchical dynamic of control and domination. The one who looks, interprets, and examines is also the one with power over the "object" of his study. As we might recall, this is the way in which social medical control works—by giving scientists and researchers the power to define, to judge, and to normalize. This is emphasized when the "object" studied is a marginalized group, since the scientist's "objectivity," "logic," and "rationality" can be used to even further marginalize the group in question.

For example, Bailey's study presumes that the researchers (Bailey and his team)—and the study itself—are objective, logical, and impartial. This presumption is then used in order to further marginalize male bisexuality by passing an allegedly "objective" judgment upon it. This dynamic stems from patriarchal values associated with science. It is also patriarchal on a material level, since the people at the top of the scientific hierarchy are often those belonging to dominant groups (especially white, cis male, and heterosexual), and who fit into the single standard of patriarchy.

In this way, Bailey's study of bisexual men perpetuates the patriarchal values of science. Such studies do so by presuming that white heterosexual men are the authority on bisexual men (rather than bisexual men themselves), and by perpetuating a hierarchical dynamic of the researcher as the "objective" observer and bisexual men as the objectified "raw material." In doing so, they are leaning on a patriarchal value system that gives positive value solely to objectivity, impartiality, and logic, while also allowing only white heterosexual cis men to be the owners of such qualities. This, in turn, further marginalizes bisexual men and reinforces the medical control of their identities and lives.

Specifically regarding trans and intersex bi men, and nonbinary bi people, it's important to note that as a patriarchal formation, science has an interest in perpetuating a binary and cissexist gender system. A binary distinction between males/men on one side and females/women on the other is the basis upon which patriarchy operates. Without a clear distinction between these two categories, there can be no clear distinction between the "superior" class (males/men) and the "inferior" class (females/women). In this way, the patriarchal character of science is inseparable from its cissexism and erasure of all nonbinary and trans genders.

COMMUNITY RESPONSE—THE SECOND STUDY

In light of all this, it is surprising (to say the least) that representatives from the American bisexual community—the heads of the American Institute of Bisexuality (AIB)—chose to contact Bailey and his team and to fund additional research on the same topic. Though their decision was controversial within bisexual movements worldwide, I still think it's worth discussing, considering the prominence of both the AIB and the second research.

The second study (published in 2011 and called "Sexual arousal patterns of bisexual men revisited") was done using the very same methods, but this time found that bisexual men actually do exist. What do you know! On the surface, it appears that the AIB has done well. Finally, there is scientific proof backing the existence of bi men. However, several problems prevent this study from being a positive achievement. In fact, despite its "positive" results, it only deepened the problem further.

The article itself was written in terms no less biphobic than the previous one. For example, Bailey and his team reused a slightly rephrased version of the opening paragraph of the previous study, writing that

Some men who have had sexual experiences with both men and women identify as bisexual. However, there is a long history of

*skepticism about whether these men also have substantial sexual
attraction toward both sexes.*

The article throughout is written with constant "doubts" (denial)
that, despite the results, male bisexuality really does exist. It concludes
by saying that "given that bisexual arousal patterns have not previously
been detected among even bisexual-identified men, an underlying bisexual orientation may be uncommon."

By funding yet another study in the same vein, the AIB reinforced
the medicalization of bisexual men. By doing so they directly contributed to the hierarchical dynamic that positions bisexual men as "a 'species' to be studied and dissected" (as Mark Simpson put it in his blog
post "Bisexual Men Exist! But Does Scientific Sex Research?"). In this
way, they contributed to the medical control of bisexual men's identities
and lives: the perception that "experts" are the authorities that get to
define bisexuality; the attempt to normalize male bisexuality; and the
isolation of bisexuality from political and social context.

They also reinforced the methods of the previous study by reusing
them in the current one. By extension, this also reinforces the results of
the previous study—if the method was problematic and produced bad
results, it wouldn't have been used again, right?

In doing so, the AIB became compliant with the idea that male
bisexuality is defined according to genital arousal, further contributing
to its sexualization. In fact, the second study used an even more reduc-
tive definition of male bisexuality—men were only allowed to participate if they have "had at least two sexual partners of each sex and a
romantic relationship of at least three months' duration with at least one
person of each sex." By doing so, AIB contributed to the erasure of *most
factors* of male bisexual identities and created a new impossible standard
for bisexual men to "qualify" as bi.

In addition and in keeping with the previous study, the second
study uses a binary, cissexist definition of masculinity that views men

only as people assigned male at birth and who are capable of having an erection. This again erases bisexual transgender, intersex, and asexual men. The study also maintained its definition of bisexuality as attraction to cisgender men and women, erasing nonbinary, transgender, and intersex people. This means that these groups were again erased from conceptions of desire since they were missing both as objects of desire and as desiring subjects. By funding this study, the AIB also became compliant with this cissexism and erasure.

On a broader perspective, by funding this study, the AIB also reinforced the patriarchal notion of the white, heterosexual male scientist as the only objective authority on matters relating to marginalized identities. It further promoted the patriarchal values of science and the systematic preference of values associated with masculinity (such as logic, reason, objectivity, and universality) over values associated with femininity (such as specificity, emotions, and empathy).

AIB's support of Bailey also extended beyond the symbolic level. On their website *BiBrain.org*, AIB even went as far as posting a full twenty-two-page document providing "information on why AIB has worked with the supposedly 'controversial' researcher(s)." In the document they actively defend J. Michael Bailey, presenting him as an ethical, responsible researcher, and supporting his transphobic theory about trans women. The document also denies all of the issues regarding his transphobic, biphobic, and homophobic biases, his support of eugenics, and his breach of ethics. It even goes as far as defending the results of the previous study and presenting them as valid (though perhaps misguided). That a bisexual organization should do all this is deeply shameful and wholly problematic.

In light of all this, one finds oneself wondering, why *did* the AIB want to collaborate with Bailey? The answer can be found in that same document: "The bisexual group that funded the study is pleased at the validation, especially coming from a former skeptic about bisexual orientation in men." In other words, they decided to work with Bailey because he is a high-profile researcher with a lot of power and media popularity. They wanted him to be the one to recant the results of the previous study *because* of his biphobia, not *despite* it.

According to AIB, they achieved their goal. The document hails: "*The New York Times* and other outlets wrote about the results ('No Surprise to Bisexual Men: They Exist'), and former skeptic and sex columnist Dan Savage penned an article entitled: 'Case Closed: Bisexual Men Exist!'"

However, taking a closer look at the media's reaction to this second study shows that its success was limited at best. While *The New York Times* did publish the follow up, it wasn't half as popular as the original article (which came to be one of the top five emailed stories on their website at the time). It also didn't get picked up as much by other press and media. For example, while the original piece got translated into Hebrew widely and at length on several newspapers (and news sites), the new study only warranted two small items on marginal news websites (and no newspapers). In fact, searching online for "bisexual" in Hebrew still brings up the "Gay, Straight, or Lying?" news item as one of the first results. Dan Savage's admittance that bisexual men exist certainly didn't make him stop being biphobic. In fact, the entire first paragraph of his column is dedicated to bashing bisexual activists and defending his "certain degree of skepticism" when meeting bi-identified young people.

As Mark Simpson writes, the previous study "was trumpeted around the world. Because of course it told people, straight and gay, what they wanted to hear, and what common sense tells them to be the case." The second study, he says, "got the result they [AIB] wanted, but I fear they're wasting their money and merely encouraging more bad science." He continues:

> *All that has been proven is that measuring penile blood-flow in*
> *a laboratory is a highly reductive and highly abnormal measure*

*of male sexuality. Men are not just penises. They are also pros-
tate glands. Perineums. Earlobes. Inner thighs. Brains. Nipples.
It also shows that you get the result you're looking for. In 2005
Bailey wanted to prove that male bisexuality didn't exist. In
2011 he didn't.*

Looking overall at this incident, it seems that by funding the second study, the AIB might have caused more damage than good. By
cooperating with Bailey, they reinforced the medicalization and sexualization of bisexual men, and the erasure of large categories of bi men.
They also reinforced patriarchal and hierarchical values of science that
objectify people from marginalized groups, and bisexual men in particular. In defending Bailey, they have supported his transphobia, biphobia, and homophobia, as well as several other problematic aspects of his
professional behavior. Instead of reinforcing all of these things while trying to prove something we all know anyway, the AIB would have done
better to fund research actually discussing bisexual men, their identities,
and their lives.

Research about bisexual men, in their complexity and multiplicity,
is important. However, the way that research about bisexual men currently works in highly problematic and harmful. In order for good and
productive research to be done in this topic, bisexual men themselves
need to be taken into account. They should be acknowledged as existing,
and as a marginalized group, their voices should be heard and respected.
Researchers should encourage bisexual men to interpret their own experiences and should endeavor to empower them through research rather
than to disempower and objectify them. Particular attention should be
paid to marginalized groups of bisexual men, such as bi trans and intersex men, bi men of color, disabled and chronically ill bi men, and many
more. Further, research about bi men should stop its nearly sole focus
on sexualized and medicalized interpretations of male bisexuality, and

instead start expanding on such wide topics as cultural studies, art studies, epistemologies, and other humanities. In this way, research might deliver male bisexuality from its current location, and create more productive and complex understandings of the topic.

"BUT WHAT ABOUT THE MEN?": BI MEN AND WOMEN

So far I've reviewed the way that other people talk about bisexual men and the meanings of these discourses. But what about bisexual men? What do they have to say about themselves? I'd like to examine the ways in which male bisexual writers explain bi male invisibility.

Before I start, I need to say that some of the things written in this section are critical in tone, in a way that may appear to contradict my position that bi men need to be listened to rather than talked about. Despite this, I'm still taking the liberty to discuss this critically, for several reasons. First of all, in terms of power, I am located differently in relation to bisexual men than most researchers of this topic. While the writings about bi men that I criticized above were written from the position of oppressor (by white, heterosexual, cisgender, middle- and upper-class, nondisabled men), my position in relation to bi men is more complex. Albeit that bi men are silenced *in general*, most bi men whom *I criticize* here are "higher up" on the chain of privileges than I am, meaning that I'm not in an oppressor position in relation to them (on the contrary). Second, as opposed to the writings criticized above, the criticism that I put forth does not echo wide biphobic perceptions in society. In fact, the point of view that I use is subversive as well as marginalized (as opposed to dominant and widespread), and does not contain biphobia. This means that I'm not feeding into negative social perceptions of male bisexuality, but trying to shed light on neglected aspects. Third, the purpose of my criticism is to empower bisexual men by suggesting new viewpoints, and offering new concepts and language to interpret their oppression (as opposed to trying to silence or disempower them).

In addition, it's important to distinguish between inner- and extra-community criticism. Where bisexual men experience biphobia and monosexism, I will fiercely stand shoulder to shoulder with them in solidarity. But where the bisexual community and internal power relations are concerned, it's very important to address these issues, so as to encourage community accountability, work, and development.

Ironically, the first thing one notices when examining bi male writing about bi male invisibility is the lack thereof. I only managed to find one published academic article about the topic (from twelve years ago), while most other references to the topic were anecdotal and in passing. That said, there seems to be a consensus about bi male invisibility within bi communities.

The consensus is that bisexual men are relatively invisible in comparison with bisexual women, and that this happens because of two reasons: that bi women can be objectified by straight men, and that bi women have had more difficulties with lesbian communities than bi men with gay male communities. These things seem to be "common knowledge" within bi communities, often repeated but rarely elaborated, perhaps presuming that it's so obvious that no further attention need be paid to it.

For example, in an online text named "Bi Men: A bi-alogue," Ron Suresha and Pete Chvany, coeditors of the anthology *Bi Men: Coming Out Every Which Way*, discuss bi male invisibility. They frequently compare between bi men and women in terms of (in)visibility: "It . . . seems that men compartmentalize our sexuality more than women, whether or not more women are fundamentally bisexual," says Suresha. Chvany continues, "Bisexual women can be threatening in lesbian communities, but straights find them compelling, and straight men's values are still dominant." In another text, this time an online article on *Salon.com* titled "The invisible bisexual man," the writer notes in passing that "One bi man observed that 'bisexual women seem to be the 'holy grail' of sexuality,' especially in the straight world, but bi guys aren't fetishized to anywhere near the same degree." As another example, we might remember the proliferation of the question "Why is female bisexuality more acceptable?" discussed in the previous chapter.

The one academic article written about this topic, "Interpreting the Invisibility of Male Bisexuality" by Erich Steinman, makes a similar point. According to the article, bisexual women are more visible than men because they've had more reason to concentrate on bisexual activism. This is because they experience more biphobia from lesbian communities than bi men do in gay male communities.

To be fair, other aspects of bi male invisibility are also discussed. For example, Suresha and Chvany also talk about heterosexism, binarism (the notion that one is "either gay or straight"), AIDS, and even mention Yoshino's article about bisexual erasure. Similarly, the *Salon.com* article mostly discusses sexual binarism, as well as negative stereotypes against bi men. However, the ubiquity of the comparison to bisexual women and the frequent references to bisexual communities are hard to ignore.

Before I go on with this argument, I need to clarify: Bi male erasure does exist, and I do not deny it. I also don't deny that bisexual women are more culturally visible than bisexual men (on the condition that they can be objectified by straight cis men). However, the terms of the discussion about this topic do not point to broad cultural erasure, but rather to inner-community disparities. The topic of bi male invisibility could be addressed in many ways. The choice of focusing the discussion on this particular aspect is significant. And it is this significance that I want to look into.

It seems that, in some way, many bisexual men perceive bisexual women as a type of oppressors, or at least as privileged in relation to them. Indeed, it seems almost impossible to raise the topic of bi male invisibility without encountering comparisons implying that bi women fare better than men. This is problematic because it makes bi male invisibility into an inner-community issue. Instead of addressing the role of heterosexist and monosexist society in erasing male bisexuality, many writers choose to focus on bisexual women, effectively scapegoating them for bi male invisibility. We can see this, for example, in Steinman's article, which focuses almost exclusively on this aspect as the main explanation for bi male invisibility. We can also see it in the way that this notion is repeated in other texts.

That this is happening is not surprising—it is well in keeping with the bisexual tradition of interpreting negative attitudes as originating from inner-community politics. As in the case of biphobia, which is interpreted as originating from gay and lesbian communities, here bi male invisibility is interpreted as originating from within bisexual communities. However, explaining different forms of biphobia through inner-community politics is limited. Like the focus on gay and lesbian biphobia while ignoring heterosexual biphobia, explaining bi male invisibility through comparisons to bi women makes us miss out on the big picture and creates both misinformation and false blame.

Another false presumption made by this line of thinking is that bi female visibility is somehow contradictory to bi male visibility. Otherwise, why compare? The constant side-by-side comparison between bi male and female visibility gives a feeling that one comes on account of the other. This outset is suspicious to say the least, and insinuates that there is more to this than meets the eye.

Judging by the constant repetition of this comparison, the real question here is not just about bi male invisibility, but about *power relations between* bisexual men and women.

In a typical, yet revealing, passage, Stephen Donaldson (in his article "The Bisexual Movement's Beginnings in the 70s: A Personal Perspective") states "one major difference" that he finds between the American bisexual movement of the 1970s and that of the early 1990s. That difference is that while in the '70s men were preponderant in the movement, in the

'90s (when he was writing) women greatly outnumbered men both on the leadership and the grassroots levels. He continues:

> *This imbalance of gender is a problem . . . The intellectual discourse of the bi movement, which often appears to be dominated by "women's issues," must be broadened, or the movement may be perceived by men as primarily a vehicle of arcane intrafeminist [lesbian-bisexual] controversies.*

As pointed out by Clare Hemmings in *Bisexual Spaces*, "Donaldson clearly deems feminism both a concern for women only and a source of tension" within bisexual communities. This passage also exposes the core issue at hand: that women dominate the bi movement, and that the bi movement is feminist.

Throughout various references to this topic, and in the quote above, the question is being framed as though it were a minority question: Men are presented as a silenced minority within bisexual communities. However, the glorious past of a bi movement dominated by men invoked by Donaldson reveals the question to be something else: Why is the bi movement no longer dominated by men? The fact that there are fewer bi men than women in bisexual communities is irrelevant to the question. For example, the fact that white cisgender nondisabled gay men are a minority within LGBTQ communities doesn't bar them from dominating our communities and politics. Likewise, the fact that bisexual men are a statistical minority within bi communities should not, according to patriarchal logic, bar them from dominating bi communities.

Likewise, if the situation were reverse (as it was in the 1970s), the question of bisexual women would be far less prevalent. Few would have wondered (as indeed few have) where the bi women are. There would be much less to wonder about since male domination is how things are "supposed to" work. The constant "need" to explain the absence of bisexual men from the movements is an indication that things are not going

224 BI: Notes for a Bisexual Revolution

the way they're "supposed to." That the question of bi male invisibility so often comes together with comparisons between bi men and women implies that this is discomforting not because bi men are *invisible*, but because bi women *aren't*.

In this way, Donaldson is not so far from the truth. To translate his second paragraph into language that is not antifeminist, he says: If the bisexual movement remains feminist in character, this will scare off the men. In practice, this seems to have been a correct historical prediction. Bi movements are feminist (and female-dominated), and this does scare off the (sexist, meaning most) men.

This "conflict," however, is not only symbolic: It has a material history in various bisexual movements. In *Bisexual Spaces*, Hemmings writes about a conflict around feminism that took place before and during the first National Bisexual Conference in the United States (in 1990). While this was probably one of many incidents, I think it can still serve as a good indication of the dynamics around feminism in bisexual movements, and of their history.

In the organizing committee of the conference, feminism was not a consensus subject, and while two organizers (Lani Ka'ahumanu and Autumn Courtney) were committed to the subject, the rest were not. However, after long discussions, it was decided that the conference would be feminist in definition. But the story continues—Hemmings writes:

> *In the early meetings (late 1988–early 1989) one of the conference committee members frequently challenged the feminist emphasis of the planning. . . . This committee member organized the first national mailing informing network members and regional bisexual groups about the 1990 Conference in San Francisco. At the last moment, he removed his name from the letter and altered its contents, adding the word* feminist *at inappropriate points. His action was intended as "an alert," to*

make people aware that "it was . . . basically 'fascist feminist people' running this organization."

This action started a debate within the community about feminism and the conference, with "for" and "against" articles published in the *Bay Area Bisexual Network Newsletter.* According to Hemmings, as the debate intensified, the feminist side became more and more apologetic and accommodating. She writes:

> *In the course of the conference [feminism] has been transformed into the assumption that men and women are equally oppressed, such that bisexual feminism becomes a unifying and healing, rather than critical, practice. The deemphasizing of male responsibility for sexist oppression is endorsed by the conference committee in the later stages of organizing.*

This attempt to accommodate bisexual cis men by altering feminism means that both men and women in the bi movement were aware of the alienating effect that feminism had on (sexist) bisexual men. Rather than insisting on a strong feminist agenda and supporting bi men in acknowledging their privileges, the conference organizers and participants chose to change what feminism means so as not to scare people off.

The tensions around feminism in bi communities are not a thing of the past, either. For example, in the International BiCon in London (in 2010), a closed women-only session caused debate in the local community as well as within the organizing committee. In the decision-making plenary toward the end of the conference, this criticism was widened to also include the "Bi people of color" session (which was people of color-only), and it was suggested to ban all "X-only" sessions in future BiCons. Although the suggestion was finally dropped, the occurrence of the debate still points out the existence of these tensions.

As another example, during the organizing stage of the first Israeli bisexual conference (in September 2012), a few men complained about the Call for Proposals. According to them, the organizers' choice to write it using feminine pronouns alienated men from the conference and the community.[35]

To return to Donaldson's quote, this dynamic might indeed explain the absence of men from bisexual movements. Since in our patriarchal world, most men are taught to fear feminism, the fact that many bisexual movements are feminist does indeed serve as a deterrent. In this way, current discourse about bi male invisibility functions as a "subconscious" outlet for antifeminist feelings. It masks the fact that the issue discussed is not really bi male invisibility, but the feminism of the bisexual movements.

It's important to note that most bisexual men using this discourse are not doing this on purpose. Indeed, many of them identify as (pro) feminist and are avid supporters of women's liberation. In no way should these men be scapegoated for sexism in bisexual movements. Despite this, it is characteristic for dominant discourses to function almost independently. From the moment they're created they are repeated and reiterated until they become "obvious" and "natural." By drawing attention to the way this discourse functions, I'm trying to shed new light on something that has become so "obvious" in bisexual communities that few actually notice what it means. It is now their responsibility to acknowledge the effect of what they've been saying and to stop it.

Yet another problem with discourses about bi male invisibility is that they almost never include references to masculinity. As mentioned above, when the topic is discussed, people talk about bisexual erasure, sexual binarism, stereotypes, and comparisons to bisexual women. Yet no specific context is offered in relation to masculinity, meaning that bi men's "maleness" becomes transparent. This means that no particular reason is offered for why it is that bi *men* are erased (the negative—"because they aren't as fetishized as bi women"—is not sufficient as such). Masculinity itself just doesn't seem like part of the equation while talking about it. This is problematic because it presumes that men don't have a gender to speak of. This gives masculinity a "default" status (no need to state it because it is the "norm"), while also preventing bi men from articulating their gender-specific experiences, including biphobia and monosexism.

In addition, this discourse erases bi trans men, since it is centered around the experiences of cisgender bi men. No specific attention is paid to the double erasure that bi trans men experience as bisexual and as trans, both within heteronormative society and within gay and bi communities. In addition, many bi trans men relate to women and to feminism in ways that are different from those of bi cis men (since they might often be more familiar with women's oppression). In this way, the comparisons between bi men and women place bi trans men in an uncomfortable "in-between" position. In addition, this discourse erases genderqueer and nonbinary people. Instead of specifically and separately analyzing bi men and women's gendered experiences, the competitive comparison between them creates a dichotomy that automatically excludes those who are neither or both.

But discussions of bi male invisibility don't have to look like this. Feminist bisexual men have—and are—creating alternatives to this type of discourse. Connecting between male bisexuality and feminism allows them to view these issues in a different way.

BI MEN AND FEMINISM

Some discussions of bi male invisibility don't repeat the mistakes of the dominant discourse. They do not compare between bi men and women and don't scapegoat bi women for the erasure of bi men. They also take masculinity into account, as well as the way that it functions in patriarchal contexts. In addition, they don't erase trans, genderqueer, and nonbinary bisexuals by setting up a male/female dichotomy. Instead, they focus on the gender-specific experience of bisexual men to explain why bi *men*, in particular, are erased or invisible.

For example, in an article called "Pansies Against Patriarchy: Gender Blur, Bisexual Men, and Queer Liberation," American "polymorphous pervert" and "poetic terrorist" Sunfrog discusses how bisexual men can relate to feminism and gender liberation. He also briefly speculates why bi men are often more closeted than women:

> *A certain locker room ideology of fear lingers with many of us from our youth, a time when being a fag was synonymous with a fate worse than death. . . . Many of us are [also] clinging to those last strands of "heterosexual privilege" . . . by falling back on the* image *provided by our heterosexual relationships, for emotional security, when the going gets rough. (Emphasis in original).*

While I dispute his second argument (also see: chapter 3), it's important to note that both of his reasons for bi male invisibility are specific to bisexual *men*. They are said in the context of an article discussing male bisexuality and patriarchy. In particular, the "locker room ideology" specifically reflects American bisexual cis men's experiences of adolescence, and connects it to current bisexual politics. In this way, it refers to cisgender male bisexuality in particular, without needing to compare or erase anyone else.

In a blog post called "Phallocentrism and bisexual invisibility," Spanish blogger and activist Michael Rosario explains bi male erasure through phallocentrism—the notion that "the sexuality of all people is determined on the basis of their relationship to 'dick.'" He writes:

> *It is very easy to receive the* gay membership card *if you're a* **boy. You touch a cock, and that's it**. *You're gay.* **Forever.** *. . . To be honest, I didn't even have to touch a cock to get*

it. Before I touched one, all I had to do was to say, hey, **I**
wouldn't mind touching one. . . . *From that very moment*
nobody ever disputed that I could be gay[,] [though] [i]t's
certainly disputed that I'm bisexual. . . . I could never be
heterosexual. Not that I'd want to, but **even if I wanted to, I**
couldn't. *I've hooked up with boys and that* **disqualifies me**.
. . . *If I request the* heterosexual membership card *I get the*
application returned with the stamp: **DENIED. REASON:**
COCKSUCKER. . . . *And I constantly have to* . . . *request*
the bisexual membership card *by special delivery, only to have*
my application returned to me . . . *(Emphases in original).*

According to Rosario, the male penis (aggrandized in our culture
as the mythic "phallus") "contaminates" those who come into contact
with it. If someone likes having sexual contact with cisgender men, then
he is perceived as liking *only* them, to the exclusion of anything and anyone else. Rosario's analysis takes patriarchy into account and examines
the way that male bisexuality relates to it. He specifically discusses bi
men and women in relation to this notion, in a way that's complementary rather than competitive. His emphasis on genitals throughout the
post exposes the cissexism that this notion is based on, and draws attention to its erasure of trans and genderqueer people.

Yet another explanation for bi male invisibility that keeps being
raised is that of the AIDS crisis and the deaths of many bisexual men.
However, just like the ubiquitous comparison between bi men and
women, this topic is often repeated but rarely elaborated—though it
should be. Addressing how AIDS has influenced the invisibility of bisexual men has the potential to account for bi *men*'s experience in particular. It could also shed light on this hugely neglected part of AIDS
and LGBTQ history. Such research could discuss bi male invisibility
without needing to compare between bi men and women, and so would
not feed into the antifeminist notions lying beneath it. It could focus on

the influence of HIV/AIDS on various groups of bi men, and on different locations, without essentializing male bisexuality as white, cisgender, and American. Such research could help contextualize bi male invisibility in history and society without suffering from the many problems currently accompanying discussions on the topic.

The connection between male bisexuality and feminism does not end with avoidance of problems, though. It goes much further than that, and can offer a powerful starting point for destabilizing patriarchal and monosexist social order.

FEMINIST MALE BISEXUALITY

As explained in the previous chapter, masculinity is perceived as singular or "one," while femininity is perceived as multiple. Men are required by society to uphold this standard by displaying decisiveness and stability, being single-minded and focused on a single goal. They are also required to comply with the patriarchal single standard, and any deviation from it is perceived as a defect in one's masculinity. Remembering bisexuality's association with multiplicity, this means that being monosexual is part of masculinity's single standard.

This gives male bisexuality the symbolic power to 'crack' masculinity's singularity on two levels: First, its noncompliance with the single standard gives bisexual men a "multiple identity." They cannot be described as singularly "men" because of their deviation from it. Second, the cultural association between bisexuality and multiplicity undermines the unity or singularity of dominant masculinity. Male bisexuality is perceived as "impossible" or a "contradiction in terms" because multiplicity is perceived as contradicting dominant masculinity.

In general, it appears that the concept of male bisexuality is so inconceivable in the eyes of society that it constantly denies that it even exists. Bisexual men "fail" at dominant masculinity; they are perceived as deficient because of the "crack" that their bisexuality creates. Being male and bisexual automatically means being a "bad" man, or failing at performing the "proper" standard of masculinity. This failure, however, is the key to the subversive possibilities that male bisexuality can offer in relation to masculinity and patriarchy.

Failure doesn't have to imply a need to "get better at it," but can instead turn into rejection and refusal. In the introduction to his book *Refusing to Be a Man*, John Stoltenberg explains that the title means disavowing the privilege that comes with being a man. He writes, "I mean the same thing as I would mean by 'refusing to be white' in a racist society." It might also mean problematizing dominant masculinity, while finding ways to enable subversive and challenging masculinities. Bisexuality's incompatibility with dominant masculinity gives bisexual men the opportunity to refuse to be men in our patriarchal society.

Here we might recall that transgender bisexual men are strategically located for this subversion, since they already inhabit a "forbidden" or "impossible" masculinity. Perhaps the most basic standard of masculinity is being cisgender; being assigned male at birth is the most direct path to dominant masculinity. Trans men's masculinity is already perceived as deficient or nonexistent, in a way that is only exacerbated by bisexuality. This is, of course, a complex position—transgender men often have to actively *fight* in order to prove themselves as "real men" in the eyes of society. For them, not being recognized as men is deeply entangled with experiences of transphobia and cissexism. What I mean here is not that trans men give up their masculine identities, but rather that they might use their symbolic location in relation to dominant masculinity in order to question and subvert it.

In "Pansies Against Patriarchy," Sunfrog suggests a similar stance. He writes:

> *Bisexual men have an important choice and responsibility.*
> *If we can transcend heterosexist power dynamics in our gay*

relationships, does this enable us to have truly liberatory rela-
tionships with wimmin? We can begin by deconstructing the
macho straightjacket of mainstream masculinity.

Sunfrog argues that bisexuality might enable bi men to subvert dominant masculinity, gender binarism, and patriarchy, and to instead construct "notions of a postpatriarchal masculinity." He writes about his cross-dressing as linked to his bisexuality, and as a method for creating "a personal subjectivity beyond the limitations of gender." As bisexuality subverts the sexual binary of heterosexual/homosexual, so can feminist and alternative masculinities subvert the gender binary of man/woman.

In order to do that, however, bisexual men must first become aware of their privileges and address them. As Sunfrog writes, many bisexual men "espouse a self-congratulatory stance." They mistake the "gender-neutral utopia for which many of us strive . . . as a given reality in the present. They get defensive at the mere suggestion that they may harbor . . . internalized sexism or homophobia."

And indeed, many bisexual men have been avoiding this responsibility in two main ways: first, by dismissing feminism entirely and trying "to do better" at performing dominant masculinity; and second, by presuming that they don't need to do any active work to address and deconstruct their privileges and internalized sexism.

For example, in a YouTube video named "5 things I hate about being a bi guy" by American vlogger Vinny Strauss, the top two items are dedicated to proving his claim to dominant masculinity. Number two: "I hate it when people assume that because I like dick then I'm not masculine. I'm as masculine as they come, motherfucker." Number one: "I hate it when girls assume that I'm going to be their gay best friend. Especially when I'm single and I have a crush on them and they say 'Oh, let's go fucking shopping.'" These two are elaborated in the video, using misogynist language and speaking derogatorily about women and femininity.

Strauss's fortification of masculinity goes hand in hand with sexism, misogyny, and homophobia. In order to prove himself as a "true man" in the face of the demasculinizing effects of bisexuality, he speaks derogatorily about women and femininity, and attempts to disconnect himself from being perceived as gay. As the video has over 100,000 views, and has garnered almost 3000 "likes," it appears that he is not the only one who feels that way.

In a well meaning but problematic essay called "Bisexual feminist man," American therapist and activist Dave Matteson discusses his feminist opinions and practices. However, in describing his life and politics, he depicts his feminism as a goal he had already achieved, something that seemingly doesn't require any further work. Male privileges or sexism do not get mentioned, creating the impression that there's no need of addressing them in the present as part of one's feminist practice. The word "oppressor" only appears once in his essay, but is mentioned in passing and quickly dismissed. For example, he writes:

> Like all change, the process was slow. But the rewards were
> many. I felt more whole. Some feminine parts I'd learned from
> my mother were now consciously accepted and integrated. . . .
> I no longer felt as protective of [my wife]; she learned to care for
> herself better, instead of focusing her care on others.

From reading his words, one might assume that, as Sunfrog puts it, gender-neutral utopia is a reality in the present.

In response to these trends, Sunfrog writes:

> Because the nature of gender socialization is so pervasive, and
> at times frighteningly subtle in our society, it is dangerous to
> deny these realities [of internalized sexism and homophobia].
> The first step for any man, regardless of class, race, or sexual
> orientation in the fight against sexism and homophobia, is to

*find those seeds of oppression rooted in his own consciousness
and to confront them.*

He continues:

*Disinvesting ourselves from the litany of power afforded to
heterosexual men in our culture will not be easy. It includes
accepting how we as men have consistently used that power
to our advantage and have hurt our friends and lovers in the
process. . . . Let's do it, brothers. We have humyn liberation to
gain. We have a world of pleasure to win.*

In the face of biphobia, monosexism, and sexism, bisexual men have a
"way out" of patriarchy, and a "way in" to creating new, "postpatriachal"
masculinities. Male bisexuality gives them the opportunity to step away
from dominant masculinity, to refuse to be oppressors and to instead
participate in the deconstruction of patriarchy. Instead of trying to "do
better" at being men, bisexual men have the opportunity to create a
sexual and gender revolution.

CHAPTER 6:

Bi and Trans

Though in some trans communities the word "feminism" has become almost synonymous with "transphobia," I would like to suggest that transgender politics is not only consistent with feminism, but is inseparable from it. If the goal of feminism is to end patriarchy and gender-based oppression, then transgender politics supplies us one of the most important perspectives from which to view—and challenge—binary gender and gender-based oppression. As mentioned in previous chapters, if no clear distinction exists between "male" and "female," it becomes impossible to oppress people according to their gender. If we have no sole criterion for determining who is "man" and who is "woman," we can't know whose role it is to be oppressor, and whose to be oppressed.

But transgender politics isn't only a "supporting argument" in favor of feminism or a "tool" for the liberation of women. Its real focus is trans and genderqueer people's identities, lives, and oppression. Of all groups that suffer from gender-specific oppression, trans people are one of the most oppressed. They suffer from discrimination in all aspects of life, including housing, health care, employment, dealings with government authorities, exposure to systematic violence, and many other things. Seen from this perspective, trans and genderqueer people can find mutual support in feminism. Again, if the goal of feminism is to end gender-based oppression, then feminism should—and does—include the fight against transphobia and cissexism.

At this point I should note that, in writing this, I am not trying to redeem cisgender feminism from its transphobia and cissexism. Indeed, many parts of the feminist movement and its history are ciscentrist at best, and blatantly transphobic at worst. But while it is important to acknowledge and address these problems, I am describing the sort of feminism that we, trans and genderqueer people, create—the kind of feminism that we feel at home with and that mutually benefits the feminist movement and us.

This type of feminism for me is also inextricably linked to bisexuality. If one goal of the bisexual movement is to end hierarchical sexual binaries, then it first needs to break down the system of sex, gender, and sexuality. Without deconstructing binaries of sex and gender, we could never deconstruct the binary of sexual orientation.

In order to truly break down this binary system, we, as a bi movement, need to begin from scratch and create something new instead.

UNGENDERING THE SYSTEM

In his post "Not Your Mom's Trans 101," American blogger Asher Bauer suggests a basic explanation of trans identities and theory of gender—but one coming from a different point of view than most. His purpose, he writes, is to "tackle the problem of explaining and defining what it means to be transgender without resorting to cissexist language," as it often does. "I am not here to make cis people comfortable," he writes, "or to reassure them that they are still the center of the gendered universe. In fact, I am totally fine with doing the opposite."

Bauer's explanation starts at the beginning, when a baby is born.

"The doctor says 'It's a boy' or 'It's a girl' based on the appearance of the child's genitals." However, not all babies are born either male or female. In cases where the doctor is unable to make a decision—that is, in cases where the child is intersex—an alternate "solution" is practiced: "Surgery is . . . performed on the unconsenting infant to render its body more socially acceptable." Following this, "[w]hether the baby is intersex or not, the child is then raised as whatever arbitrary gender the doctor saw fit to assign." This is referred to as the *sex* or *gender assigned at birth*.

Cisgender people, Bauer explains, are those who feel comfortable with the gender they've been assigned at birth. "No one really knows," he writes, "why so many people are capable of fitting into such arbitrary categories." Transgender people are those who do not: "We know that there is a different way, a way of autonomy, self-creation, and self-definition . . . because we can never be happy with the parameters that have been mandated for our behavior and our bodies."

In fact, despite appearances, sex is *not* determined by bodies:

> *[H]ormone levels vary wildly within the categories of cis male and cis female. Chromosomes, too, vary. If you thought "XX" and "XY" were the only two possible combinations, you have some serious [research] to do. In addition to variations like XXY, XXYY, or X, sometimes cis people find out that they are genetically the "opposite" of what they [thought] they were— that is, a "typical" cis man can be XX, a "normal" cis woman can be XY.*

Moreover, what is often called "secondary" or even "primary" gender traits are all fragile and mutable: "Many of these traits do not always appear together, and before puberty and after menopause, many of them do not apply." Consider, for example, a woman who'd had her breasts removed due to cancer, or a man who'd lost his penis in an accident. Does losing these body parts mean that they also lose their gender? "Sex," Bauer

concludes, "is as much a social construct as gender," and just as much subject to self-identification. Self-identification, he notes, is therefore "the *only*
meaningful way to determine gender" (emphasis in original).

In terms of identity, not everyone identifies as either a man or a
woman. Many people identify as both, neither, or something completely
different. For example: genderqueer, androgyne, agender, bigender, mul-
tigender, and pangender are all terms describing such nonbinary gender
identification. Bauer emphasizes that gender is not a two-dimensional
"spectrum," ranging between masculinity and femininity. Instead, gender is "a huge three-dimensional space too big to be bounded by the concepts of 'male' and 'female.' Being trans," he continues, "is not always
about falling 'in between' binary genders, and as often as not, it's about
being something too expansive for those ideas to have meaning at all."

If bodies are defined by identification, and identification (as well as
bodies) is not always binary, then no real female or male bodies actually
exist anywhere outside of our cultural imagination.

> *This being the case, I believe the most sensible way to look at
> the question of sex now is this: A male body is a body belonging
> to a male—that is, someone who identifies as male. A female
> body is a body belonging to a female—that is, someone who
> identifies as female. Genderqueer bodies belong to folks who are
> genderqueer, androgynous bodies belong to androgynes, and so
> forth, and so on.*

It's important to note that none of these things is meant to minimize the necessity of physical changes that many trans people wish to
perform. As Bauer says:

> *Many trans people do experience body dysphoria. Many of us
> do seek hormones, surgery, and other body modifications. But
> the point is that, while such modifications may be necessary for*

*our peace of mind, they are not necessary to make us "real men"
or "real women" or "real" whatevers. We're plenty real right
now, thank you.*

This leads us to two additional concepts that are usually left out
of "Trans 101" texts: cissexism and transphobia. Bauer defines cissexism
as "the system of oppression which considers cis people superior to trans
people." He explains:

> *Cissexism is believing that it is "natural" to be cis, that being
> trans is aberrant. . . . Cissexism is defining beauty and attrac-
> tiveness based on how cis people look. Cissexism is prioritiz-
> ing cis people's comfort over trans people's ability to survive.
> Cissexism is believing that cis people have more right to have
> jobs, go to school, date and have sex, make decisions about their
> bodies, wear the clothes they want, or use public restrooms than
> trans people do.*

He defines transphobia as "irrational fear and hatred of trans people."

> *Transphobia is referring to transgender surgery as self-
> mutilation. . . . Transphobia is believing that we are out to
> rob you of your hetero or homosexuality. Transphobia is trans
> people being stared at, insulted, harassed, attacked, beaten,
> raped, and murdered for simply existing.*

And as Bauer takes care to emphasize: "If you want to be a good ally,
you need to start taking cissexism and transphobia seriously right now."

CONNECTIONS AND INTERSECTIONS

Bisexuality and transgender share a lot of common ground, which places
them in symbolic proximity and provides enormous potential for alliances

between them. Note that in writing these things, I am not trying to equate the oppression of trans and bi people or to create a false sense of symmetry between them. Rather, I am trying to draw attention to the intersections and common ground between our experiences in order to highlight the option for solidarity and shared struggles. In addition, it should be noted that in talking about these two issues, I am not addressing particular trans and bi people and identities. Rather, I am exploring symbolic and meta-phorical meanings of the two terms in society.

First of all, perhaps the most obvious common ground that bisexu-ality and transgender share is that of subverting binaries. While neither of these identities is automatically subversive (indeed, many people who identify as bi or trans consciously support sexual and gender binaries), the response that they cause in society and culture points to the deep anxieties that they trigger. Bisexuality raises social anxieties concerning the hierarchical binary of gay and straight, and transgender raises anx-ieties concerning the hierarchical binary of woman and man. As men-tioned above, these subversions threaten to blur—and confound—the "clear cut" borders between oppressor and oppressed classes. In addition, they also expose the fact that a hierarchy exists, since by crossing that metaphorical "border," they reveal its very existence.

The bisexual side of this is thoroughly explained in previous chap-ters. On the transgender side, for example, one might recall the 2011 controversy around American company J. Crew's catalog showing the company's president and creative director, Jenna Lyons, painting her son's toenails pink. The backlash to this image included attacks against the ad's "blatant propaganda celebrating transgendered [sic] children." It continued with a fortification of binary gender roles, to the extent that some critics called the ad "an attack on masculinity." This story illus-trates the kind of panic that society (and in particular, American society) responds with when encountered with subversion of gender binaries. The fact that such response was created reveals how much weight minor-ity-world society puts into such divisions.

Both bisexuality and transgender offer alternative understandings of identities. In a world that presumes one is born a certain way (male, female, gay, straight) and cannot change, both bisexuality and transgender offer the options of mutability and change. Bisexuality encompasses changes that happen throughout lengths of time, as opposed to isolating moments in people's lives and essentializing their identities. Transgender requires long-term viewpoints that allow for change over time, as opposed to the assignment of a single, immutable gender that "can never be changed."

For example, if isolated to one moment in her life, a bisexual person might be identified according to her current desires, as either gay or straight. But looking at the same person over time might reveal that she also desires other genders. Likewise, one might isolate a trans person to one moment in his life and presume that he is female. But looking at the same person over time might reveal that he is male, or something else completely. In general, both trans and bi identities also allow room for broader forms of change: Not only might one's desires or gender identities simply "switch," but they might also be multiple, complex, contradictory, and fluid.

Bisexuality and transgender also share a complex experience of passing (both voluntary and coercive). In order to survive, members of both these groups are obliged to pass as something they are not—cisgender or monosexual. People who do wish to be recognizable as trans or bi are often coercively passed off as cis or mono anyway. The price of both these things is the erasure of those particular identities from the knowledge and experience of everyday life. People who do pass as trans or bi (intentionally or not) are then forced to deal with the consequences in the form of social policing, discrimination, and other forms of violence. (I discuss many examples in chapter 3).

Despite the severe oppression that each group suffers, it has also been a custom—especially in queer communities—to accuse trans and bi people of seeking straight privilege. Bisexuals have been accused of wanting to lead heteronormative lives while enjoying the side benefits of queer sex or communities. Trans people have been accused of actually being gay men and lesbians who change their genders in order to become straight and avoid homophobic oppression. In addition, transgender men in particular have been accused of seeking male privilege, changing their gender as a cowardly act of internalized misogyny. Trans women have been accused of seeking the "side benefits" of femininity while maintaining their "male privilege." Note that all of these points of view necessitate actively cisgendering and monosexualizing trans and bi people: assuming that all people in both groups are actually monosexual (gay or lesbian), and that the genders we've been assigned at birth determine who and what we are.

[Trigger warning: direct quotes containing transphobia and biphobia]

For example, in "Bisexual politics: A superior form of feminism?" Australian writer Sheila Jeffreys presents a biphobic manifesto meant to incriminate the entire bisexual movement as antifeminist and male-identified. Among her many other accusations, she describes bisexuality as "a way not to identify as lesbian or gay." This is because the "loss of privilege involved in identifying as lesbian [is] significant and likely to encourage women to . . . avoid such a definition." Likewise and unsurprisingly, she didn't spare trans people either. Her article "Transgender Activism: A Lesbian Feminist Perspective" is a transphobic manifesto meant to incriminate the entire transgender movement as (you guessed it) antifeminist and male-identified. In the article, she describes trans men as "women" who are hopelessly oppressed by internalized misogyny and lesbophobia. She describes trans women (whom she calls "male-to-constructed-female") as invaders seeking to exploit feminist movements for their own selfish needs, as a result of internalized male supremacy. Note that in both cases Jeffreys cisgenders and monosexualizes trans and bi people, presuming that we're all "really" gay or lesbian.

[End of trigger]

Following suit, both groups have also been accused of maintaining gender binaries. As described more fully in chapter 1, people who identify as bisexual have been accused of reinforcing the gender binary by identifying as bi (which literally means "two," but in fact holds no reference to gender). Trans people—and especially transexuals—have been accused of reinforcing the gender binary by seeking physical changes and "imitating" binary gender norms.

On the other side of the same coin, both bisexuality and transgender have been used in queer theory as "proofs" or "illustrations" for the so-called "inherent" instability and fluidity of sexuality and gender. According to Clare Hemmings, this has been done by separating bisexual identity from practice, and by separating transexuality from transgender. Bisexual behavior has been widely written about as the "ultimate subversion" of sexual binaries, especially in the copious writing that exists about sexual desire between gay men and lesbians. Transgender has likewise been applauded as the "ultimate subversion" of gender binaries, again focusing on behavior and performance (rather than identity). In this way, Hemmings suggests, queer writers have used bisexuality and transgender in order to demarcate the boundaries of gay and lesbian identities—behavior and performance as positive "boundary subversions" and identities as negative "boundary preservers."

For example, in her article "Confessions of a Second Generation . . . Dyke?" Katherine Raymond discusses her desire for men as well as women, while strongly rejecting bisexual identity, to the extent of expressing biphobic opinions. Within the framework of the book, *PoMoSexuals: Challenging Assumptions About Gender and Sexuality*, this is presented as challenging and subversive. Bisexual desire or practice is separated from bisexual identity, while the former is labeled "subversive" and the latter "preservative." From the transgender side of things, Hemmings criticizes American writer Judith/Jack Halberstam for viewing transgender performance as "transgressive spectacle," while treating

244   BI: Notes for a Bisexual Revolution

transexuality as something that fails to "challenge notions of natural gender." Transgender performance is separated from transexual identity, while the former is labeled "subversive" and the latter "preservative."

Another point of similarity is noted by U.K. researchers Merl Storr and Jay Prosser. In their article "Transsexuality and Bisexuality," they explain that bisexuality and transgender have often been conflated. This type of thinking began with late-nineteenth-century sexology, but it is certainly still happening today. As Hemmings explains in her reading of their text, bisexuality and transgender are often used interchangeably. This happens because of their "common association with hermaphroditism, gendered inversion, and sexual ambivalence." They are both (reductively) perceived as incorporating or transcending two binary poles, as either "somewhere in between" or "two in one."

For example, as we saw in chapter 4, transgender women in mainstream porn are often perceived as "inherently" bisexual. This happens as a result of viewing trans women as a combination of "both sexes," assuming that a trans woman's "male part" desires women and that her "female part" desires men.

As we've seen in the two previous chapters, bisexuality creates "gender trouble," which places bisexual people outside the culturally legitimate boundaries of male and female. In addition, bisexuals have often been imagined as being psychologically "both male and female" since their "male side desires women" and "their female side desires men." Trans people have also been imagined as inherently bisexual because of the transphobic presumption that they are necessarily "both man and woman in one." In addition, they have been imagined as carrying a bisexual threat into society since, according to transphobic thought, desiring trans people means you're secretly into "both sexes." As Julia Serano writes in her poem "Cocky," "My penis changes the meaning of everything. And because of her, every one of my heterosexual ex-girlfriends has slept with a lesbian. And every guy who hits on me these days could be accused of being gay."

To conclude, transgender and bisexuality share many common meanings and intersect almost inseparably. This closeness gives us the potential to create alliances between our communities, as well as creating shared bi-trans communities and struggles.

That said, it is hard to admit that not much of this potential has been used at all. In fact, many bi communities are ridden with transphobia, and many trans communities abound with biphobia.

THE PLIGHT OF THE BI-TRANS

As a bisexual trans person, I constantly find myself at odds with both bisexual and transgender communities. Not only are trans and bi people always discussed as separate and distinct groups, but we are also doubly erased as bi in trans communities, and as trans in bi communities. Unfortunately, the "strong alliance" often identified between bi and trans is in many cases imaginary.

CISSEXISM AND TRANSPHOBIA
IN BISEXUAL COMMUNITIES

Within mainstream bisexual movements, the links between bisexuality and transgender have always been thought of as close. These have been written about and applauded by mainstream bisexual movements (especially in the United States) since their very beginnings. However, the efforts of these communities to be trans-inclusive have been lacking.

Before I go on, I need to clarify: If asked on any occasion, I would say that the bisexual movement, as a whole, is light-years ahead of most other activist communities (not just gay and lesbian) as far as it concerns transgender and genderqueer inclusion. I think the movement deserves every bit of respect when it comes to acknowledging these things, and this should not be dismissed in light of the critique I put forth below.

For example, volume seventeen of the American bisexual zine *Anything That Moves* was dedicated to "Forging a Bi-Trans Alliance," and included texts from bi and trans writers, discussing the connections and intersections between these two topics. Likewise, the anthology *Bisexuality and Transgenderism: InterSEXions of the Others* was edited by bisexual scholars, includes bi and trans writers, and engages with the same themes. Clare Hemmings devotes one out of four chapters of *Bisexual Spaces* for discussing intersections between bi and trans in a highly ethical and enlightening way. The *Transcending Boundaries* annual conference in the United States is a shared bi, trans, intersex, and polyamory project that originally grew out of a *BiNet USA* project. And those are just a few examples.

But alongside awareness, declarations, and actions that encourage trans and genderqueer inclusion, the mainstream bi movement has also long been suffering from many problems around transphobia and cis-sexism. In general, it seems that the proportion of *speaking* about how trans-inclusive the movement is, is larger than *actual* trans-inclusion taking place. On the other side of the same coin, actual incidents of transphobia and cissexism remain largely unaddressed.

Note that when I talk about "the" mainstream bi movement, I am referring mostly to mainstream movements within North America and Western Europe—and within those, I'm referring only to hege-monic discourse. While it's worth remembering that a lot of differ-ent bi communities exist all over the world, and that not all of them behave in similar ways, it should still be acknowledged that there's a huge body of bisexual work that nonetheless comprises a dominant discourse for these communities: books, zines, articles, essays, papers, blogs, mailing lists, online groups, etc. The fact that I do not live in any of those places and only experience them "second hand" only serves to emphasize this: I am more likely to be exposed to hegemonic discourse *because* it is hegemonic.

And hegemonic discourse about bisexuality, that I see from my own vantage point, is cissexist: often referring to "both genders" or "both sexes," treating bisexual and transgender people as if we're two discrete populations, generally being led by cisgender people (making it de facto a cis movement), engaging in tokenism, and many more things—all while talking about trans-inclusion and patting ourselves on the back.

Hemmings talks about this in *Bisexual Spaces* and says that, in general, bisexual communities in the United States and the U.K. often speak of themselves as if they're "already inclusive" without concerning themselves with the dirty details of actually working to include marginalized groups (not just trans/genderqueer people, but also people of color, working-class people, disabled people, and many others).

Speaking about these issues is not easy. Because of the frequent biphobic accusations that the word "bisexuality" reinforces the gender binary, any attempt to engage with actual cissexism or transphobia in bi communities may be seen to justify those accusations. Indeed, many bi activists and communities have tried glossing over these problems in attempt to avert these accusations. Many also seem to find it difficult to separate these biphobic accusations from legitimate, concrete inner-community criticism. To suggest that cissexism and transphobia are present in bisexual movements seems tantamount to accusing all bisexual people of being transphobic simply by identifying as bi.

However, these are not the same. Calling out specific problems within bisexual communities is an attempt to address existing issues and to encourage working on them. It promotes accountability and responsibility for power dynamics and forms of oppression existing in our communities. Addressing these issues is an act of solidarity with marginalized groups and part of our ongoing struggle to end oppression in all its forms. In contrast, making blanket accusations against all bisexual people because of the word that we choose to identify with is a biphobic act drawing from a general notion that bisexuality is a negative or harmful identify. The criticism put forth below should not be read as an act of biphobia, but as one of community accountability and empowerment.

Perhaps the most obvious example for cissexism in bisexual communities is binary definitions of bisexuality. While many people in mainstream bi movements have defined bisexuality as attraction to same and different genders or as attraction to more than one gender, binary definitions of bisexuality (as attraction to "both genders" or to "men and women") still abound in both past and present activist and academic bisexual writing.

For example, the anthology *Bi Any Other Name* (of 1991) contains about forty mentions of binary expressions such as "both genders" or "both men and women." In contrast, the expression "more than one gender" does not appear at all. Likewise, Marjorie Garber's book *Vice Versa: Bisexuality and the Eroticism of Everyday Life* (of 1996) contains over twenty mentions of gender-binary terms, while "more than one gender" does not appear at all. More recently, the anthology *Getting Bi* (first edition, 2005) still contains forty binary expressions, though it also includes eight mentions of nonbinary expressions such as "more than one gender." Even in the most recent anthology that came out about bisexuality, *Bisexuality and Queer Theory: Intersections, Connections and Challenges* (of 2011), most of the writers still use binary definitions and cissexist language, while only a minority employ a nonbinary tool set. Notably, in an article from this volume called "Thirteen Ways of Looking at a Bisexual," American researcher David Halperin suggests *thirteen* different definitions of bisexuality—*all of which* are written in gender-binary and cissexist language!

On a personal note, while reading any kind of book or anthology about bisexuality, *ever* (with the exception of Hemmings's *Bisexual Spaces*)—and I've read a whole lot—I've often needed to curb my irritation and frustration with the amount of gender-binary and cissexist language that I had to read just to get through a single text. It's stopped me several times from reading bisexual anthologies fully in one batch—I needed whole months of breaking them down. Even while reading a single piece, I often have to stop, take a deep breath, and make a conscious effort to move forward. I've read very few published texts about bisexuality that are written throughout using nonbinary or trans-positive language. Despite the bi movement's insistence that binary definitions are a thing of the past, even today they are hard to avoid.

Another problem is gender essentialism, an argument ironically popularized through Julia Serano's article "Bisexuality does not reinforce the gender binary." According to Serano, bisexuality doesn't reinforce the gender binary because, whatever their *gender*, most people have one of two "general types of *sexed bodies*: female and male" (emphasis mine). In addition, she writes, most people are automatically "read" as either male or female by society. For Serano, bisexuality denotes attraction to male and female bodies or to people gendered by society as either male or female. It should be noted that Serano's general perception of sex and gender, as put in her book *Whipping Girl*, is that although "male" and "female" are unstable and nonexclusive categories, they should still be recognized because of their social importance. And so, despite this argument's binarism, it cannot be called transphobic.

However, many bi people reading this article have used it to justify their own cissexism and erase the need for bi communities to account for their transphobia. Instead of making the term about the *gender* binary, these people have made it about the *sex* binary. Thus, people have used it to claim that "attraction to males and females" is, in fact, inclusive of everyone. This presumes that people's gender identities are irrelevant, and that what *other people* think about their bodies determines who and what they are. This erases an entire spectrum of nonbinary genders and sexes, and feeds into the cissexist notion that we're all "really" cis "underneath the labels."

Note that I am not trying to claim that bisexuality, as a word, is inherently transphobic, or that all bi people are cissexist simply by identifying as bi. As explained in chapter 1, both of these claims are false and related to biphobia. What I am trying to point out is that many people in mainstream bisexual communities *use binary definitions* for bisexuality, or otherwise employ binary and cissexist language while talking about it. To put it simply: *It's not the word; it's how we use it.*

In response to such criticism, some people suggest that defining bisexuality as binary is really okay, because some people actually *are* attracted only to cisgender men and women. While I don't think that they are deliberately transphobic, I do find that this tendency resonates with cissexist social standards.

People often think about attraction as an apolitical, inborn quality that is somehow a given. But in fact, more often than not, our desires are shaped by social standards of beauty and attractiveness—of who or what is considered attractive, and who or what is not. These standards of attractiveness are deeply political, since they are shaped by dominant social beliefs and structures. To name just a few: White people are considered more attractive than people of color, thin people more than fat people, nondisabled people more than disabled people—and cisgender people more than trans and genderqueer people.

In her book *Read My Lips*, American writer Riki Wilchins argues that transgender people are considered unattractive because their bodies are unintelligible in terms of sexual attraction, to a culture that constructs its sexuality around cisgender bodies. In order to be considered attractive, one must possess a body that "matches" their gender identity. This means that cisgender bodies are structurally privileged in terms of sexuality and desire—and we know what structural privileging of cisgender identity is called (that's rights, cissexism).

Yet another facet of transphobia in bi movements is tokenism: mentioning trans and genderqueer people in passing without really engaging with the topic, or including one or two trans people (in an event, an anthology, or whatever else) while all the rest is dominated by cis people and ciscentrist content. For example, the anthology *Bisexual*

Politics contains only two essays by trans and genderqueer people, while the rest of the texts in the book are not only written by cis people, but also use cissexist language and largely ignore trans issues. Another example is the *Bisexual Invisibility* report, which defines bisexuality as attraction to "more than one sex or gender," but uses cissexist and gender-binary language throughout the text. Out of the forty-one pages of the report, only three paragraphs are dedicated to discussing transgender issues, and these treat bi and trans as two separate and distinct groups. One "personal story" of a bi trans person is combined in the report, but stands alone as the single (and isolated) reference to bi trans people.

The exclusion of trans and genderqueer people in bi movements doesn't end with text. In my first encounter with a "real life" bi community outside my own (in the U.K.), after years of reading self-congratulatory "inclusive" texts from minority-world bi movements, I was shocked by the lack of actual trans and genderqueer inclusion. For example, on the spoken level, many people were using the acronym "LGB" instead of "LGBT," or used the term "both genders." Some discussion topics never seemed to incorporate viewpoints or issues related to transgender people. Very few workshops and spaces explicitly targeted trans and genderqueer people or issues—only two scheduled workshops (in a five-day conference) specifically targeted trans people. The other two trans-only spaces, during lunch breaks, were a last-minute effort organized by my girlfriend. One evening I sat with quite a few other trans people (most of whom were local), and we had a long conversation about transphobia at the convention and in bi communities in general. People were definitely feeling marginalized. Yet, throughout the convention, many cis people were still praising the bi community for being so trans-inclusive. Although I understand that BiCon has recently been improving on trans and genderqueer inclusion, these issues still need to be addressed.

Of course, that these token inclusions exist at all is a shining success in relation to other movements. Indeed, most other movements blatantly erase trans people and think nothing of it. Bisexual communities (including the U.K. BiCon) deserve every bit of respect for the inclusion that is taking place. However, token inclusion is not enough. Tokenism means that although bi communities in general are aware of the need to be trans-positive, they mostly worry about appearance and lip service. It means that bisexual communities might not be as committed to inclusion of trans and genderqueer people as they say or think they are.

Part of the problem is that these issues are generally unspoken in minority-world bi communities. Moreover, in my experience, when they *are* mentioned, they are generally silenced or met with heavy criticism. For example, in a certain thread in an online bi group (serving mostly people from North America), some people actually argued that acknowledging that some bi people were attracted to more than just two genders might make others "feel uncomfortable." As another example, when I posted an early version of this text to my blog, most commentators ardently denied the fact that cissexism and transphobia existed at all in bi communities, and refused to accept any suggestion that the bi movement is anything but flawless on that regard. But rather than taking this criticism as an assault, bisexual communities should take this opportunity to check themselves, grow, learn, and improve.

To conclude, despite thinking of themselves as trans and genderqueer inclusive, bisexual movements unfortunately share much of the cissexism and transphobia of mainstream society and of lesbian and gay communities. As a movement that largely proclaims its solidarity with transgender movements and people, we are responsible to take up these points of criticism and turn them into productive work aimed toward eliminating transphobia and cissexism in our communities. If our bi communities truly want to be trans-positive, we need to start taking transphobia and cissexism seriously right now.

BIPHOBIA IN TRANS COMMUNITIES[36]

If bi communities only concern themselves with transgender tokenism, then transgender communities are completely unconcerned about bisexuality. In fact, it is disturbing to admit that the considerable amount of writing that exists about intersections between bi and trans *all* comes from bisexual movements, and *none at all* from the other way around. Bi trans people looking for inclusion in trans communities or writings will find little: They will be accepted on the premises of being trans or genderqueer, but their bisexuality will be considered anything from irrelevant to suspicious (depending on where they are).

Before I continue, it's important to note that two wrongs don't make a right. Just because biphobia exists in trans communities, it is not "okay" for bi communities to be transphobic. Nor the other way around. By writing about these two topics, I am not trying to create a fake "balance" between biphobia and transphobia, in which shitty attitudes justify one another. What I am trying to do is to draw attention to two things: the huge waste of revolutionary potential that these two groups could have by being allied, and the double erasure experienced by people who are both bi and trans.

Though most bisexual anthologies and books that I've read address transgender issues on some level (ranging from tokenism to serious engagement), most trans anthologies and books erase bisexuality completely. For example, in the anthology *Gender Outlaws*, the word "bisexuality" appears a total of four times. It is also unsurprising to note that in all four cases, the word is mentioned in passing and as part of a longer list of identities. The anthology *GenderQueer* might be considered a little bit better, with a total of nineteen appearances of the "B-word." This is because one essay in the volume does engage somewhat seriously with bisexuality—though, again unsurprisingly—ends up rejecting it as a viable identity.

In many cases in trans writings, when bisexuality does appear, it happens in a negative context. For example, in Riki Wilchins's book

Queer Theory, Gender Theory, bisexuality's first appearance happens when she talks about limiting identity words. All other appearances of the word in the book (eight in number) can be described as anecdotal at best, most cases being as part of the list "lesbian, gay, bisexual, and transgender." Kate Bornstein does the same in her book *Gender Outlaw* (not to be confused with the anthology *Gender Outlaws*), which only mentions bisexuality when she criticizes sexuality models based on the gender of one's partner(s). Again, all other mentions are either anecdotal or part of a longer list of identities.

Much transgender writing conflates bi communities with gay and lesbian ones while discussing exclusion of trans people. As mentioned in chapter 1, many trans writers have adopted the form "LGB" when speaking about transphobia, implying that bisexuals have an equal part in the GGGG hegemony, and erasing the exclusion that is shared by both our groups.

Biphobia in trans communities doesn't end with text, either. In fact, one of the main reasons why I started doing bisexual activism was the exclusion I felt in my trans community. Back then in that community, being bisexual was completely transparent. To be considered "queer," you needed to be either gay or lesbian—and if you weren't, you were suspected or simply assumed to be straight. Bisexuality was rarely discussed, or if it was, it mostly came in the context of "reinforcing the gender binary." For example, I remember one trans community party where I made an announcement about a new bisexual support group that opened in Tel Aviv (the first one ever in the city). After I was done, the party's host had only this to say: "But pansexuality is cooler." Though these attitudes have slightly changed in recent years, the basic food chain of "queerness" or "coolness" still largely bars bisexuality from being considered as "cool" or "queer" enough in this community (as well as others). Likewise, I doubt that things are better in other trans communities abroad.

To conclude, though an alliance between bi and trans communities certainly exists, it is definitely lacking and needs much more work. Though bi communities have often attempted to be trans-inclusive, they have also often failed. On the part of trans communities, not only have they failed to reciprocate these attempts at inclusiveness (limited though they were), but they have often also supported biphobic ideas. This situation means that instead of using their shared subversive potential together, both communities end up reinforcing oppressive ideologies. It also means that bi trans people find themselves excluded from both communities: in bi communities for being trans or genderqueer, and in trans communities for being bisexual.

Bi communities need to start taking transphobia and cissexism seriously, to confront and address their cisgender privileges and internalized cissexism. We need to deconstruct the cissexist language currently in use, and to start constructing an alternative, trans-positive language. This means stopping the usage of binary cissexist terms such as "both men as women" or "both sexes" (try "all genders" instead). We need to stop speaking as if cisgender men and women are the only genders worth addressing (saying "all genders" and then talking only about men and women is still cissexist). We need to stop referring to bi and trans as if they were two separate groups. We especially need to inform ourselves about what cissexism is, what transphobia is, and to start subverting it—both on the level of communities, and individually.

All this requires a deep commitment for doing this type of work. It is worth remembering that the purpose of doing it is not only "being nice to other people." It is not about appearances and it's not about goodwill. It's about working toward everyone's liberation from cissexism and transphobia—trans and cis people alike. It's also about the fact that the bisexual movement could never create true change in society while still reinforcing oppressive binaries. If a bi revolution could happen, it could only happen shoulder to shoulder with our trans and genderqueer siblings.

Likewise, trans communities need to start taking biphobia seriously, to confront and address our own monosexual privileges and internalized biphobia. We, in trans communities, need to start learning about and understanding the experiences of bi people and the character of mono-sexism. Instead of throwing the bisexuals in with oppressor groups, trans communities need to start emphasizing the similarities between our two identities. This does not mean we no longer hold bi people and communities accountable for transphobia, but it does mean ending the pattern of ceaselessly accusing them of it. Trans communities need to understand that the "bi is binary" accusation does not in fact address existing cissexism in bi communities, but originates in a type of biphobia. This biphobia closely resembles transphobia and was created at around the same time (as described in chapter 1). We need to understand that many trans and gender-queer people identify as bi, and that these identities are not mutually exclusive. (In fact, assuming so not only erases these people's bi identities, but also our identities as trans and genderqueer). A trans revolution that reinforces the oppression of bisexuals is no revolution at all.

CASE IN POINT: THE BI COMMUNITY IN ISRAEL/OCCUPIED PALESTINE

Seeing evidence of cissexism and transphobia in bi communities abroad was all the more shocking to me because of my local context. As alluded to above, the bisexual community in Israel/Occupied Palestine grew out of the transgender community. In this, our community inherited much of the discourse and politics of the Israeli transgender movement. The bi community here is led mainly by trans and genderqueer people, and many people in the community itself also identify as such. In a way, it might be said that our community is also a trans community. In particular, it has been a home for many genderqueer people (rather than transexual people, who are the main focus of the trans community). Thus, our community fills two gaps left by other queer and trans spaces: one for bisexuals, and one for genderqueer people.

This atmosphere also means that the community serves as a learning space for people who are new to trans issues and politics. For example, for many people, the bi community was the first place where they met trans and genderqueer people. This means that in joining the community, many people also become allies to the trans movement. Many others also get to explore their own gender identities within and through the community, as it serves as an enabling and nonjudgmental space for all gender identities. As a result, many start identifying as trans, genderqueer, or nonbinary after joining the community. Language and politics in our community incorporate multiple gender identities and trans issues—this is our local "hegemonic discourse"—there's no such thing as "both genders."

In writing these things, I don't mean to suggest that the community is a perfect bi-trans utopia or that full equality has been achieved between cis and trans people within it. Indeed, there are many incidents of cissexism and transphobia within the community—both by people who are new and uninformed (cissexism, after all, is the norm), and by people who simply do not accept that cissexism is a problem.

What I do mean to say, though, is that the community is constantly and regularly working against cissexism and transphobia. People who say cissexist things or act in transphobic ways are routinely called out. Cissexism and transphobia are not tolerated. In this way, the community actively produces itself as a safe and politicized space for trans and genderqueer people.

For example, a memorable discussion took place in one online bisexual forum where a straight-identified man wrote that he is curious about sex with "trannies" (a transphobic term for describing trans women). He stated that although he was curious, he might "be disgusted," and then asked for places where he could get to meet "such people." This objectifying and transphobic message sparked up a flame war, which spread across at least three different threads, all discussing transphobia and cissexism. Trans people and allies in the forum explained how and why the message (and the attitude behind it) was transphobic[37], while some cis people (including the original poster) continued throughout the discussion to insist upon their right to define everyone else's gender identities (for example, to claim that trans women were actually a type of "men"). While transphobic attitudes were certainly called out and criticized in this discussion, it nonetheless emphasized the constant tensions our community faces. It also emphasized the fact that, as mentioned above, the community constantly needs to do active work against transphobia and cissexism, in order to produce itself as a safe space for trans people.

The trans-positive atmosphere in the bi community has, in turn, also lead to greater acceptance of bi people within the trans community. This happened as a result of a change happening on two levels: One, as the bi community was created, trans and genderqueer people increasingly started coming out as bi, increasing bi visibility within the trans community; and two, the bi community became populated with trans and genderqueer people, in a way that couldn't be missed by the trans community. Due to these two things, attitudes toward bi people have slowly changed in the trans community, and this in turn encouraged more alliance work. For example, in April 2011 the first-ever bi-trans panel was held in Tel Aviv, where a group of bi and pan trans and genderqueer activists (including myself) spoke about links between those two identities in front of an audience of trans people and allies. As another example, in June 2011 a radical pride march was held in Tel Aviv (in response to the commercialized, Zionist, municipality-sponsored "Gay Pride"). As we took over the stage that the municipal parade had left behind, the first flags that we hung there were bi and trans. In the open stage that then took place, about half of the speakers were either bi, trans, or both.

The radical march is a particularly good example of the great things that can be done through the alliance between trans and bi communities.

Though the march was certainly not organized or attended solely by trans and bi people, our alliance was nonetheless one of its strongest supporting columns. This is because the organizing committee included leaders from the trans and bi communities working together for what might have been the first time. Another contributing factor was the fact that the march was not based on identity politics. Rather, it focused on a common goal shared by all the groups involved (opposing gay assimilationism, capitalism, and Zionism, and giving voice to marginalized LGBTQ groups). It also allowed enough space for each group to articulate its unique point of view. The march itself was a great success and might serve as an example for the type of solidarity work that can be done together by diverse groups.

In light of the tensions existing between bi and trans communities, it might be useful for these communities to learn from the bi-trans solidarity work done in Israel/Occupied Palestine. The Israeli bi community provides an example for the kind of behaviors and actions necessary to make bi spaces safe for trans and genderqueer people. It also provides an example for working toward a radical (pertaining to the root, *radix*— rather than superficial) trans-bi alliance.

An alliance between bi and trans communities has the potential to subvert the entire system of sex, gender, and orientation. Acknowledging common issues, as well as common forms of oppression, might provide our movements with the tools, the language, and the power to deconstruct these hierarchical binaries. Instead, we can create radical alternatives, to form our own spaces free of oppression, cissexism, and monosexism, and to join hands in our common fight for gender and sexual liberation.

CHAPTER 7:

Bisexuality and Racialization

As is the case with other identities, bisexuality both intersects and shares common ground with racialized identities. *Racialization* is a word describing the process in which certain groups of people come to be understood as a "race." It suggests that "race" is not a natural or inherent phenomenon, but something actively created by society through discourse and power distribution. For example, "blackness," as understood in minority-world cultures, only receives its meaning in a social context that differentiates certain people according to their skin color and heritage. It receives further meaning when this differentiation is used to marginalize these people, and to distribute privileges to those unmarked by "race" (white people).

In this chapter, I'd like to discuss the connections and intersections between one particular racialized identity—Mizrahi—and bisexuality. The way Mizrahis are racialized bears resemblance to the way that bisexuality is characterized by society. Mizrahis are Arabic Jews: Jews who are descended from Arabic or Islamic countries (for example, Iraq, Iran, Morocco, Yemen, Lebanon, and other Middle Eastern and North African countries). Though they are not the only two descent-based identities in Israel/Occupied Palestine, Mizrahis are usually contrasted with Ashkenazis, Jews who are descended from Europe. Ashkenazis, as a group in Israeli society, occupy the space of "white." In contrast, Mizrahis occupy a racialized space, and are marginalized in various ways.

A BIT OF HISTORY

[Trigger warning: general descriptions of systematic racism]

The state of Israel was founded in 1948 after a lengthy and continuous process of colonizing Palestinian territories and ethnically cleansing its geographical space (a process which goes on to this day). This ethnic cleansing, in turn, created a need to replace cheap Palestinian labor with new workers, as the Palestinians either were massacred or expelled, or fled from their homes (in what is known today as *Al Nakba*, the disaster). At that point, nearly 80 percent of the Jewish population in Israel was Ashkenazi, not fit for "dirty" manual work according to their own supremacist values. The need for cheap labor, then, gave birth to the idea of importing Jews from Arabic countries: On the one hand, their Jewishness meant that Israel's hold on Palestinian land would be strengthened; on the other hand, their Arabic descent meant that (similar to their Palestinian sisters and brothers) they were perceived as fit for hard labor and economic exploitation.

It's important to note that while Ashkenazis came to occupy Palestine as a result of a severely oppressive antisemitic reality—ranging from pogroms (violent antisemitic riots) to the holocaust—the state of Mizrahis in their respective countries was hardly as severe. In fact, many Mizrahis were prosperous, well-educated, and in some cases even reached central positions of power in their countries. This is not to say that Jews in Arabic countries did not suffer from anti-Semitism or oppression (they certainly did), but things for them were hardly as desperate as they were for Ashkenazis. This meant that in order to convince people from these countries to immigrate, Ashkenazis needed to send agitators to Arabic countries. These agitators told Jewish populations in these countries lies about the "better life" that they would have in Israel. They also often agitated for anti-Semitism in the Muslim communities surrounding the Jews, so as to encourage them to leave. By these means and others, they fed these communities Zionist ideology and convinced people to join their cause and immigrate to Israel/Occupied Palestine.

The Mizrahis were brought to the country mostly during the 1950s. Upon their arrival, they were put in "temporary" housing called *Ma'abarot*—low-standard shantytowns. While Ashkenazis received priority in relocating to permanent housing, for Mizrahis the wait often lasted for years. This resulted in a constant ratio of 80 percent Mizrahis and only 20 percent Ashkenazis living in Ma'abarot during the '50s. When Mizrahis were finally relocated to permanent housing, they were put in peripheral geographical areas, which often lacked many services and opportunities that central cities could offer. Ashkenazis, on the other hand, were sent mostly to central areas.

[Trigger warning: direct quotes containing extreme racism]

All this, of course, was accompanied and supported by copious amounts of racism, characterizing Mizrahis as primitive, ignorant, and backward—attitudes which linger to this day. Ashkenazis, in contrast, were imagined as "enlightened saviors" whose jobs were to save Mizrahis from themselves by instilling European values and standards into them. For example, in 1949 a prominent Israeli journalist wrote:

> *[The Mizrahis are] a race the likes of which we've never seen in our country. They are exceedingly primitive people. Their education level borders on utter ignorance, and worse, they completely lack the ability to understand anything spiritual. In general, they are only slightly better than the Arabs . . . amongst whom they lived. In any case, they are inferior to Israel's Arabs whom we've gotten used to . . .*

David Ben-Gurion, Israel's first prime minister, wrote in the same year:

This tribe . . . is distanced from us by two thousands years, if not more. They lack even the most basic and rudimentary concept of civilization . . . They treat children and women as primitive men. The state of their health is poor. Their physical strength is meager and they are unable to detect even the most minimal hygienic needs.

[End of trigger]

In order to maintain an Ashkenazi majority in Israel/Occupied Palestine, the government also created immigration quotas, which limited the number of Mizrahis who could be received in Israel. This was done so that the "superior" Ashkenazi culture would not be "dragged down" by this potential mass of Mizrahis. Despite those efforts, however, Mizrahis today comprise over half of Israel/Occupied Palestine's Jewish population.

[Trigger warning: descriptions of violence, coercive human subjects research, and systematic kidnapping]

In addition to these blatant forms of discrimination, Mizrahis suffered much worse forms of oppression. For example, during the 1950s, the Israeli government performed medical experiments on one hundred thousand Mizrahi children (mostly Moroccan). These children, affected with mild illnesses, were imprisoned and exposed to lethal levels of radiation, which often caused them to die in agony. Those who survived often also died prematurely, of cancer and other diseases. A major hospital in Israel is, to this day, named after the doctor who performed these horrors, Dr. Chaim Sheba.

Also during the 1950s, Mizrahi (mostly Yemenite) children were systematically kidnapped from their parents by the government. When parents would arrive to hospitals with their children, the children would be taken away and reported dead to the parents, even in cases where the original malady was mild. The hospitals refused to show the parents the bodies of their children or to produce a death certificate. In some cases graves were shown to the parents—these were later revealed to be empty. In thirty known cases, children were returned to their parents after being declared "dead" by the hospital, following protest by the parents. In the other seventeen thousand known cases, the children were lost forever. It is thought that the kidnapped children were either adopted by Ashkenazi families or sold abroad. This was considered a "favor" done to the children, since Mizrahi mothers were thought "unfit" to raise them.

[Trigger warning: descriptions of systematic racism]

One more major form of oppression experienced by Mizrahis was—and is—race-based educational tracking. Under this system, Mizrahi students were—and are—tracked into vocational education, meaning that instead of receiving academic education, they learn manual professions such as carpentry, tailoring, car mechanics, and cosmetics. This creates a strong gap between the academic achievements and professional opportunities of Mizrahi and Ashkenazi students, resulting in a situation where many Mizrahis end up working dead-end jobs and being structurally barred from higher-paying work and positions of power. While in previous decades this was done openly, since the 1980s a myth that tracking is a thing of the past has settled in dominant discourse. In fact, however, not only has tracking continued, but the educational and economic gaps between Mizrahis and Ashkenazis have only increased throughout the years.

Today, most of the Mizrahis in Israel/Occupied Palestine still live in peripheral areas and suffer from enormous gaps in economy, education, housing, health, and many other factors. The racist perceptions of Mizrahis as primitive, ignorant, and backward remain, in addition to other stereotypes imagining us as inherently violent, racist, sexist, criminal, uneducated, uncultured, and more. On the other hand, Ashkenazis as a group keep imagining themselves as progressive, enlightened, educated, and cultured. They also enjoy many privileges typical to white people, including better education, better jobs, access to power, lack of discrimination, etc. Despite this, it's a dominant perception in Israeli society that racism towards Mizrahis is a thing of the past. Thus racism is normalized, and can run rampant while drawing little attention in culture and discourse.

[End of trigger]

BISEXUALITY AND MIZRAHINESS

As mentioned above, bisexuality and Mizrahiness are imagined and constructed by society in similar ways. By viewing these two identities in proximity, I hope to shed light on both these groups and on the ties between them. By this I hope not only to promote alliances between bisexuals and racialized groups, but to also encourage critical readings of bisexuality as it intersects with race. What I hope to show is that constructions of race and racialization have a function within—and parallel to—discourses of bisexuality. In order for bisexual movements to be race-aware and antiracist, it is vital to be aware of these workings.

It's also important to note that, while I'm specifically discussing Mizrahi identity, many other racialized identities might share some of the experiences discussed. In this, I am hoping that my discussion of Mizrahi identity will help shed light not only on Mizrahiness in particular, but also on other forms of racialization. In particular, many of the things I describe below derive from a broader attitude toward East Asian, Middle Eastern, and North African people called *orientalism*, in which "the East" (and people from it) are imagined as barbaric, backward, and "exotic."

It's important to note that while I will be addressing similarities and intersections between these two identities, I do not mean to suggest that they are the identical, or that bisexuals and racialized people suffer from oppression in the same ways. Indeed, suggesting this would cancel out the specificity of either of these identities. What I do mean to do is to create an informed understanding of these connections to encourage race-critical bisexual politics (alongside bi-aware antiracist politics).

Perhaps the most obvious common ground between Mizrahi and bisexual identities is their erasure. As discussed in chapter 2, bisexuality is routinely erased from discourses and cultural production. Similarly, Mizrahiness routinely undergoes massive erasure in Israeli culture—especially as it concerns Mizrahi cultures and histories. A rich multitude of philosophies, poetry, literature, art, sciences, histories, and religious traditions are all erased by Zionist (Ashkenazi) culture.

Historically, this has been done deliberately and explicitly by the Israeli government. For example, David Ben-Gurion famously said: "We don't want Israelis to be Arabs. It is our duty to fight the spirit of the Levant, which corrupts individuals and societies." While today the language around this erasure has changed (into "They created nothing valuable"), the erasure of Mizrahiness nonetheless continues on many levels, from schoolbooks through media to movies and TV shows. For example, a famous 1997 photograph by Mizrahi artist Meir Gal shows the artist holding out nine pages dedicated to Mizrahi history out of a four hundred-page school history book. An additional photo from 2010 by Mizrahi feminist Ortal Ben-Dayan (made as a gesture to Meir Gal), shows Ben-Dayan holding out six pages dedicated to Mizrahi art, out of a two hundred-page book about Israeli art.

Similar to bisexuality, when Mizrahiness does appear, it mostly does in negative and stereotypical contexts, presenting Mizrahi people and cultures as ignorant and barbaric. This alienates Mizrahi people from their own identities and cultures, while also encouraging them to instead identify with Ashkenazi values. This is similar to the way that monosexual culture presents bisexuality in negative and stereotypical contexts, encouraging people to identify as monosexual regardless of their actual desires. These representations respectively help perpetuate racist perceptions of Mizrahi people and biphobic perceptions about bisexuals. The erasure of these groups then continues since it replaces actual engagement with those identities with superficial and uninformed caricatures.

Both identities also share the experience of denial. In the case of bisexuality, as mentioned in chapter 1, this denial is often used as a tool of erasure, a method of obliterating the "problem" without having to engage with it. Bisexuality is constantly denied as a valid or existing identity; as the infamous sayings go, "There's no such thing as bisexuality" or "We're all bisexual, really."

Likewise, Mizrahiness is often denied existence by dominant discourses in Israel/Occupied Palestine. Frequently, in discussions about Mizrahi issues, people claim that "There's no such thing as Mizrahis or Ashkenazis," since we're all "mixed-race" anyway. Both cases feature an attempt to deny an identity out of existence, out of fear of the threat that it holds against the mainstream. In particular, Ashkenazis often use this argument in order to avoid examining their own positions as beneficiaries of the racist Israeli system. In both cases, this denial involves simultaneously claiming the identity doesn't exist and that everyone belongs to it anyway. As a result, in both discussions about bisexuality and about Mizrahiness, one is forced to validate the identity's existence as a first step before being able to engage with the oppression working against the group. This barrier hinders both bisexual and Mizrahi activists from being heard, and allows monosexuals and Ashkenazis (respectively) to conveniently dismiss the topic at hand.

Both bisexuality and Mizrahiness are consigned to a "primitive" past. As discussed in chapter 1, bisexuality is often imagined as an early developmental stage from which an individual develops a "stable" sexual orientation (also known as "We're all born bisexual," and "You have to choose eventually"). In biology, bisexuality is associated with early physical development stages of fetuses ("bisexuality" here is used to denote the originary "intersex" condition of the fetus) as well as with "lower" life forms such as snails or flowers. Mizrahiness is likewise imagined as a "primitive" category, existing in the past but never in the present. People often argue that in the 1950s the Mizrahis might have been an actual category, but that since then, the group has become too dispersed to be recognized (the same "We're all mixed-race now" argument mentioned above). This means that Mizrahiness is accepted (albeit dubiously) as a category in the past for the sole purpose of rejecting it in the present.

This similarity goes well beyond the surface level. According to the Forum for Social and Cultural Studies in Van Leer Institute in Jerusalem, while Mizrahiness is imagined as a primordial category, at the same time it is also imagined as transitive and therefore "curable." According to this logic, by turning the "savage" into a "cultured" person, the Mizrahi problem will disappear into a Zionist melting-pot utopia. As explained above, the purpose of categorizing Mizrahiness as a "primitive" identity is to dismiss concerns about the here and now. It is also meant to secure minimum opposition to Ashkenazi Zionist hegemony by assuring the notion that "they can change."

According to U.K. theorist Merl Storr, this type of colonial discourse has been used in discussions of bisexuality. In her article "The Sexual Reproduction of Race: Sexuality, History and Racialization," Storr discusses nineteenth-century German sexologist Richard von Kafft-Ebing's writings about bisexuality from a critical race perspective.[38] She concludes that his theory of bisexuality perpetuates colonial discourses in two ways (among others): One, monosexuality is perceived as characterizing "civilized races" while bisexuality is perceived as characterizing "less developed races." Two, "the dynamic of bisexuality itself is articulated . . . in the language of conquest and racial struggle. A conflict between opposing forces properly ends in the conquest of one by another" (by this she means that monosexuality "wins over" the "basic" bisexuality that we're allegedly born with). Thus, in addition to being racially charged, and likewise to the perception of Mizrahiness as "primitive," the perception of bisexuality as primitive gives way to the convenient presumption that "it will pass." The "problem" of bisexuality can then be resolved in the same way as the "problem" of "uncivilized races," receiving its "cure" in the form of "superior" white monosexuality.

Yet another similarity between bisexuality and Mizrahiness is that both identities are nonbinary. As explained in previous chapters, bisexuality disrupts the binary structure of sex, gender, and orientation by drawing attention to the instability of these categories and opening up the space "in between" them. Mizrahiness, on its part, disrupts the Jewish/Arabic binary, which is essential for the maintenance of Zionist ideology in Israel. This dichotomy structures an enormous basis for Zionist ideology by providing a reason for the occupation and colonization of Palestine.

According to this reason, Ashkenazis have founded a "safe haven" for themselves in a previously uninhabited and primitive land. Within this perception, the Palestinians play a double role: first, the role of the colonized "other," to whom the "white man" must allegedly bear the torch of "culture" and "civilization"; and second, the role of impending threat to the Zionist state (a "ticking bomb" as the phrase goes in Hebrew), whom the state must oppress for the sake of its own "safety." These roles are also extended to include all Arabic countries of the Middle East, presenting Israel as the "white" extension of the "West" in the area, or "the only democracy" there. At the same time, the Arabic states surrounding Israel are perceived as a constant threat to its existence, and thus as a justification for the military violence routinely performed by the IOF (Israeli Occupation Forces).

According to the Forum for Social and Cultural Studies, since Jewishness and Arabness are produced as conflicting and dichotomous terms, the Mizrahis—Arabic Jews—are forced to choose between an anti-Zionist "Arab" identity and a racist Zionist "Jewish" identity. When they do not, Mizrahiness becomes a problem for Zionist ideology. The coexistence of these two identities within a single person or a group reveals the false separation between them and exposes the colonial and racist Zionist ideology for what it is.

Following from this, both bisexuality and Mizrahiness also serve as boundary markers between the binary categories that they relate to. As explained in the previous chapter, bisexuality serves as a boundary marker between gay and straight identities by separating bisexual behavior from identity. Bisexual behavior coupled with gay identities receives the status of "subversive," while bisexual identity is labeled as "preserving" or "reinforcing" heterosexism.

Likewise, Mizrahiness is used as a boundary marker between Zionist Ashkenazi Jewishness on the one hand, and Arabness on the other. This is done by separating Mizrahiness into "good" and "bad" kinds. The "good" kind of Mizrahi is imagined and represented as someone who's accepted the Zionist ideology and his role within the system—for example, representations of "successful" Mizrahis who have "made it through hard work" under the racist and capitalist system, and who bear no ill will toward the Ashkenazi institution. As another example, it's frequent to see representations of Mizrahi people (especially men, and especially in commercials) as "happy workers," all too pleased to serve their Ashkenazi patrons. A third and ubiquitous example is that of the "heroic soldier," praised for his exploitation by the State for the sake of the occupation. These representations are all used as positive boundary markers. They reinforce and justify the racist Zionist Ashkenazi ideology by showing compliance and identification with the values of the system. They also reinforce this ideology by erasing Mizrahis' Arabness, creating a fictional image of an Ashkenazi Zionist "melting pot," where the "Jews" are on one side and the "Arabs" on the other.

"Bad" Mizrahis, on the other hand, are used as projections for "Western" colonial Ashkenaziness to "purify" itself from noncompliance. According to Israeli researcher Raz Yosef in his article "The Invention of Mizrahi Masculinity in Israeli Film," traits that aren't considered compatible with the Ashkenazi Zionist vision of valuable personhood are projected onto Mizrahis. In this case, Mizrahis serve as a negative boundary marker when they are identified with their Arabness, characterized according to racist stereotypes as violent, savage, ignorant, racist, sexist, and homophobic. In this way, Mizrahis come to symbolize Arabic Middle Eastern cultures that Ashkenazi Zionism rejects and seeks to erase by colonization. The contrast, in turn, reinforces the perception of Ashkenaziness as cultured, enlightened, and peaceful.

As identities located on the boundaries of other categories, bisexuality and Mizrahiness also share a common sense of partiality. As explained in chapter 3, bisexuality is a partial identity since it exists "everywhere and nowhere," always imagined in relation to something else. Therefore bisexual identity is both a patchwork and a scavenger, taking what it can, where it can.

Likewise, Mizrahi identity is partial because it's constructed, erased, included, and excluded all at once. According to the Forum for Social and Cultural Studies, "The Mizrahi person [simultaneously] experiences her being a 'problem' and a 'victim,' 'one of us' and 'threatening other.'" The erasure of Mizrahi cultures and histories, along with the production of very specific forms of Mizrahiness in Zionist culture, turns it into a patchwork identity where one is always both inside and outside. We are included by Ashkenazi culture inasmuch as it is the only culture available to us, yet are constantly excluded from it by the fact that it is ultimately not "about us." We are included by Mizrahi cultures inasmuch as we were been born into them, but at the same time, the erasure of our cultures, histories, and languages means that we remain ignorant about what is "ours." (This applies in particular to third-generation Mizrahis, born to non-immigrant, Hebrew-speaking parents).

In addition to all these similarities, bisexuality and Mizrahiness are also mutually bisexualized and racialized. As mentioned above, in nineteenth-century sexology, bisexuality was imagined in colonial terms as a "primitive" characteristic that one later "conquers" by achieving monosexuality. As Storr explains, "The logic of bisexuality is a racial logic" in the sense that the suppression of it in favor of monosexuality is, for nineteenth-century sexologists, a mark of evolution and "racial superiority."

On the other hand, racialized groups are often bisexualized. In particular, Mizrahis and Arabs are often imagined as bisexual and

contrasted with the "cultured" monosexual/heterosexual "West." For
example, in 1983 a prominent Israeli researcher wrote:

[Trigger warning: direct quote containing racism]

> *The Levantine tries his best to prove his heroics and masculin-*
> *ity to himself and others in various ways: He treats women as*
> *if they were objects for his use . . . he walks proudly wearing*
> *colorful clothes, enjoying every display of sentimentalism.*
> *Sometimes he even becomes addicted to homosexual relations,*
> *although he is not truly homosexual.*

[End of trigger]

As we might notice, the Arab man imagined in this paragraph is
hypermasculinized, feminized, and bisexualized all at once. In concur-
rence with orientalist perceptions of Middle Eastern cultures, this man is
imagined as savage, sexist, and hypersexual. His bisexuality here emphasizes both his imagined hypersexuality and his "savageness," creating
an image of a carnal existence made up of exploitation of women and
homosexual addiction. Also note that this is contrasted with the "truly
homosexual" notion, a quality that we are to presume only belongs to
the "cultured" white people of the "West."

As another example, in the same article as mentioned above, Yosef
discusses an Israeli gay movie by the name of *Baal Baal Lev (A Husband
with a Heart)*. The movie revolves around the lives of two Ashkenazi gay
men, both of whom desire the Mizrahi bisexual Marito.[39] According
to Yosef, the character of Marito is constructed in keeping with orientalist perceptions of Mizrahi men, as a hypersexualized fetish for the
Ashkenazi men. He writes: "The homosexual gaze [in the film] objectifies Marito's body, which is inscribed with colonial fantasies about the
wild and animalistic nature of Mizrahi sexuality." Marito's bisexuality
is used doubly in this movie, both as a marker of his hypersexualized
Mizrahiness and as a marker of his "homophobia." At the end of a sex

scene between him and one of the movie's heroes, Marito is seen scrap-ing his body from the "filth" of the "homosexual" sex that just took place.[40] This internalized "homophobia" also goes hand in hand with the perception of Mizrahis as naturally or inherently homophobic.

To conclude, bisexuality and Mizrahiness are often imagined in similar ways, and are used for similar functions in various discourses. They are both erased in society and culture because they expose and sub-vert binary structures that relate to them. They are both used as bound-ary markers between those binary categories, by being separated into "good" and "bad" kinds in the case of Mizrahiness, or to "subversive" and "preservative" kinds in the case of bisexuality. Due to their erasure and their "in-between" location, they are also both partial or patchwork identities, always located as both insiders and outsiders. And finally, both these identities are specifically imagined as related to one another in white colonial thought. Bisexuality is imagined in racist terms, as being a mark of "inferior" races, while monosexuality is perceived as a mark of the "cultured West." Likewise, Mizrahiness is imagined as bisexual, as bisexuality emphasizes orientalist perceptions of Arab and Mizrahi people as hypersexualized and homophobic savages.

DECIPHERING THE POWER, CREATING A NEW WORLD

In a seminal article by this same name, Mizrahi feminist Vicky Shiran writes about Mizrahi identity as inherently political and subversive. I'd like to explain her perception, and examine what bisexual identification and politics can draw from it.

According to Shiran, identifying as a feminist is a militant act. She writes:

> *Such a woman says very personally, I decipher the social reality in which I live from a rebel's point of view. . . . Further, she*

says she knows that the world is designed by men, for their point
of view, to their benefit, and that in order to change it . . .
she needs to fight to remove her chains with her own hands.

Similarly, identifying as Mizrahi is a militant political act challenging existing order.

A woman who chooses to identify as Mizrahi is a brave woman
willing to fight against hatred, denial, shaming, and mockery.
Using one word, she says that she is going through personal
and internal liberation as well as political liberation. She says
she knows that the Mizrahi collective she belongs to has been
marginalized. . . . She says she knows that Mizrahi culture has
been blatantly erased. . . . She also speaks more than one or two
hard truths about Zionism. . . .
  In other words, when a woman identifies as Mizrahi she
says that she's learned to decipher the power structure. . . .
Such a woman begins to dream, to create, a new world.

According to Shiran, both feminist and Mizrahi identities cause
discomfort to people of the privileged groups relating to them. Mizrahi
identity, in particular, is perceived as a "defiant and threatening political
act, and it provokes much hostility and hatred." She continues:

Among Ashkenazis it tends to provoke discomfort, anger,
revulsion, nervousness, and cautious patronage. Many
Ashkenazis tense up to the person identifying as Mizrahi,
because in their eyes this self-identification conceals an imagi-
nary narrative, blaming them for the oppression and disprivi-
leging of the Mizrahis.

The lived experiences of Mizrahi feminists is complex, multifocal, and often contradictory. Shiran writes:

> *The life of a Mizrahi feminist is an intersection of gender,*
> *race, and often also class oppression. Because of this she also*
> *finds herself fighting a number of fronts: against male oppres-*
> *sion, Mizrahi male oppression, racial oppression by Ashkenazi*
> *women and men, and her oppression as a daughter of the lower*
> *class. In addition, a Mizrahi feminist is aware of her location*
> *as part of the Jewish majority oppressing the Palestinian-Arab*
> *minority, both women and men. All of these things require*
> *of her an ability to understand a complex overview of life,*
> *to observe herself and her actions critically, to move between*
> *patches of conflicting identities, and especially, to create a new*
> *world by nonviolently destroying the old oppressive one.*

According to Shiran, the power of feminist and Mizrahi identifications stems from the threat that they hold against existing patriarchal and Ashkenazi order. Identifying by these terms means reversing the system that privileges certain groups over everyone else and using their own power against them. Taking a militant, subversive stance exposes the power structure by proudly taking on an identity that, to the existing order, should be trodden and erased. This position is defiant precisely because it dares to create a counterpoint in the face of hegemony, to intentionally reverse the values of the oppressive system.

Seen from this perspective, it's of little surprise that Mizrahi and feminist identities provoke such intense reactions. Privileged people can feel the way these identities threaten their privileged status and the benefits that they receive as a result. For this reason also, trying to reassure hegemony that these identities are not a threat to it (for the purpose of being "accepted" into society) is moot. Hegemony is right to feel threatened, because there's no way one could change social order without deconstructing power.

This defiant journey of subversion, however, doesn't end with the external world. According to Shiran, a woman taking on these political identities has also taken upon herself to be accountable to her own privileges and oppressor status. This means that her attempt to deconstruct power isn't only limited to the types of power that oppress her, but expands to include the types of power that she benefits from. Doing so requires an ability to examine oneself honestly and then to work on taking apart one's privileges and internalized oppression. This comes from the understanding that deconstructing only one patch of power while preserving others only creates a different kind of hegemony and oppression. Since the goal of these politics is to create another world, we could be satisfied with nothing less than everything.

According to Shiran, a woman who identifies as feminist or Mizrahi exclaims that she has learned to decipher the power structure as patriarchal and racist. Identifying in this way, then, becomes a political tool to communicate these understandings. Likewise, bisexuality can be used as a defiant political tactic for destroying existing order and subverting power structures. It can be used as a political tool to communicate our understanding of the social power structure as monosexist, acknowledging that the collective one belongs to has been marginalized and erased. Just like Mizrahi or feminist identities can symbolize a personal and political journey of liberation, so can bisexual identity.

This means that bisexual identification can be a reversal of the system placing sole value on monosexuality, validating an identity that, according to this power structure, should be trodden and erased. Bisexuality can be a defiant, rebellious identity, marking a dangerous and subversive point of view.

As in the case of feminism and Mizrahi identity, bisexuality's subversive potential can be seen through people's responses. Just as in the case of feminism and Mizrahiness, monosexual people often become defensive or even hostile when encountering bi identities. They often feel the need to clarify that *they are not* bisexual (even when nothing's been said about their sexuality). These people often seem to imagine that the bi person in front of them is accusing them personally of erasing and oppressing bisexuals. That, in turn, means that, similar to Mizrahi identity, bisexuality makes many people feel discomfort, anger, revulsion, and nervousness.

Like Mizrahi identity, using bisexuality in this way is also closely tied with accountability and with being able and willing to examine one's privileges as well as oppressor status and behaviors. It means understanding that different kinds of oppression are interlinked, and that one can't liberate only one group without the others. It means acknowledging kyriarchy and intersectionality—the fact that along different axes, we're all both oppressed and oppressors, privileged and disprivileged. In this way, taking on a bisexual identity also means taking on the responsibility for taking apart all oppression, starting with our very selves.

Using bisexual identity in this way, as inspired by Vicky Shiran, makes bisexual identity into a defiant political statement. No longer just a form of sexuality and desire, but active resistance to systems of monosexism, sexism, cissexism, racism, and others. It means creating bisexuality not as a plea to be accepted by the same systems that reject us, but to destroy these systems and build something new.

Using bisexuality like this also means acknowledging that identities alone can't create a revolution. Rather, it means being committed to acting on the political statement borne by bisexual identity, and actively working to dismantle systems of oppression by doing activist, community, and personal work. It means being willing to look at all the dirty details and work on addressing these issues specifically and radically.

Of course, using bisexuality in this way also means acknowledging the source of this suggestion, respecting and being accountable to feminism and Mizrahiness. It means not only being committed to resisting all oppression in general, but also being specifically committed to supporting women and racialized people.

Following Vicky Shiran's writings about feminist and Mizrahi identities, bisexual people and movements can take on the same ideas and apply them to bisexuality. Just as feminist and Mizrahi identities can mark resistance, defiance, and radical politics, so can bisexuality be used to imply the same things. Doing so would make bisexuality into a militant political identity, stating rebellion against social order and all forms of oppression, and serving as a constant reminder for the need to work on deciphering power, and creating a new world.

BISEXUALITY AND WHITENESS

Despite the fact that bisexuality shares much in common with racialization, we must also remember that ultimately, bisexuality is a white identity, invented and maintained mostly in minority-world counties. As discussed in chapter 1, bisexuality was invented by European sexologists in order to categorize and pathologize human behavior. As we've seen above, it has also been used in the framework of colonial and racist discourses in order to preserve the superiority of white minority-world cultures.

Another connection between bisexuality and whiteness is described by Clare Hemmings in her article "What's in a Name? Bisexuality, Transnational Sexuality Studies and Western Colonial Legacies." She explains that within the field of transnational sexuality studies, bisexuality is often relegated to minority-world and white cultures, and perceived as an oppressive identity, irrelevant to majority-world people, and preserving minority-world binaries (while gay and lesbian identities, are, of course, just fine). On the other hand, Hemmings writes, bisexuality is often also used as a "neutral" term, while obscuring its history and context as a white minority-world term.

Regardless of the fact that both these things are problematic, situating bisexuality as inferior in various ways, we must also acknowledge these uses of the term, and take them into account when discussing bisexuality and racialization. As much as we may want to believe it, bisexuality is not, in fact, a purely "antiracist" identity, and is not always and inherently on the "good side." On the contrary, it has often been used in order to maintain hierarchical divisions between "East" and "West," as well as the idea of white supremacy.

This is particularly important to remember because mainstream bisexual movements often like to present themselves as "natural allies" to racialized groups, sometimes even going as far as equating between the oppression of racialized people and that of bisexuals, as if they were the same. In *Bisexual Spaces*, Hemmings notes that the "bisexual community is considered uniquely positioned to provide a home, and a parallel to [issues] of race." "In these ways," she continues, "bisexuality is produced as either inherently or culturally situated in unique relation to communities and discourses of race." However, "while white bisexuals may see bisexual identity as incorporating racial diversity, bisexuals of color apparently do not."

If this notion sounds familiar at this point, it must be due to the similarity between this and the issue of transgender and bi communities. In both cases, bi communities often seem to engage in a type of wishful thinking that renders them "already inclusive," while ridding them of the responsibility to do actual work to ensure that they really are so. As with the case of trans people, the good intentions of bi communities are not always sufficient in order to make the space truly inclusive.

As a case in point, Hemmings examines the 1990 National Bisexual Conference (NBC, mentioned in chapter 4) and writes that "there is a marked gap between the conference committee's desire for bisexual space to be inherently racially diverse and their certain knowledge that it will not be." In planning the conference, the committee went to great length to try and ensure racial diversity. Importantly, they formed a People of Color caucus, intended to influence conference decisions and provide a voice for racialized bisexuals. In addition, the conference included a People of Color workshop track, including nine sessions, while all the other workshops and panels were also instructed to be inclusive of racial issues and racialized people. In addition, at the stage of planning, the committee decided to allocate any surplus funds as scholarships for people of color to be able to attend.

Despite these commendable efforts, the conference itself still proved to be predominantly white. As Lani Ka'ahumanu notes (and Hemmings quotes), "while 'the representation of people of color from the stage was very well thought out,' the majority of (white) workshop presenters still presumed a white bisexual audience." In addition, "According to Ka'ahumanu, members of the People of Color caucus were amazed at the lack of 'sophistication around challenging white supremacy' from white bisexual participants." Hemmings writes:

> In the course of the conference . . . the caucus's role shifted to become one of highlighting how the conference space consistently fell short of [its race-inclusive] intentions—how, in fact, racial diversity remained marginal rather than central to bisexual community.

And indeed, the lack of racial diversity was called out by people of color many times throughout the conference. Some people walked out of workshops in protest, while others wrote about the issue in the conference evaluation sheets. In addition, a major debate spanned over several days concerning the naming of the new "National Bisexual Network In-Formation," as the word "multicultural" was added and then dropped from the network's title.

Despite this, in an article in the *San Francisco Bay Times*, Greta Christina praises the conference's racial diversity, writing that:

> Although the crowd was largely white, middle class, educated, and able-bodied, it was not overwhelmingly so: There was a strong presence of disabled people and people of color,

*in significantly more than token numbers. An entire track of
workshops focused specifically on bisexual people of color, and
organizers and participants alike expressed a strong interest in
creating a bisexual community that is multicultural and hospi-
table to any and all bisexuals and bi-friendlies.*

As Hemmings notes, readers are obviously meant to be impressed
by the "entire" track of workshops dedicated to bi people of color. In
addition, one wonders for whom the conference was not "overwhelmingly white," and who gets to decide "what constitutes 'token numbers,'
'strong interest,' or indeed 'hospitality.'"

In this passage, the conference's failure to hold up to its own
inclusive standards is concealed by wishful rhetoric. Christina seems to
tell us that *Yes, the conference was white and non-inclusive, but let's not
think about that too much. After all, it wasn't that bad, and it's better to
think about the happy side.* In this way we are soothed by the rhetoric to
think that things are not as bad as they seem to appear, and as racialized
attendees of the conference experienced them. Instead of addressing and
working on these problems, the text encourages us to replace reality with
an inclusive fantasy that never happened, but which nonetheless pacifies
us into thinking that nothing is actually wrong.

As alluded to in chapter 4, race-based tensions were also apparent
twenty years later, at the International BiCon in London, 2010. The conference itself was predominantly white, both in attendance and content.
In fact, the predominance of white people was so noticeable that one
could easily tell apart between conference attendees and students of the
University of East London (which served as the venue) simply by the
color of their skin (the students were mostly people of color). At the same
time, almost no content was dedicated to addressing race issues—most
presenters in the workshops and panels were white, and presumed a white
audience. A unique exception was the "Bi People of Color" workshop, the
only session in the entire five-day conference devoted to this issue.

As a visible person of color, who was also visiting from a Middle Eastern country, I felt consistently marginalized both by people's behavior and by the structure of the conference. From relatively "trivial" matters, like people constantly being surprised at my fluency in English, through the silent presumption that "they" (white people) "knew better" than I did about anything discussed, to the fact that all rooms in this "international" conference were named after European countries. As a matter of fact, when I tried to briefly raise this issue in a lecture I gave, a person from the audience interrupted me to ask how I could possibly refer to English culture as "white," seeing as so many people of color lived there.

As mentioned in chapter 4, the Bi People of Color session, along with the feminist women-only session, caused a controversy within the local bi community, to the extent that it was suggested to ban "X-only" sessions. The rejection of this suggestion by the decision-making caucus later created space for a proliferation of such workshops. The BiCon code of conduct currently includes a paragraph about respect for such spaces. The Bi People of Color workshop later grew into a group called Bi's of Color, which has been recently active in the U.K. bi and LGBTQ communities. Following BiCon 2012, Bi's of Color cofounders Camel and Jacqui wrote, "There was a consensus that things were slowly improving for us, but there was still plenty of work to be done before BiCon became a truly welcoming and supportive place for all bisexuals of color."

It's unfortunate to say that the bisexual community in Israel/Occupied Palestine doesn't fare much better. In September 2012, the country's first bisexual and pansexual conference took place in Tel Aviv. The conference lasted for a day and a half, and included four panels, one lecture, and three workshops. At the stage of planning, the organizing committee took care to ensure that multiple racialized groups would be represented as speakers and workshop facilitators. However, even after our efforts to include these groups, only five presenters in the conference were Mizrahi, and only two were Russian-speakers (another consider-able racialized group in Israel). All the rest, however, (twelve in number) were Ashkenazi. Try as we might, we could not secure any Palestinian presenters, nor did we have the resources to outreach to any other racialized groups, such as Ethiopian Jews, African asylum seekers, migrant workers, etc. In terms of content, race issues were addressed by only two of the presenters, and were only mentioned in passing or completely left out everywhere else.

In the planning stage, the committee also took care to make the conference financially accessible, so as to enable people of economically marginalized groups to attend. The conference was completely free of charge, wheelchair accessible, included free vegan meals, and took place in a central part of the city accessible by public transportation. Despite this, the attendance of the conference, too, was overwhelmingly Ashkenazi. Few visible Mizrahis and Russian-speakers attended, and no Palestinians, Ethiopians, or people of other groups were to be seen.

Though it might be tempting to think that the fault in this case (as well as in the case of the NBC) was not with the leadership, but with the racialized people who didn't show up, this is not so. Despite the prior work done to ensure that the space would be structurally inclusive, more basic problems remain with the structure of the community and its human composition. While the organizing committee could control structural elements of the space, it couldn't do the same regarding the character of the community itself.

Here we return to the fact that bisexuality is an identity originating in white and minority-world cultures. This is especially relevant in Hebrew, where the foreign word "bisexual" has been adopted into the language as-is. This means that even on the linguistic level, Israeli bisexual identity is mediated and negotiated by—and through—North American and Western European discourses. While there is a word for *bisexual* in Hebrew ("Du-Meenee"), this is often frowned upon by people in the bi community for reasons of linguistic elitism. On the level of politics as well, while certainly local and unique, our bi political discourse is none-theless heavily influenced by those of minority-world countries.

What all of this means is that in order to participate in the bi community, one must first possess at least a basic level of understanding regarding these cultures and discourses. This, in turn, creates a struc-tural exclusion of people who do not have access to these systems of knowledge, or indeed the English language. In addition, much of the bisexual discourse here leans upon radical queer, trans, and radical left discourses, all predominantly Ashkenazi communities that similarly require good levels of understanding of minority-world discourses and cultures. Here again people are barred from fully participating in the community if they don't possess access to this knowledge. All of this works to create a situation where even though the community leadership is Mizrahi or race-aware, the community itself is nonetheless exclusive of Mizrahi and other racialized people.

This problem, however, is not inherent to bisexual communities, nor is it unavoidable. As with any other problem, it needs to be addressed through community and activist work. For example, one thing that can be done is more outreach to racialized bi people. Specifically in the Israeli context, this might include creating or utilizing existing con-nections with Mizrahi, Russian-speakers', or Palestinian organizations (queer, feminist, or others), creating collaborative projects, hosting com-mon meetings, or simply requesting that these organizations pass on information about the bi community. This, of course, is also relevant to other countries and contexts, replacing these groups with ones relevant to the community in question.

Another method would be increasing the bi communities' acces-sibility—not only in terms of finances or physical conditions, but also in terms of discourse and language. Explaining terms and knowledge, using accessible language, and never speaking over people's heads, in any situation, are all primary steps to ensure this. Further, conversation and discourse topics need to address and engage with people's lives and lived experience—including racialized people. When writing, speaking, or even just talking, we must always remember that people's lives might be very different from what is often considered the "standard." Once people feel that they are being addressed at eye level (rather than patronized, belittled, or ignored), they will also start feeling more comfortable inside the community.

In addition, no community work on race issues can be complete without working on internalized racism, within the community as well as individually. In particular, white people must continually acknowledge, address, and work on deconstructing their racist perceptions, feelings, and behaviors. This includes those who feel that they don't need to, who believe that they're not racist, or who consider themselves allies to racialized people. Living in a racist culture, no one can help but internalize that culture's problematic perceptions and viewpoints. In fact, denying that we possess them only serves to further obscure their existence, and allows us to continue with a privileged existence, never being accountable to our own oppressive patterns. Working on this, among other things, means organizing workshops, talks, and lectures about race issues, writing about it in community-related media, in blogs and online groups, thinking and talking about it with members of the community, and doing personal as well as collective work. Addressing and seriously engaging with race and racism is the only way to counter our racist conditioning. It is the only way to ensure that bi communities are truly welcoming to racialized people.

To conclude, bisexuality and racialization intersect and share similarities on multiple points. These points can serve as a fruitful basis for alliances between bisexual and racialized groups, and can encourage and highlight race awareness in bi communities. Despite this broad potential and best intentions, however, bisexual communities are often overwhelmingly white, and exclude racialized people in various forms. In order to live up to their inclusive standards, bisexual communities must actively work at deconstructing the racism and default whiteness that are present in them. Such work would make bisexual communities not only more welcoming toward racialized people, but also more accountable, radical, and revolutionary.

CHAPTER 8:

Bisexuality and the GGGG Movement

Throughout this book, I've discussed various political issues, and the way that they intersect with, or work within, bisexual communities. In this chapter I'd like to move one step back and look at the mainstream bi movement from "outside"—at how it does activism, its reasons, and its goals. In general, this could be described as *bi assimilationism*—a long-term and encompassing attempt by the mainstream bisexual movement in minority-world countries to assimilate into the assimilationist gay movement.

The assimilationist gay movement is the same movement usually simply called "the gay movement" or "the LGBT movement." It is the movement whose goal is to cater for the interests of mostly white, middle-class, cisgender and nondisabled gay men, leaving out most everyone else. For this reason, I also call it the *GGGG movement*, meaning the Gay, Gay, Gay, and Gay movement. This movement is called *assimilationist* because its method of catering to GGGGs is assimilating

Homonormativity is the acceptance of heteronormative values by gay people and movements. It guides the ideology of the GGGG movement and is often used to further marginalize marginalized LGBTQ groups.

into the heteronormative mainstream. This is done by adopting the mainstream's conservative values, trying to prove to the heteronorm that GGGGs are "just as normal" as straight people. Instead of challenging straight life and helping straight people out of the unfortunate structures culture has built all around us, the GGGG movement tries to gain access into the same oppressive structures that are keeping everyone locked in.

Bi assimilationism, on the other hand, seems to stem from a perceived need in bisexual communities to "redeem" bisexuality and bi people through "good behavior." Since being bisexual is considered an insufficient reason to belong to LGBTQ movements, bisexual movements, as a whole, might feel as if they need to fit into **homonormativity**. This includes rejecting such things as radical or "unpalatable" opinions, criticizing assimilationist ideology, speaking too much about specifically bisexual issues, and so on. Many bi movements behave as if such opinions or activism might damage their chances for acceptance within GGGG communities (much in the same way that assimilationist gays feel that bisexuals might damage *their* movement by tarring their normative image). In this way, normativity, which is the condition for entrance into the GGGG movement, is "inherited down" into bisexual movements whose goal is assimilation with the assimilationist gay movement.

In the past decade, the GGGG movement in the United States has walked two main paths into the heart of the white mainstream, both cornerstones of conservative American ideals: marriage and the military. That it has done so is hardly surprising given its ultimate goal— to become indistinct from the norm. Concurrently, the campaigns for "marriage equality" and the "right to serve" in the U.S. military are not progressive struggles for human rights, but deeply conservative attempts to be accepted into heteronormative society by strengthening two of its most oppressive systems. (I will return to this later.)

However frustrating it may be for everyone else, the fact that those with white, middle-class, cisgender, and other privileges would want to fight for their full access to the one privilege they don't own (straight) is understandable. That the mainstream bisexual movement, usually ideologically aligned with marginalized groups—and doubly marginalized itself—would want to join in that fight is neither understandable nor tolerable. In this chapter I'll try to understand how and why this happened, and what we can do to change it.

In his 1995 essay "Pimple No More," American writer Mykel Board pins down the problem—and the reason for it— accurately and poignantly:

> *[Many people] say that because bisexuals face discrimination mainly on the basis of the homosexual part of their identity, bisexuals should align ourselves with the homosexual rights movement. Often this alignment becomes a plea for inclusion. "Oh please let us be a tagline," we beg. "Just add us at the end of your titles and events. We'll be happy.* Lesbian, Gay and Bisexual. *That's all we want."*
>
> *Most of the lesbian and gay movement considers bifolks a pimple on the butt of their struggle. In truth, bisexuals haven't made it that far. Most of us* want to be *pimples on that butt. (All emphases in original).*

First of all, it needs to be said that this problem is obviously not a new one, having been written about nearly twenty years ago. Surprisingly, though, despite its being an ongoing debate in the American mainstream bi movement for many years, discourse around it has developed very little, and the movement largely remains the same.

The very first reason for bi assimilationism starts with the presumption mentioned (and made) by Board in this paragraph—that bisexuals experience oppression not as bisexual people, but as "quasi gays and lesbians." As explained in chapter 3, this notion divides bisexual identity into "gay" and "straight" parts. It presumes that bisexuals are only oppressed by heterosexism inasmuch as they live a "gay" life, and that they gain privileges inasmuch as they live a "straight" life. This is compounded by the presumption, explained in chapter 2, that bi people only experience *biphobia* from gay and lesbian communities and not from straight populations.

With these two presumptions as the basic premises for bisexual politics and activism, it only makes sense that the goals of the bisexual movement would be: 1. joining the gay and lesbian movement, and 2. gaining acceptance within it. In fact, the two are almost indistinct, since one cannot be done without the other. Historically, this is what the mainstream bi movement in the United States has been doing all these years. Its main struggles have focused on supporting assimilationist GGGG struggles on the one hand, and on assimilating into the GGGG movement on the other.

As Board mentions, in the 1990s the one great campaign of the U.S. mainstream bisexual movement was becoming a tagline to the ubiquitous "gay and lesbian" title. Simply put, most of bisexual activist effort was devoted to adding "and bisexual" to titles of gay and lesbian organizations, groups, events, etc. As explained above, this happened because it was presumed that bisexuals mostly experience biphobia in gay and lesbian communities. On the other hand, it was also presumed that bisexuals needed to join the gay and lesbian movement if they wanted to fight heterosexism. As a result, not only was the tagline perceived as bi people's most burning problem, it was perceived as the only one.

In fact, however, bi people face issues far more burning than the twofold assimilationist goal. As described in chapter 2, depression, poor physical and mental health, poverty, and violence are only a few of the issues that many bisexuals are forced to face in their daily lives. Because of this, reducing monosexism and biphobia to nothing but named inclusion in gay communities is inaccurate at best and negligent at worst.

In addition, the presumption that fighting heterosexism can only be done through GGGG communities erases the power that bi communities can have in fighting it themselves. Since bi people face different issues than gay people, we might also develop our own unique perspectives about how to fight oppression (as done throughout this book). In this way, even if we are combating the same structures, we still get to address our own issues rather than being subsumed under something else.

Concurrently, setting this twofold goal prioritizes the issues of privileged white gay men above and beyond those of bi people. By seeking to assimilate into the assimilationist gay movement, the mainstream American bi movement seems to presume that GGGG issues are more important than our own. In fact, it might even suggest that bi people have no unique issues at all (or else, why would it be so urgent for us to fight the struggles of the privileged?). Accepting this, it's easy to conclude, as many do, that the role of bi people in the GGGG movement is only that of allies, and that bisexuality itself is a non-issue.

At this point, though, it is essential to take a step aside and examine what exactly is so wrong with the assimilationist gay movement. I'll do so by examining the two issues which have been hailed as *the* issues embodying and defining the GGGG rights struggle in the past decade: marriage and the military. As mentioned above, both these issues embody a movement that is conservative, privilege-seeking, and exclusionary.

FUCK MARRIAGE, FUCK EQUALITY

For about a decade, same-sex marriage has been the flagship issue of the GGGG movement.[41] Marketed as the single-issue battle that would bring equality and solve GGGG-phobia for all, it has been the main focus of GGGG activist and political effort. The struggle for same-sex marriage has been presented to us as a struggle for full equality and citizenship. We are told that the one step separating between us—"the gays"—and perfect rainbow utopia is the ability to register our same-sex relationships with the state. As soon as this right is won, apparently, we'll all be able to walk away into the sunset.

But before we start with the walking away, we first need to examine what it is that we are asking. Marriage, as an institution, is and has been a tool of patriarchy, capitalism, and government for about as long as it's existed. It is and has been used to control women, divide and consolidate money and resources, and strengthen the power of states over their subjects. All in all, for most of history and until today, it is and has been one of the most dangerous institutions created by society.

Note that my discussion of marriage and patriarchy refers to minority-world cultures. Though the things I write might not always be convenient, I ask my readers not to make the mistake of attributing them to majority-world cultures or to racialized people. Patriarchy and its violence influences everyone's lives—including those who perceive ourselves as living in "equal" societies.

At its very base, marriage is a patriarchal institution. Its goal is to decide and maintain male ownership and control of women, transferring the woman from her father to her husband. A dash of linguistics might be enlightening here, as the original meaning of the word *husband* relates to husbandry—ownership of land and animals, while one of the original meanings of *wife* is "bitch" and contains a root indicating shame.[42] Last names are also relevant here, as even today most women in minority-world cultures bear the names of their fathers, their husbands, or a combination of both.

[Trigger warning: general discussion of familial violence]

Most violence perpetrated against women, as well as children, happens within heteronormative families. Intimate violence, sexual violence, spousal rape, spousal murder, incest, violence against children, and economic violence are only some of the horrors that marriage is designed to contain. This is all the more relevant to bisexual women, since studies indicate that they have an elevated risk for experiencing intimate violence and sexual violence.

This happens because the man is considered the head and owner of the family, and thus as entitled to treat his "property" in any way that he sees fit. Not so long ago, all of these things were also perfectly legal in most minority-world countries. For example, up until 1993, spousal rape was a legal act in most U.S. states. To this day, even though they are *technically* illegal, these phenomena are considered minor and marginal, especially when compared to other issues, such as theft, drug use, or "illegal" immigration. This is despite the fact that each of the issues mentioned above, and certainly all put together, happen more frequently, and influence more people than the ones just listed.

[End of trigger]

But even if one's particular marital arrangement doesn't include any form of direct violence, marriage still constitutes symbolic violence against women in and of itself. This is a structure meant to secure women's unpaid labor on behalf of men. When a woman enters a marriage, she also enters a presumed and unspoken contract, one she has been trained for all her life. She is to be her husband's cook, cleaner, psychologist, personal assistant, secretary, and sex worker, to bear him children and be their caretaker, educator, nurse, entertainer, and driver, and a handful of other jobs. No matter what a married woman does in her life outside marriage—career, education, social life, hobbies, and any other pursuit—at the end of the day, she is expected to begin the infamous "second shift," serving the family in their home. That many women do this willingly and gladly still doesn't change the point—this is their designated role within the marital structure, whether they want to or not.

[Trigger warning: general discussion of familiar anti-queer/trans violence]

In addition to perpetrating violence against women, heteronormative families are also one of the most difficult sites in the lives of queers and trans people (especially youth). The lack of acceptance that so many of us experience from our families often also turns into homelessness, physical and sexual violence, punishment, imprisonment at home, and conversion treatments. Even for those whose parents avoid direct violence, surviving inside the family often means keeping secrets, avoiding trust, and being isolated and distant. It also means having to deal with our parents' and relatives' disappointment with "how we turned out," having to constantly navigate the shifting balance between wanting to please our parents and wanting to live our lives, and knowing that the two will often contradict. This, too, is one of the functions of marriage: making sure that the children raised within them will follow the same "straight" path.

[End of trigger]

Yet another function of marriage is the maintenance of capitalism. Marriage is a financial contract, deciding who gets what and how much. It's a means to allocate money and possessions between men through— and on the backs of—women. Marriage determines lines of succession. It also pools up the money for those who have it, making sure that it doesn't get distributed to others who do not. In other cases, marriage is used to consolidate money and possessions, or to exchange status for money and vice versa. Since most people marry within their class as well as race, marriage keeps capital, status, and privilege concentrated in one place while ensuring that it doesn't "leak out."

As mentioned above, marriage also functions as a tool for financial exploitation of women's labor. In this way, money doesn't have to be "lost" on paid services, and men can reap the benefits both materially and financially. Notwithstanding, marriage also maintains the capitalist yoke around men's necks by expecting them to be the main financial supporters of the family. In this way, men are pressured into being productive, earning citizens, while reducing their lives to their jobs (albeit for the benefit of increased financial gain and status).

Marriage is also used as an instrument of control by the state and government. Dividing its subjects into minimal units keeps people as separate from one another as possible. This applies in particular to minority-world countries and white populations, where one's family only includes the nuclear unit. Minimizing communities in this way makes it harder for people to oppose the state or government, keeping it safe from civil uprisings. In addition, heteronormative families serve as convenient production units, manufacturing productive citizens, workers for the capitalist system, and soldiers for the military (through the bodies of women). The role of families in producing these functions in people is critical, because families are responsible not only for birth rates, but also for the education of their young. Indeed, most people learn to love and serve their governments first and foremost within their families, through "educational values" such as patriotism, nationalism, militarism, and capitalism.

Seeing as such, it is unsurprising that states and governments place such high value on marriage. Marriage and heteronormative families are in many ways necessary for their "proper" function—maintaining patriarchy, capitalism, and government itself. It only makes sense, then, that states would want to privilege those who comply with the system while punishing those who do not. The many privileges granted to married couples by the state serve as a reward for their compliance; withholding those privileges from those who do not, serves as their punishment for disobedience.

As we can see, then, marriage is a useful institution for upholding oppressive structures. It's not, however, very good for most people. For this reason, among other things, a huge cultural apparatus exists for the sole sake of convincing us to get married. From legal privileges through romantic comedies and dating shows to wedding ceremonies and social treatment, almost every piece of dominant culture relating to relationships and love is pushing us in this one direction. I often wonder: If all these things were nonexistent, would people want to get married at all?

Minority-world culture being what is it, however, marriage is one of the biggest entry tickets to the heart of the mainstream. Because it plays such a huge role in the maintenance of several oppressive systems, it is also granted enormous value by them. To be married is to be a proper citizen, a mature adult, and a productive part of society. Compliance with the system is rewarded, while disobedience is punished. It only makes sense, then, that a movement such as the GGGG, whose ultimate goal is to be accepted into the mainstream, should want to take such a direct path.

But in taking this "straight" path to the mainstream, the GGGG movement also pays a dear price: It reinforces the very structures that work against it and that oppress many others. In choosing this campaign, the GGGG movement has made a choice. It chose to prioritize the needs and values of the privileged at the expense of everyone else. It chose to validate the mainstream and to "redeem" itself from marginalization by reinforcing its values. Instead of fighting to bring these structures down, the GGGG movement chose to fight in pursuit of the exclusive privileges that these structures offer.

The campaign for same-sex marriage leaves behind almost everyone who isn't already privileged. People with more urgent needs than marriage are neglected from the resources and activist efforts of the GGGG movement. GGGG organizations spend many millions of dollars on the struggle for marriage, while organizations addressing the issues of queer and trans homelessness youth, HIV+ queers, queer and trans people of color, queers in poverty, queer and trans survivors of violence, and many others suffer from a constant lack of money and resources.

Some claim that for many of these populations, legalizing same-sex marriage is the very path to justice, as the governmental marriage package includes so many economic and other privileges. But as long as these privileges continue being distributed only to married people, the problem will remain. Marriage will continue to be used as the carrot with which to divide and conquer populations, keeping people under control and barring their access to those privileges. Same-sex marriage will not help the ones who cannot or will not get legally married. It will not solve poverty, it will not solve violence or sexual violence, it will not open borders or keep people out of imprisonment. Instead of fighting for universal rights for everyone—or indeed the abolition of government control—the fight for same-sex marriage reinforces the oppression of all those who are left outside.

In addition, whole LGBT populations get thrown overboard from the struggle in fear that they might "tar" the clear and normative image that the GGGG movement presents. Bisexuals, trans and genderqueer people, queer and trans people of color, disabled queers, and many others are among the first to get tossed away in sight of the golden promise of assimilation into the system. Since this campaign is based on access to privilege, and similarity to the privileged, it only makes sense that those who cannot fit also don't get to enter.

Specifically in the case of bisexuals, it is necessary to erase us from the campaign because we fail to fit in with heteronormativity, or indeed homonormativity. The promiscuous and traitorous image of bisexuals is likely to cause difficulties for the campaign. As GGGGs try to rid themselves of the "dangerous" specter of gay cruising, casual sex, and other deliciously indecent spectacles, bisexuality looms around the corner to return all of this and more back into the picture.

In this way, by supporting the GGGG campaign for same-sex marriage, bi activists participate in bisexual erasure on several levels: First of all, they choose the maintenance of the systems that oppress them, instead of fighting those systems. Second, they prioritize privileged GGGG issues over more burning issues suffered by bisexuals (and other queer and trans people). Third, they participate in the bisexual erasure performed by the GGGG movement for the sake of appearing "normal" to the mainstream public. Lastly, as explained in chapter 1, they reinforce the same values of normalcy, and police bi people who do not comply with the normative image. Instead of earning "rights" and aspiring for "equality," bi movements should agitate for liberation and aspire for a revolution.

DON'T ASK TO KILL,
DON'T SAY IT'S JUSTICE[43]

The repeal of the U.S. military policy of Don't Ask, Don't Tell (DADT) on September 20, 2011, was celebrated by the American GGGG movement as if another neocolonial war was just won. And in many ways, it was. As the second most important GGGG campaign in the United States, the issue of DADT has further exposed the conservative and oppressive face of this movement. While radical queer activists around the world have been fighting *against* wars, military, and white neocolonialism, privileged white GGGGs in America have been fighting for their right to *participate*.

As someone growing up and living in one of the most militarist countries in the world, I must confess that for many years I remained unsurprised about this struggle. In Israeli society, the most direct path into the heart of the Zionist mainstream is the military—and opposition to the military the most direct path out. The GGGG movement, as we've established, is a movement concerned with being accepted into oppressive structures rather than deconstructing them. As such, even in its particular, local, American context, it only made sense to me that a movement concerned with assimilation would want to "fight for (assimilation in) its country."

Though I was right (this struggle was indeed being fought, after all), I was also in many ways wrong. Not until much later did I realize that American movements considering themselves "progressive" (a patronizing term that implies linear motion along a self-defined scale of morality) have had a long history of opposing war and the military. As a result, I did not experience the heartbreak that many queer activists went through as the movement that they founded and helped build betrayed them as it changed and begun to move in the opposite direction.

For example, in her article "'Community Spirit': The New Gay Patriot and the Right to Fight in Unjust Wars," American activist and writer Mattilda Berstein Sycamore writes:

*As a 19-year-old queer activist surrounded by grieving, lone-
liness, desperation and visionary world-making in 1993, I'll
admit that I held some hope that universal healthcare might
become a central issue for queer struggle. What could have built
more beautiful and far-reaching alliances, what could have
held a greater impact not just for queers, but for everyone in
this country? My hopes for a broad struggle based on universal
needs were dashed at the March on Washington, which felt
more like a circuit party than a protest: a circuit party with a
military theme. Except that this wasn't just drug-fueled bac-
chanalia or straight-acting role play—brushing aside the ashes
of dead lovers, the gay movement battled for the right to do its
own killing.*

Though I consider myself lucky for not having to experience this,
I think this anecdote nonetheless expresses a grave understanding: that
not only did the American GGGG movement betray its queer roots of
antiwar and radical struggles, but also that it has done so in a way that
makes militarists and governments proud. Moreover, this GGGG fight
has also taught me about American militarism, and the way that it isn't
really lesser, but simply different, from the notorious Israeli militarism.

In order to understand how this works, we must first explain how the
U.S. military functions, what it does, and how intimately close it is to
the maintenance of American domination over its subjects, as well as
the world. The United States is the most predatory country in recent
history, putting any other competitors to shame with its scope, greed,
and murderousness.

[Trigger warning: general discussion of war and murderous attacks]

For example, it is a well-known fact that out of its 236 years of
existence, the United States has been at war for 215 years. In 236 years,
there have only been twenty-one aggregated calendar years in which

the United States has not waged war against anyone. The longest time
the United States has gone without doing so has been five years (1935
to 1940, otherwise known as the great depression). The United States
has also attacked a multiplicity of countries, including Korea, Vietnam,
Laos, Cambodia, Cuba, Nicaragua, Iraq, Somalia, Afghanistan, Serbia,
Pakistan, and Yemen. As a result, it has been responsible for the deaths
of dozens of millions of people all over the world. For example, while
2,977 Americans died in the 9/11 terrorist attack on the World Trade
Center in New York City, about 13,000 people died in Afghanistan, and
about 100,000 in Iraq as a result of the U.S. military response.

[End of trigger]

As opposed to popular opinion, this is not done for "freedom and
democracy" but for capitalism and financial gain. The United States has
been known to attack and then occupy countries with desired resources
such as oil, gas, metals, and other coveted merchandise. It has also been
known to set up client states and banana republics in such countries.
In fact, the very term "banana republic" is partly originated with the
American-backed coup against Guatemalan president Jacobo Árbenz
Guzmán in 1954, setting up a pro-business government that cooper-
ated with the U.S. interest in maintaining the banana trade. The United
States has given similar treatment to several other governments around
the world, including Indonesia, Iran, Egypt, Congo, Haiti, Uruguay,
Chile, Argentina, Brazil, and others. This has also caused the deaths
of hundreds of thousands of people, who died at the hands of terrorist
regimes instated by the United States.

To justify these horrors, the United States has been using the rhetoric of "freedom and democracy," claiming that rather than massacring,
colonizing, and exploiting other countries, it has actually been spreading justice and peace. For that end, and especially in recent years, the
American mainstream has been consistently portraying its target countries as symmetrically opposite to it. If the United States is the bringer
of light, justice, democracy, and freedom, then these countries are

invariably war-mongering, antidemocratic threats to world freedom and the "American way of life." This, of course, is also consistent with the type of racist and orientalist discourses discussed in the previous chapter. The United States portrays itself as the white savior of the savage "East," arriving to deliver the savages from their own backwardness using their higher and whiter morals.

Note that this is not to say that these countries are morally perfect or that they don't have their own oppressive structures. Indeed, as the United States is ridden with sexism, racism, heterosexism, and other forms of oppression, so do many other countries suffer from their own versions of these structures (according to their histories, conditions, and circumstances). But the type of discourse portraying the United States as morally superior erases the existence of oppression within it, while creating a false dichotomous vision of reality where the United States is labeled "good," and its target countries "bad." This type of discourse is not only symbolically racist, but is also materially blood-drenched. It has justified murderousness, exploitation, and other acts of horror performed by the United States in its name.

As part of its self-labeling as "good" or "progressive," the United States has also used the topic of GGGG, portraying itself as a GGGG-phobia-free haven while its target countries are portrayed as inherently GGGG-phobic. In her article "The end of DADT, State Violence and National Belonging," American writer Karma R. Chávez explains:

> Homonationalism, a term coined by [American scholar] Jasbir
> Puar, refers to the practice of including certain gay and lesbian
> subjects in order to justify nation and empire-building foreign
> policies. Usually, in the name of modernity and tolerance, the
> nation wants to protect the good citizen gay from the dangerous
> Muslim other. This can be seen when the U.S. uses the supposed
> intolerance towards gays and lesbians as one of the reasons
> to invade Muslim countries. Homonationalism has . . . been

> *adopted as state policy in Hillary Clinton's pronouncement*
> *that "gay rights are human rights," during a December 2011*
> *speech to the United Nations. . . . In putting these phenomena*
> *in conversation with the DADT repeal and the celebration*
> *surrounding it, it becomes clear that gays and lesbians have not*
> *only become active members of the state's violent arm, but they*
> *have also become a willful participant in a far-reaching logic*
> *and ideology of U.S. imperialism.*

This brings us back to the GGGG movement, as this institutional bear hug has obviously come about as a response to the courtship made by the GGGG movement toward the U.S. government. What we have here is a relationship of mutual exploitation: The U.S. government uses "the gays" in order to appear morally superior to military target countries, while the GGGGs for their part use the military as a gateway into American consensus.

However, as in the case of marriage, the support of this campaign and the celebration of this dubious "victory" means supporting one of the most oppressive systems in the world. In fighting for the repeal of DADT, the GGGG movement has chosen to side with the racism, violence, and neocolonial murderousness that is enacted by the United States and its military. It has fought—and won—the right to participate in killing and destruction, and has dared to name that "freedom." It's reinforced the American and minority-world ideology of orientalism and has justified all the horrors done under the guise of "freedom and democracy." And lest we forget, many LGBTQ people in those countries have suffered and died as a result of these wars, and the local backlash against U.S. occupation has put them in danger. The GGGG movement has helped the United States to purge itself of its many crimes, and to justify its international terrorism. But being gay doesn't make it okay, and all the pinkwashing in the world cannot erase the bloody stain that the GGGG movement now has on its hands.

Similar to the campaign for same-sex marriage, the GGGG movement has also tried to paint this issue as one of economic justice. This is because the military is often the only option for impoverished queers, queers of color, and working-class queers. But the fact that the United States keeps education, housing, jobs, and other opportunities in a constant state of neglect can lend no justification to its overbudgeting of the military. As American writer Larry Goldsmith writes in his article "Bradley Manning: Rich Man's War, Poor (Gay) Man's Fight":

> *The U.S. manages, in the midst of an international economic crisis, to spend half a billion dollars every day on the wars in Iraq, Afghanistan, and Libya, but the federal and state governments have drastically cut funding for education, and public as well as private universities have reacted to funding cuts with astronomical increases in tuition and fees. Publicly-funded financial assistance to poor students is a thing of the past—except as part of a military recruitment package.*

In fact, it is a military and state interest to keep the army as the sole gateway for people of marginalized groups. As Goldsmith puts it, "Military recruiters do not spend much time in middle-class neighborhoods. . . . In its recruitment it has always observed the time-honored and deeply discriminatory precept of 'Rich man's war, poor man's fight.'" Simply put, it's good for the army that many people literally have no other options. It increases the army's numbers and provides it with good fresh cannon fodder. By keeping it this way, the United States gets to exploit these people's labor, bodies, and lives, serving the interests of the government and the country's ruling class.

The military itself, even after the repeal of DADT, is not a safe environment for queers to say the least. For some soldiers, LGBT-phobic bullying and abuse are daily experiences. For example, a survey by the American Department of Defense, performed in 2000, found that 80 percent of service members heard derogatory LGBT-phobic remarks in the preceding year. Thirty-seven percent experienced or witnessed LGBT-phobic harassment, and 14 percent reported LGBT-phobic threats or physical violence. The risk for such occurrences is higher for women in the military, as women routinely suffer from sexual violence and harassment from other soldiers as well as their superiors. According to the U.S. Department of Defense, over 19,000 incidents of sexual assault happened in the military during 2010. It is unlikely that the repeal of DADT has caused any significant decrease in those numbers.

In addition, and in likeness to the campaign for same-sex marriage, the campaign for the repeal of DADT had diverted much-needed money, resources, and energy from other, more urgent fights. Like the campaign for same-sex marriage, it abandons anyone who cannot or will not join the militarist killing machine. Instead of fighting against poverty, capitalism, and lack of opportunities for queers of marginalized groups, the GGGG movement has preferred to align itself with the government and its oppressive regime.

Likewise, this struggle has routinely erased bisexuals, causing bi activists involved in this campaign to actively participate in their own erasure. They have also actively supported the killing and colonizing of majority-world bisexuals, presuming that having poor black and brown American bis killing brown majority-world bis can somehow be named "progress." They have in fact prioritized this right to kill beyond and above struggles for enabling life for bisexuals in their own communities and the rest of the world, ignoring the severe oppression working against bisexual people everywhere (and detailed in chapter 2).

Perhaps now that this campaign is over, the queer and bi communities can concern themselves with more urgent struggles. In particular, they should take the opportunity to begin fighting against the U.S. military and its multiple crimes, to oppose wars, killing, and the racist neocolonialism of the United States.

BACK TO BI

As we recall, the American mainstream bisexual movement in recent years has established a twofold goal: Assimilating into the GGGG movement, and becoming accepted within it. Though this pattern has slowly started changing over the last couple of years, things have largely remained the same in minority-world bisexual movements. In the next section I'll examine two recent bisexual campaigns—one from the United States and one from Canada. These two campaigns can provide examples for bi assimilationism and its twofold goal.

Before I start criticizing, however, I first need to say that over-all, the existence of these two campaigns is both positive and exciting. Despite the problems I discuss, they were both well-intended, passion-ate, and touching. Their attempts to empower bi people were both nec-essary and important. My critique of them is not meant to detract from that. In addition, by addressing these two campaigns, I do not mean to single them out or to accuse them of being the source of bi assimilation-ism. Rather, my intention is to highlight an existing trend in minority-world bi politics that these two campaigns reflect. I appreciate both the work put into them and the people behind them. That they were done at all shows that there are people who care enough about bisexuality to invest their efforts and energy into the movement, no small thing in a monosexist reality.

But in order to improve future activist work, and to prevent our-selves from repeating the same mistakes, I think it's vital that we also address what went wrong along with the positive parts. Such a perspec-tive allows us to appreciate the work done, while still drawing conclu-sions and improving for the future. This enables us to learn from past mistakes, to develop and grow as a movement.

"I AM VISIBLE"

Since the particular "tagline" goal has largely been achieved—"LGBT" being the most common acronym these days—the bisexual movement has become somewhat static. The struggle for adding "and bisexual" to "gay and lesbian" titles certainly stirred a lot of hidden biphobia to the surface in queer communities. This made the problem tangible and provided a clear target for investing bi activist energy. Ever since this struggle succeeded, the number of opportunities decreased for tangible biphobia to raise its head. Following this, and in conjunction with the presumption that biphobia only (or mainly) exists in gay and lesbian communities, bisexual activists were faced with a new problem: There was nothing left to fight.

From the turbulent 1990s, when a tangible struggle was being fought, the mainstream bi movement in North America has moved into a different phase. In the first decade of the 2000s, bi discourse lost some of its focus on named inclusion, and instead focused on invisibility and stereotypes. While both these issues were strongly present even previously, during the 2000s they started taking up more relative space. From here on, it became "known" that the greatest problem bi people faced was invisibility, and that what we needed to do about it was create more visibility for bis.

The "I am Visible" campaign was launched in November 2010 by the American *Bi Social Network* website founder and bi activist Adrienne Williams, and ran for one year. According to Williams, the goal of the campaign was to increase bisexual visibility and to draw attention to biphobia and bi erasure in LGBT as well straight communities. A press release announcing that Hollywood actor Alan Cumming had joined the campaign also states that:

> The 'I am Visible' campaign is for many [who have] been
> bullied, [accused of] not being real, or hated . . . for speaking
> on bisexual rights regarding key issues on equality—causes
> such as "Don't Ask, Don't Tell," marriage rights, bullying for
> being bisexual and all causes that our allies in all communities
> seek justice for. These in fact are the causes that bisexuals feel

strongly in representing and yet are [accused of] not being [a
part] of the cause . . .
> *The campaign is for bisexuals . . . to be allowed to speak out*
> *in national campaigns where gay and lesbians [sic] are offered*
> *. . . to attend as guest speakers . . .*

The campaign itself consisted of photos and YouTube videos. The photos feature portraits of bisexual people alongside short texts counting some of their personality traits, hobbies and professions, and finally their bisexuality. The YouTube videos (six in number) are mostly short personal stories reminiscent of the viral "It Gets Better" campaign.

This campaign was positive in that it allowed bisexuals the space to identify and talk about their experience of erasure. While bisexuals are normally silenced, it empowered them to tell their own stories and find their own voices. It encouraged them to phrase their own language, to recognize and be recognized for what they are. Its attempt to counter bisexual erasure was important, courageous, and touching. In addition, the campaign did well on the diversity aspect—especially concerning disability, which appeared in two of the six campaign videos.

But despite its good intentions and passionate organizing, this campaign was also problematic. While it enabled bi people a space to speak, listen, and be heard, it also somewhat missed its original purpose: It opened a space too wide to be used on the one hand, and too narrow to include everyone who needed it on the other.

The very outset of this campaign asumed that invisibility is the most burning issue for bi people. Given this presumption, it also assumed that the solution for this problem is straightforward visibility. By doing so, the campaign engaged with bisexuality on a superficial level. Instead, it could have asked questions such as: What does invisibility cause? What causes it? What are the material results it creates in the lives of bi people, and especially young bisexuals? Following this, it could have also asked:

Which of these results are the burning issues bi people face? How can an online campaign effectively address them?

As important as visibility is for bisexuals, invisibility alone is not their most burning problem, and visibility in and of itself is hardly the solution. For instance, one of the most severe results of bisexual erasure on the lives of bis is isolation. Isolation, in turn, might cause people to feel deeply lonely. They might feel friendless, unloved, unappreciated, and unseen. In addition with biphobic treatment within their environments or the necessity to remain closeted for personal safety, this in turn could cause depression—and as we've seen in chapter 2, depression is no stranger to many bisexuals.

A more focused campaign could have thought about this problem and addressed it in a clearer way. Instead of "I am Visible," such a campaign could use a more direct or engaging name (for example "You Are Not Alone," or indeed "It Gets Better"[44]). Its focused goal would have provided material for content, a sense of purpose for participants, and a sense of being acknowledged or understood for the audience of the campaign (while remembering that the latter two wouldn't necessarily be mutually exclusive).

This is, of course, just a random example. There are many issues that are burning, important, and ready for bisexual activist work. This example isn't here to set up a standard burning issue for all bisexual campaigns, or to insinuate that the "I am Visible" campaign is flawed because it didn't address this specific topic. This example is here to illustrate the "step beyond" missing from the campaign's visionary outset, and the resulting oversimplification of its message.

This oversimplification and lack of focused direction is also a symptom of the same problem mentioned in the beginning of this section: Since achieving its one goal of the tagline in the '90s, the mainstream bi community in the United States hasn't generally known which way to go and what to fight next. This oversimplification could also be cited as the reason why this campaign didn't reach far beyond the online American bi community. The campaign was supposed to be based on community participation—members of the community sending images, texts, and videos. But participation first requires motivation, a feeling that one is doing something valuable and important. A campaign with an unclear message and an unfocused purpose is not likely to inspire people to action.

Another problem with the campaign is its reinforcement of the twofold goal of bi assimilationism: joining the GGGG movement, and becoming accepted within it. The campaign's press release claims that same-sex marriage and the repeal of "Don't Ask, Don't Tell" are "*the* causes that bisexuals feel strongly in representing" (emphasis mine). It then continues to explain that the goal of the campaign is for bisexuals to be allowed to represent these issues together with GGGG activists.

By doing this, the campaign created a paradox of erasing bisexuality even as it attempted to address bisexual erasure. On a superficial level, the message of the campaign indeed demands recognition and visibility. But on a more basic level, it demands to participate in bisexual erasure by prioritizing GGGG issues over bisexual issues, and seeking to reinforce the oppressive structures working against bi and queer people. The wording of the message also erases the existence of bisexuals who are opposed to these ideologies by presenting these struggles as "*the*" causes that bisexuals are interested in. By doing so, it is pushing bisexuals to comply with bi assimilationist ideology and binormative behavior.

For example, in a thread on an American bi mailing list concerning the campaign's press release, I noted that I, as a bi activist, did not feel included by the wording of that sentence. I suggested that the sentence be changed instead into something less definitive. But instead of acknowledging my need to feel included by bisexual texts, the participants on the mailing list began criticizing my political stances. They continued doing so even after I clarified that I wasn't interested in debating my opinions— that it was, in fact, beside the point. From this discussion, I concluded that most participants preferred to see me change my opinions rather than

seeing the text change. This is an example of the type of binormative policing caused as a result of this bi community's assimilationist goals.

The campaign goal of being allowed to represent the GGGG movement is again a sign of assimilationism. Even given the limited scope
of the campaign, setting such a goal seems defeatist at best. Is being
allowed to represent the assimilationist and conservative campaigns of
the GGGG movement really our most urgent problem? This goal seems
to imply that what bisexuals really want is to disappear into the gay
and then straight mainstream (via gay assimilationism). The campaign's
ultimate goal, then, comes out as counterproductive: It seeks to erase bis
and bisexuality by allowing them to assimilate.

The language of the videos and images was also assimilationist in
that it emphasized normalcy and erased differences between bi people
and the heteronormative mainstream. For example, one of the images in
the campaign features a portrait of a young white man along with the
text: "I am [an] **actor**. . . . I am [an] **activist**. . . . I am a **good friend**. . . .
I am **bisexual**. . . ." and finally: "**I am visible**" (emphases in original).
This type of language insinuates to the audience of the campaign that
this person is actually just like them. This form of representation seeks
to create an assimilationist illusion that no differences exist between bi
people and everyone else. One is to conclude that since everyone now
realizes that we're all just people, we can proceed to kiss, make up, and
continue with our happy, normal existence.

But this type of attitude doesn't account for actual differences in
lifestyles, nor for power and structural oppression. American activist
and writer Amber Hollibaugh discussed the will to emphasize similarity
rather than difference in a piece called "Sexuality and the State: The
Defeat of the Briggs Initiative and Beyond." She writes:

> *A woman in the audience looked at me and said, "What you're
> saying really makes me angry because you make it sound like
> there's nothing different in homosexuality and heterosexuality*

except the sex of the person you are lovers with. I don't know a lot about it, but I suspect that's not true. I think there is something different about it." And I sat there and realized of course there's something different. She hit it right on the head. Was I going to be safe if I pretended to be just like her only married to a woman? Is that the image I wanted to present of homosexuality? So I said, "No, you really are right and have called me out correctly. I'm scared to talk about what I think is unique in a homosexual experience. I don't know how to talk about that because I don't know what you'll think. It's hard for me to explore that because it's my life and something I protect carefully because of people like Briggs and how they describe what it means to be a homosexual. I want you to understand that there are things that are common in our lives. I keep thinking if I talk about my life in ways that are common to yours, you'll see me not as an enemy. But, be that as it may, let me say I do think homosexuality is different."

It seems that the mainstream American bi movement has been suffering from the same type of fear: afraid to speak about or acknowledge differences out of fear of upsetting the mainstream and losing what little acceptance it has already gotten. While certainly understandable, such politics nonetheless prove problematic, presuming an apologetic standpoint. It assumes from the outset that we are the ones needing to fit into the mainstream comfort zone, and that we need to tone down our identities for the sake of acceptability. This is yet another form of subtle bisexual erasure: By choosing to emphasize similarity over difference, this campaign contributed to erasing the unique aspects of bisexual experience and oppression of bisexuals.

"THIS IS OUR COMMUNITY"

"This is Our Community" was a Canadian campaign launched in October 2011 by the Re:searching for LGBTQ Health group. Defined as a "Bisexual Anti-stigma Poster Campaign," the campaign was an initiative following a pilot study about bisexual health issues performed by the group. According to information from the group, this campaign was one of three responses made by them following their study, in effort to make mental health care more accessible to bi people. In addition to the campaign (and to their ongoing work on bi health-related education and networking), the group also opened a new bisexual support group, as well as a new mailing list dedicated to bisexual health. The purpose of the campaign, however, was to "address the issue of bisexual inclusion in LGBTQ communities." This was meant as an indirect way of addressing the feelings of isolation that many bi people reported within the study.

The campaign consisted of four images of different people: one white pregnant woman, representing bisexual mothers; one Eurasian man, representing bi trans people; one two-spirit woman, representing racialized people; and one black man, representing bi youth.[45] The images were overlaid with a text reading: "LG**B**TQ—This is my community," continued by a specific phrase for each person: ". . . because I'm bi even if you think I look straight" for the pregnant woman, ". . . because I'm bi and trans" for the trans man, ". . . because homophobia hurts me too" for the two-spirit woman, and ". . . because I fight for all our rights" for the young person.

The campaign's online page describes the mental health disparities suffered by bisexuals, and explains that "One possible reason for this may be experiences of stigma, prejudice and discrimination that create a hostile social environment." It describes four main forms of biphobia and monosexism that might contribute to those mental health disparities. It explains the campaign as a response meant to counter these problems and create more acceptance of bisexuals in the LGBTQ community:

> The "This is Our Community" posters address the issue of
> bisexual inclusion in LGBTQ communities and provide much
> needed positive images of bisexuals. The four posters provide

visibility to groups identified in our pilot study, and in the
literature on bisexual health, as strongly impacted by biphobia.

It goes on to describe the specific types of biphobia working against each of the groups represented.

What's positive about this campaign is that it tries (albeit in an indirect way) to address a highly important topic. Its message is focused and concrete, addressing a material issue. It also relies in part on feedback from the group's local bi community and their particular needs (via their study). It features activists from the community as well, showing this project's grassroots sensibility. Its attempt to represent diverse groups within the bi community is also commendable. Rather than lumping bisexuals in together as a single group (as is normally done), this campaign decidedly acknowledges the diversity and difference within their bi community—not only racially, but also in other ways. By providing visibility for bisexuals, the campaign also counters bisexual erasure. Its attempt to counter negative stereotypes is also positive, in that it tries to provide a positive image of bi people and promote their inclusion in the LGBTQ community.

However, this campaign, too, suffers from problems around bi assimilationism, and can serve as an example of the twofold "tagline" goal.

Before I continue, it's important to clarify that by criticizing this campaign's sensibility I am not trying to dismiss bi people's need for acceptance within their communities. This need is real, tangible, and has severe effects on the lives of many bi people, and it needs to be addressed. I do, however, question its placement as bi people's *most burning problem*—a notion which this campaign reinforces by choosing this topic over others. I also question the particular way in which this is done, and especially the presumption that in order to become accepted within LGBTQ communities, bi people need to assimilate.

The campaign seems to locate acceptance and assimilation into LGBTQ communities as a central or burning problem for bisexual people. In particular, it seems to take a detour, from bisexual mental health to something else entirely. While many participants of their pilot study did express concern about this issue, they also expressed concern regarding other issues, no less severe. That the group chose this particular topic of all possible options speaks to a possible assumption that lack of acceptance in these communities is the most central, or urgent, issue to start a campaign about (otherwise, why not take up something else?).

The way in which this is done also testifies to the campaign's bi assimilationist sensibilities. First of all, its literal use of the "tagline" trope through the acronym "LG**B**TQ" is reminiscent of Mykel Board's observation. Seemingly, the central issue here isn't *bisexuals* as a group unto themselves, but bisexuals as an *appendage* of LGBTQ communities.

The content of the campaign also suggests that bisexuality by itself cannot justify acceptance or inclusion—it needs a legitimizing agent, namely homo- or binormativity. This can be observed in such declarations as "Homophobia hurts me too," or "I fight for all our rights." First of all, these statements insinuate that biphobia and monosexism are not considered valid reasons for inclusion. Rather, they use homophobia and GGGG rights in order to show that bi people "deserve" to be included. At the same time, they also insinuate that bisexuals need to "redeem" ourselves by providing "GGGG community service," by participating in GGGG, rather than bisexual, struggles. All of the posters emphasize bisexuals' similarity to other LGBTQ communities while toning down bisexuality itself. In this way, the campaign accepts and reinforces the fact that inclusion of bisexuals is conditioned, and never granted on the premises of bisexuality itself.

These things clearly reflect the twofold goal of bi assimilationism: to become accepted within GGGG communities, and to assimilate within them. The use of the "LGBTQ" acronym, as well as the emphasis on bisexuals' *similarity* to LGBTQ communities, suggests that bi people are, or should be, indistinct from other LGBTQ people. It erases the ways in which bi people's experiences or lives might be different from those of other LGBTQ people, implying that there's actually little to no difference, and that this should be the basis on which bi people are accepted.

In addition, the visibility of this campaign is problematic in terms of racial diversity. Though three racialized people are included within, only the black man passes as racialized while the other two pass for white in the photos (apparently as an adverse effect of the bright lighting). Since the text on their images has no mention of their racialized identities, the audience of the campaign has no way of knowing that these people are not white. As a result, the black man appears to be tokenized in an otherwise all-white campaign. Here too the campaign seems to have missed its purpose.

TOWARD A BISEXUAL REVOLUTION

So what does a radical bisexual movement look like? It looks as big and expansive as one might imagine, and it can make our dreams come true. Such a movement would be devoted not only to bisexual liberation, but also to the liberation of all other groups. In fighting for its goals, it would not forget how all forms of oppression are interlinked. It would not desert other groups in its chase after the golden rainbow dream of normalcy, and it would not throw them overboard. It would not make alliances with those who would perpetuate oppression, and it would not reinforce oppression itself. It would not seek to assimilate but rather to multiply and expand.

Instead, such a movement would be critical, aware, accountable, and passionate. It would acknowledge difference and diversity within bisexual communities as well as without. It would struggle against monosexism, sexism, cissexism, heterosexism, racism, ableism, classism, and any other form of oppression both within and outside the movement. In fighting its own battles, it would tear apart power structures, including the hierarchies that bis themselves enjoy. By using the power that bisexuality has in threatening and destroying hegemony, such a movement could create a revolution indeed.

In order to do that, bisexual movements need to change. While they already have a long tradition of doing exactly this kind of work, there's still much that needs to be done. Bisexual movements need to remember their own power—not apologize for what they are or try to fit into constrictive notions of normalcy, but to stand up for their identities and the threat to normalcy that comes along with them: fighting for liberation rather than privilege, for the destruction of the system rather than a place at the table, for the revolution rather than for rights.

A radical bisexual movement would be aware of monosexism and biphobia, of their structural character and their enormous influence on everyone's lives. It would know how to identify and then dismantle them, not by reassuring society of its own docility but by wielding its power. Such a movement could empower bi people by doing grassroots work, developing a radical bisexual language, acknowledging shared experience and oppression, and directly addressing bi people's urgent needs. By providing safe spaces for bi people to learn, express themselves, and listen to others, such a movement could counter the isolation, depression, loneliness, and disempowerment that so many bis suffer. By taking the fight outside and to the streets, such a movement could also influence the lives of people on a wide scale. By organizing groups, actions, protests, and rebellion, such a movement could make the world all the more bi-fabulous.

Such a movement would embrace the inauthenticity, impurity, and hybridity that comes along with bisexuality. It would not try to present itself as pure but would rather continue to pollute and invade society and its binary categories. It would use these trespasses in order to destroy the purity and homogeneity of monosexism, as well as binary hierarchies as a whole.

A radical bi movement would also be committed to feminism and to fighting against all women's oppression. It would remember the threat that women's bisexuality poses to patriarchy, and use it to bring patriarchy to an end. It would also remember that bisexual women suffer from particular forms of misogyny. It would fight against the oppression of bi women, and all other women, while creating alliances and shared struggles between multiple groups.

The same movement would also acknowledge the way that patriarchy simultaneously privileges and hurts men. It would hold men accountable to their privilege while helping them dismantle it. Such a movement would remember that bisexuality gives men a "way out" of dominant masculinity, and would use this as an opportunity for creating subversive, antipatriarchal masculinities. Instead of competing with bi women, or trying to prove that bi men can be "real men" too, such a movement would support bi men—and all men in general—in refusing to be oppressors and participating in creating a feminist revolution.

A radical bi movement would also seek to deconstruct the binaries of gender along with those of sexuality. It would not only be an ally to the transgender movement, but also trans-positive and inclusive in and of itself. Such a community would stop using binary definitions of bisexuality and instead start taking transphobia and cissexism seriously. It would put time and effort in confronting cis bisexuals' privileges and in empowering trans and genderqueer bis. It would remember and act on the many common issues that it shares with transgender movements and join forces in fighting for gender and sexual liberation.

Such a movement would also remember the many ways in which bisexuality intersects with issues of race. It would remember not only the ways in which bisexuality resonates with racialized identities, but also the ways it has been used as a tool of racism. It would be race-aware and race-sensitive, opposing racism and white supremacy both within and outside the movement. Such a movement would deconstruct white privilege, transform the bi community into a racially inclusive space, and join in the fight for racial liberation.

This vision of a movement is not a fantasy or a dream. It's not utopian, nor is it naive. Such a movement can be real and tangible. It can be strong, loud, and powerful. What it requires is energy, work, and passion. It requires a change and new beginnings. This work will not be easy, but it will be fun. It will create a community of learning, sharing, destroying, creating, difficulty, complexity, joy, pride, friendship, accountability, solidarity, and passion. By doing this work, we can create something new, and in creating it, we can create a revolution.

Glossary

Ableism is the social system according to which everyone is, or should be, nondisabled, including social rewards for nondisabled people and punishments against disabled people.

Ashkenazis are European Jews; Jews who are descended from European or white countries.

Bi assimilationism is mainstream bi movements' attempt to assimilate into the assimilationist gay movement.

Biphobia is fear, hatred, or prejudice against bisexual people.

Cisgender is someone whose gender identity is "appropriately" aligned with the sex one was assigned at birth, i.e. men who were assigned a male sex at birth, and women who were assigned a female sex at birth.

Cissexism is the social system according to which everyone is, or should be, cisgender, including the social system of privilege for those who are cisgender, and punishment for those who are not.

Disability should not be understood as relying on physical "impairment," but rather as referring to a situation of being actively dis-abled by social standards of ability and the "failure" to achieve them.

Discourse is a term coined by French philosopher Michel Foucault. It means everything spoken, written, or otherwise communicated about a certain topic. An important derivative is **dominant discourse**, meaning a discourse created by those in power and which dominates social understandings about a given topic.

False consciousness is a term originally coined by Karl Marx. It denotes a situation in which an oppressed group identifies with the values of its oppressors.

Gay assimilationism is the gay ideology of assimilation into heteronormative society, through acceptance and mimcry of its values and standards.

The gender binary refers to the minority-world gender system, in which only two opposing and mutually exclusive genders are recognized (woman and man).

Genderqueer (or *nonbinary*) is a name for gender identities other than "woman" or "man." For example, people who identify as both man and woman, neither man nor woman, fluid, third gender, etc., might identify as genderqueer.

The GGGG movement is the Gay, Gay, Gay, and Gay movement (also known as the "LGBT" movement). This term attempts to expose the power hierarchy within LGBT movements, in which middle class white cisgender gay men are the main focus, while erasing everyone else.

Hegemony means dominance, power, and control.

Heteronormativity is a set of cultural and social norms, according to which there are only two binary sexes and genders (man and woman), and the only acceptable form of sexuality or romance is between one cisgender man and one cisgender woman. According to heteronormative standards, any lifestyle or behavior deviating from the above is abnormal and should change to fit.

Heteropatriarchy literally means "straight male rule." This term seeks to acknowledge the fact that heteronormative values are an inseparable part of patriarchy.

Heterosexism is the social system under which everyone is, or should be, heterosexual, including systematic rewards for straight people, and punishment for queers.

The heterosexual matrix is a term coined by Judith Butler. In biology, "matrix" is the material existing between cells, meaning that it is an all-present environment. This term emphasizes how heteronormativity comprises an all-present environment in minority-world cultures.

Homonationalism is a term coined by Jasbir Puar, referring to the state practice of including some gay and lesbian groups in order to justify nation- and empire-building foreign policies. It might also refer to LGBT cooperation with the practice.

Homonormativity is the acceptance of heteronormative values by gay people and movements. It guides the ideology of the GGGG movement and is often used to further marginalize marginalized LGBTQ groups.

Hypermasculinization means imposing an exaggerated masculinity on a person or a group of people.

Hypersexualization means imposing an exaggerated sexuality on a person or a group of people.

Internalized biphobia (or *internalized monosexism*) is the acceptance and internalization by bisexuals of negative stereotypes about bisexual people and bisexuality itself, and belief in the superiority of both monosexual people and monosexuality. This is often done subconsciously, meaning that most bi people are unaware of their internalized biphobia.

Intersex is a spectrum of biological sexes that don't fit medical definitions of "male" or "female."

The Kinsey scale is a seven-point scale (from 0 to 6) created by sexologist Alfred Kinsey in order to measure sexual attraction, ranging from complete heterosexual (0) to completely homosexual (6).

Kyriarchy is a term coined by Elisabeth Schüssler Fiorenza as an elaboration on the term *patriarchy*, stating a complex system of multiple and intersecting hierarchies (for example, gender, class, race, sexual identity, ability, and so on).

The male gaze is a term coined by Laura Mulvey. It describes any form of media which puts the viewers into the presumed perspective of a heterosexual cisgender man. Following this, the male gaze is also voyeuristic and objectifying towards women.

Masculinism is a social system attributing superior value and power to masculine people, masculinity, or anything perceived as having masculine traits.

Minority world is a term denoting the geographical areas and countries usually imagined as the "West" (west of what?). It corresponds with the term **majority world**, which comes to replace the use of the problematic term "third world".

Misogyny means hatred of women.

Mizrahis are Arabic Jews; Jews who are descended from Arabic or Islamic countries (for example, Iraq, Iran, Morocco, Yemen, Lebanon, and other Middle Eastern and North African countries).

Monosexism is the social system according to which everyone is, or should be, monosexual, including social rewards for monosexual people and punishments against bisexual and other nonmonosexual people.

Monosexual means someone who is attracted to people of no more than one gender.

Orientalism is a term coined by Edward Said, describing a white cultural attitude in which "the East" (and people from it) are imagined as barbaric, backward, and "exotic."

Pathologization means imposing a medical viewpoint on certain human feelings, thoughts, or behaviors (which are otherwise normal), in a way which views them as pathological.

Patriarchy literally means "male rule." It reflects a social structure in which men have both material and symbolic control in society.

Phallocentrism is a cultural and social system privileging masculinity and the phallus (the symbolic erect penis), and granting it power and value above other things.

Pinkwashing is similar in meaning to *homonationalism* and refers to the way in which states use a discourse of "LGBT rights" in order to justify militarist actions and policies.

Polyamory is a nonmonogamous practice or lifestyle, which involves being open to more than one (sexual or romantic) relationship at the same time, with the knowledge and consent of everyone involved.

Racialized means someone perceived as having a "race." This term comes to replace "people of color," which presumes whiteness as default (as white people are rarely imagined to be "of color" or to have a "race").

Rape culture means dominant cultural attitudes that promote rape and sexual violence against women.

The sex/gender assigned at birth is the sex/gender attributed to a person at the time of birth based on the appearance of their genitals.

Symbolic capital is a term coined by Pierre Bourdieu. It refers to the symbolic (intangible) resources that a certain person has, such as prestige, reputation, and acknowledgement, all of which give a person more value in the eyes of society and culture.

Transgender is anyone whose gender identity is not "appropriately" aligned with the sex one was assigned at birth. In addition to being an adjective, "transgender" can also be used as a noun in place of "transgenderism," which bears negative connotations.

Transmisogyny is hatred of trans women.

Transphobia means fear, hatred, or prejudice against transgender and genderqueer people.

Whorephobia means fear, hatred, or prejudice against sex workers.

For Further Reading

BOOKS, ZINES, AND REPORTS

Alexander, Jason, and Serena Anderlini-D'Onofrio. *Bisexuality and Queer Theory: Intersections, Connections and Challenges.* Routledge, 2011.

Alexander, Jonathan, and Karen Yescavage, eds. *Bisexuality and Transgenderism: InterSEXions of the Others.* Routledge, 2004.

Anzaldúa, Gloria. *Borderlands/La Frontera: The New Mestiza.* 3rd ed. Aunt Lute Books, 1987/2007.

Bailey, Michael J. *The Man Who Would be Queen: The Science of Gender-Bending and Transsexualism.* Joseph Henry Press, 2003.

Baumgardner, Jennifer. *Look Both Ways: Bisexual Politics.* Farrar, Straus and Giroux, 2007.

Bernstein-Sycamore, Matt, ed. *Nobody Passes: Rejecting the Rules of Gender and Conformity.* Seal Press, 2006.

Bi Academic Intervention, eds. *The Bisexual Imaginary.* Continuum, 1997.

Bornstein, Kate, *Gender Outlaw: On Men, Women and the Rest of Us.* Vintage, 1995.

Bornstein, Kate, and S. Bear Bergman, eds. *Gender Outlaws: The Next Generation.* Seal Press, 2010.

Bryant, Wayne M. *Bisexual Characters in Film: From Anais to Zee.* Routledge, 1997.

Burleson, William E. *Bi America: Myths, Truths, and Struggles of an Invisible Community.* Routledge, 2005.

Butler, Judith. *Gender Trouble: Feminism and the Subversion of Identity.* Routledge, 1990/2006.

Chamberlain, Brent. *Bisexual People in the Workplace: Practical advice for employers.* Stonewall Workplace Guides.

Chomsky, Noam. *Failed States: The Abuse of Power and the Assault on Democracy.* Holt Paperbacks, 2007.

Chomsky, Noam, and David Barsamian. *Imperial Ambitions: Conversations on the Post-9/11 World.* Metropolitan Books, 2005.

Davis, Madeline, and Elizabeth Kennedy. *Boots of Leather, Slippers of Gold: The History of a Lesbian Community.* Penguin (Non-Classics), 1994.

Douglas, Mary. *Purity and Danger: An Analysis of Concepts of Pollution and Taboo.* Taylor & Francis, 1966/2002.

Foucault, Michele. *The History of Sexuality, Vol. 1: An Introduction.* Trans. Robert Hurley. Vintage, 1976/1990.

Forging a Bi-Trans Alliance. Spec. issue of *Anything That Moves* 17 (1998). Retrieved Tue 9 Oct 2012. http://web.archive.org/web/20021020035411/ anythingthatmoves.com/ish17/index17.html.

Friedan, Betty. *The Feminine Mystique.* W. W. Norton & Company, 1963/2001.

Garber, Marjorie. *Vice Versa: Bisexuality and the Eroticism of Everyday Life.* Simon & Schuster, 1995.

Hemmings, Clare. *Bisexual Spaces*. Routledge, 2002.

hooks, bell. *Feminism Is for Everybody: Passionate Politics*. South End Press, 2000.

Hutchins, Loraine, and Lani Ka'ahumanu, eds. *Bi Any Other Name: Bisexual People Speak Out*. Alyson Books, 1991.

Kinsey, et al. *Sexual Behavior in the Human Male*. Indiana University Press, 1948/1998.

Klein, Naomi. *The Shock Doctrine: The Rise of Disaster Capitalism*. Picador, 2008.

Lee, Reba. *I Passed for White*. P. Davies, 1956.

MacKinnon, Catharine. *Toward a Feminist Theory of the State*. Harvard University Press, 1989/1991.

National Center for Injury Prevention and Control Division of Violence Prevention. (2013). *The National Intimate Partner and Sexual Violence Survey (NISVS): 2010 Findings on Victimization by Sexual Orientation*. Atlanta, Georgia.

Nestle, Joan, Clare Howell, and Riki Wilchins, eds. *GenderQueer: Voices From Beyond the Sexual Binary*. Alyson Books, 2002.

Ochs, Robyn, and Sarah Rowley, eds. *Getting Bi: Voices of Bisexuals Around the World*. 1st ed. Boston: Bisexual Resource Center, 2005.

Ochs, Robyn, and Sarah Rowley, eds. *Getting Bi: Voices of Bisexuals Around the World*. 2nd ed. Boston: Bisexual Resource Center, 2009.

The Open University Centre for Citizenship, Identities and Governance and Faculty of Health and Social Care. (2012). *The Bisexuality Report: Bisexual inclusion in LGBT equality and diversity*. London, U.K.: Meg Barker, Christina Richards, Rebecca Jones, Helen Bowes-Catton & Tracey Plowman with Jen Yockney and Marcus Morgan.

Puar, Jasbir. *Terrorist Assemblages: Homonationalism in Queer Times*. Duke University Press, 2007.

Reba-Weise, Elizabeth, ed. *Closer to Home: Women and Bisexuality*. Seal Press: 1992.

Roper, Moses. *Narrative of the Adventures and Escape of Moses Roper from American Slavery (1846)*. Kessinger Publishing, LLC., 2007.

San Francisco Human Rights Commission LGBT Advisory Committee. (2011). *Bisexual Invisibility: Impacts and Recommendations*. San Francisco, California.

Serano, Julia. *Whipping Girl: A Transsexual Woman on Sexism and the Scapegoating of Femininity*. Seal Press, 2007.

Servicemembers Legal Defense Network. (2001). *Conduct Unbecoming: The Seventh Annual Report On "Don't Aask Don't Tell, Don't Pursue, Don't Harass."* Washington D.C., United States: Stacey L. Sobel, Jeffery M. Cleghorn, and C. Dixon Osburn.

Suresha, Ron Jackson, and Pete Chvany. *Bi Men: Coming Out Every Which Way*. Routledge, 2005.

Stoltenberg, John. *Refusing to Be a Man: Essays on Sex and Justice*. Routledge, 1989/2000.

Stonewall. *Unseen on screen; Gay people on youth TV*. 2010.

Stryker, Susan. *Transgender History*. Seal press, 2008.

Tucker, Naomi, ed. *Bisexual Politics: Theories, Queries and Visions*. Routledge, 1995.

Wilchins, Riki Anne. *Queer Theory, Gender Theory: An Instant Primer*. Alyson Books, 2004.

Wilchins, Riki Anne. *Read My Lips: Sexual Subversion and the End of Gender*. Firebrand Books, 1997.

ARTICLES AND BOOK CHAPTERS

Allison, Dorothy. Introduction. *My Dangerous Desires: A Queer Girl Dreaming Her Way Home.* Amber L. Hollibaugh. Duke University Press, 2002. xi-xix.

Anzaldúa, Gloria. "La Prieta." *The Gloria Anzaldúa Reader.* AnaLouise Keating, ed. Duke University Press, 2009.

Armstrong, Elizabeth. "Traitors to the Cause? Understanding the Lesbian/Gay 'Bisexuality Debates.'" *Bisexual Politics: Theories, Queries and Visions.* Ed. Naomi Tucker. Routledge, 1995. 199-218.

Ault, Amber. "Ambiguous Identity in an Unambiguous Sex/Gender Structure: The Case of Bisexual Women." *The Sociological Quarterly* 37:3 (1996): 449-463.

Ault, Amber. "Hegemonic Discourse in an Oppositional Community: Lesbian Feminists and Bisexuality." *Critical Sociology* 20 (1994): 107-122.

Blaisingame, Brenda. "Power and Privilege Beyond the Invisible Fence." *Bisexual Politics: Theories, Queries and Visions.* Naomi Tucker, ed. Routledge, 1995. 229-233.

Board, Mykel. "Pimple No More." *Bisexual Politics: Theories, Queries and Visions.* Naomi Tucker, ed. Routledge, 1995. 281-288.

Callis, April S. "Playing with Butler and Foucault: Bisexuality and Queer Theory." *Journal of Bisexuality* 9:3-4 (2009): 213-233.

Carroll, Traci. "African American Bisexual Narrative." *RePresenting Bisexualities: Subjects and Cultures of Fluid Desire.* Maria Pramaggiore and Donald E. Hall, eds. NYU Press, 1996. 180-206.

Chedgzoy, Kate. "'Two loves I have': Shakespeare and bisexuality." *The Bisexual Imaginary.* Bi Academic Intervention, ed. Continuum, 1997. 106-119.

Cixous, Hélène. "The Laugh of the Medusa." Trans. Keith Cohen and Paula Cohen. *Signs* 1:4 (1976): 875-893.

Conrad, Peter. "The Discovery of Hyperkinesis: Notes on the Medicalization of Deviant Behavior." *Social Problems* 23:1 (1975): 12-21.

Conrad, Peter. "Medicalization and Social Control." *Annual Review of Sociology* 18 (1992): 209-232.

Diamond, Lisa. "Female Bisexuality From Adolescence to Adulthood: Results From a 10-Year Longitudinal Study." *Developmental Psychology* 44.1 (2008): 5-14.

Donaldson, Stephen. "The Bisexual Movement's Beginnings in the 70's: A Personal Perspective." *Bisexual Politics: Theories, Queries and Visions.* Naomi Tucker, ed. Routledge, 1995. 31-45.

du Plessis, Michael. "Blatantly Bisexual; or, Unthinking Queer Theory." *RePresenting Bisexualities: Subjects and Cultures of Fluid Desire.* Maria Pramaggiore and Donald E. Hall, eds. NYU Press, 1996. 19-54.

Eadie, Joe. "Activating Bisexuality: Towards a Bi/Sexual Politics." *Activating Theory: Lesbian, Gay, Bisexual Politics.* Joseph Bristow and Anglia R. Wilson, eds. Lawrence & Wishart Ltd., 1994. 139-165.

Eisner, Shiri. "Love, Rage and the Occupation: Bisexual Politics in Israel/Palestine." *Journal of Bisexuality* 12:1 (2012): 80-137.

Ellis, Henry Havelock. "Extracts from *Studies in the Psychology of Sex, Volume I: Sexual Inversion* (1879) and from *Studies in the Psychology of Sex, Volume II: Sexual Inversion* (1915)." *Bisexuality: A Critical Reader.* Merl Storr, ed. Routledge, 1999. 15-19.

Fahs, Breanne. "Compulsory Bisexuality?: The Challenges of Modern Sexual Fluidity." *Journal of Bisexuality* 9:3-4 (2009): 431-449.

Farrimond, Katherine. "'Stay Still So We Can See Who You Are': Anxiety and Bisexual Activity in the Contemporary Femme Fatale Film." *Journal of Bisexuality* 12:1 (2012): 138-154.

Fox, Ron C. "Bisexual Identities." *Psychological Perspectives on Lesbian, Gay, and Bisexual Experiences*. 2nd ed. Garnets, Linda, and Douglas Kimmel, eds. Columbia University Press, 2002.

Fraser, Mariam. "Lose Your Face." *The Bisexual Imaginary*. Bi Academic Intervention, ed. Continuum, 1997. 38-57.

Ginsberg, Elaine K. Introduction: The Politics of Passing. *Passing and the Fictions of Identity*. Elaine K. Ginsber, ed. Duke University Press, 1996.

Goldman, Emma. "Marriage and Love." *Anarchism and Other Essays*. Dover Publications, 1969. 133-140.

Halperin, David. "Thirteen Ways of Looking at a Bisexual." *Bisexuality and Queer Theory: Intersections, Connections and Challenges*. Alexander, Jason and Serena Anderlini-D'Onofrio, eds. Routledge, 2011.

Haraway, Donna. "A Manifesto For Cyborgs: Science, Technology & Socialist Feminism in the 1980s." *Feminism/Postmodernism*. Linda J. Nicholson, ed. Routledge, 1990.

Hemmings, Clare. "A Feminist Methodology of the Personal: Bisexual Experience and Feminist Post-Structuralist Epistemology." *Feminist Methodology: Gender Theory, Feminist Epistemology, Sex and Gender, Cross-Cultural Feminist Ethics, Politics of Gender, Ethnography of Gender*. Channa Subhadra, ed. Cosmo, 2006.

Hemmings, Clare. "Resituating the Bisexual Body: From Identity to Difference." *Activating Theory: Lesbian, Gay, Bisexual Politics*. Joseph Bristow and Anglia R. Wilson, eds. Lawrence & Wishart Ltd., 1994. 118-138.

Hemmings, Clare. "What's in a Name? Bisexuality, Transnational Sexuality Studies and Western Colonial Legacies." *The International Journal of Human Rights* 11:1-2 (2007): 13-32.

Herek, Gregory M. "Heterosexuals' Attitudes toward Bisexual Men and Women in the United States." *The Journal of Sex Research* 39:4 (2002), 264-274.

Highleyman, Liz A. "Identity and Ideas: Strategies for Bisexuals." *Bisexual Politics: Theories, Queries and Visions*. Naomi Tucker, ed. Routledge, 1995. 73-92.

Hollibaugh, Amber. "Sexuality and the State: The Defeat of the Briggs Initiative and Beyond." *My Dangerous Desires: A Queer Girl Dreaming Her Way Home*. Duke University Press, 2000. 42-61.

Irigaray, Luce. "This Sex Which Is Not One." *This Sex Which Is Not One*. Trans. Catherine Porter and Carolyn Burke. Cornell University Press. 1985.

Izakson, Orna. "If Half of You Dodges a Bullet, All of You Ends up Dead." *Bisexual Politics: Theories, Queries and Visions*. Naomi Tucker, ed. Routledge, 1995. 251-256.

Jeffreys, Shiela. "Bisexual politics: A superior form of feminism?" *Women's Studies International Forum* 22:3 (1999): 273–285.

Jeffreys, Sheila. "Transgender Activism: A Lesbian Feminist Perspective." *Journal of Lesbian Studies* 1:3-4 (1997): 55-74.

Kaufman, Michael. "Men, Feminism, and Men's Contradictory Experiences of Power." *Men and Power*. Joseph A. Kuypers, ed. Fernwood Books, 1999. 59-83.

Kessler, Suzanne J. "The Medical Construction of Gender: Case Management of Intersexed Infants." *Signs* 16.1 (1990): 3-26.

Ku, Chung-Hao. "The Kid Is All the Rage: (Bi) Sexuality, Temporality and Triangular Desire in Leslie Marmon Silko's Almanac of the Dead." *Journal of Bisexuality* 10:3 (2010): 309-349.

Lingel, Jessa. "Adjusting the Borders: Bisexual Passing and Queer Theory." *Journal of Bisexuality*, 9:3-4 (2009): 381-405.

Llyod, Genevieve. "The Man of Reason." *Metaphilosophy* 10:1 (1979): 18-37.

MacDowall, Lachlan. "Historicising Contemporary Bisexuality." *Journal of Bisexuality* 9:1 (2009): 3-15.

MacKinnon, Cathatine A. "Sexuality, Pornography, and Method: 'Pleasure under Patriarchy.'" *Ethics* 99:2 (1989): 314-346.

Matteson, Dave. "Bisexual feminist man." *Bi Any Other Name: Bisexual People Speak Out*. Hutchins, Loraine and Lani Ka'ahumanu, eds. Alyson Books, 1991. 43-50.

McIntosh, Peggy. "White privilege: Unpacking the invisible knapsack." *Peace and Freedom* (July/August 1989): 10-12.

Mulvey, Laura. "Visual Pleasure and Narrative Cinema." *Screen* 16:3 (1975).

Obradors-Campos, Miguel. "Deconstructing Biphobia." *Journal of Bisexuality* 11:2-3 (2010): 207-226.

Ochs, Robyn. "Biphobia: It Goes More Than Two Ways." *Bisexuality: The Psychology and Politics of an Invisible Minority*. Beth A. Firestein, ed. Sage, 1996. 217-239.

Ochs, Robyn. "What's in a Name? Why Women Embrace or Resist Bisexual Identity." *Becoming Visible: Counseling Bisexuals Across the Lifespan*. Beth A. Firestein, ed. Columbia University Press, 2007.

Piper, Adrian. "Passing for White, Passing for Black." *Out of Order, Out of Sight, Volume I: Selected Essays in Meta-Art 1968-1992*. MIT Press, 1996. 275-308.

Pritchard, Mark. "Liberating Pornography." *Bisexual Politics: Theories, Queries and Visions*. Naomi Tucker, ed. Routledge, 1995. 171-178.

Prosser, Jay, and Merl Storr. "Transsexuality and Bisexuality." *Sexology Uncensored: The Documents of Sexual Science*. Lucy Bland and Laura Doan, eds. University of Chicago Press, 1999. 75-77.

Queen, Carol. "Sexual Diversity and the Bisexual Community." *Bisexual Politics: Theories, Queries and Visions*. Naomi Tucker, ed. Routledge, 1995. 151-160.

Rapoport, Esther. "Bisexuality in Psychoanalytic Theory: Interpreting the Resistance." *Journal of Bisexuality* 9:3-4 (2009): 279-295.

Raymond, Katherine. "Confessions of a Second Generation . . . Dyke?" *PoMoSexuals: Challenging Assumptions About Gender and Sexuality*. Carol Queen and Lawrence Schimel, eds. Cleis Press, 1997.

Rich, Adrienne. "Compulsory Heterosexuality and Lesbian Existence." *Signs* 5:4 (1980): 631-660.

Rieger, Gerulf, Meredith L. Chivers, and J. Michael Bailey. "Sexual Arousal Patterns of Bisexual Men." *Psychological Science* 16:8 (2005): 579-584.

Robinson, Amy. "It Takes One to Know One: Passing and Communities of Common Interest." *Critical Inquiry* 20:4 (1994): 715-736.

Rosenthal, A.M., D. Sylva, A. Safron, and J.M. Bailey. "Sexual arousal patterns of bisexual men revisited." *Biological Psychology* 88 (2011): 112-115.

Rubin, Gayle. "Thinking Sex: Notes for a Radical Theory of the Politics of Sexuality." *Pleasure and Danger: Exploring Female Sexuality*. Carole S. Vance, ed. London: Pandora. 1992. 267-293.

Rust, Paula C. "Two Many and Not Enough." *Journal of Bisexuality* 1:1 (2000): 31-68.

Samuels, Ellen. "My Body, My Closet: Invisible Disability and the Limits of Coming-Out Discourse." *GLQ* 9:1-2 (2003): 233-255.

Sollors, Werner. Chapter Nine: Passing; or, Sacrificing a Parvenu. *Neither Black Nor White Yet Both: Thematic Explorations of Interracial Literature.* Oxford University Press, 1997.

Spade, Dean. "Fighting to Win." *That's Revolting!: Queer Strategies for Resisting Assimilation.* Mattilda Bernstein Sycamore, ed. Soft Skull Press, 2008. 47-53.

Steinman, Erich. "Interpreting the Invisibility of Male Bisexuality." *Journal of Bisexuality* 1:2-3 (2000): 15-45.

Storr, Merl. "The Sexual Reproduction of Race: Sexuality, History and Racialization." *The Bisexual Imaginary.* Bi Academic Intervention, ed. Continuum, 1997. 73-88.

Sunfrog. "Pansies Against Patriarchy: Gender Blur, Bisexual Men and Queer Liberation." *Bisexual Politics: Theories, Queries and Visions.* Naomi Tucker, ed. Routledge, 1995. 319-324.

Sweeney, Syreeta J. *Normative Monosexism, Biphobia, and the Experience of Bisexual Women: A Content Analysis of an Online Community.* MA thesis. University of Texas, 2011. ProQuest Dissertations and Theses. Web. 15 Oct 2012.

Tucker, Naomi. "Bay Area Bisexual History: an Interview with David Lourea." *Bisexual Politics: Theories, Queries and Visions.* Naomi Tucker, ed. Routledge, 1995. 281-288.

Wald, Gayle. Introduction: Race, Passing and Cultural Representation. *Crossing the Line: Racial Passing in Twentieth-Century U.S. Literature and Culture.* Duke University Press, 2000.

Walker, Lisa. "How to Recognize a Lesbian: The Cultural Politics of Looking Like What You Are." *Signs* 18:4 (1993): 866-890.

Weiss, Jillian Todd. "GL vs. BT: The Archaeology of Biphobia and Transphobia in the U.S. Lesbian and Gay Community." *Journal of Bisexuality* 3 (2004): 25-55.

Wittig, Monique. "One Is Not Born a Woman." *The Lesbian and Gay Studies Reader.* Henry Abelove, ed. Routledge, 1981/1993. 103-109.

Yoshino, Kenji. "The Epistemic Contract of Bisexual Erasure." *Standford Law Review* 52.2 (2000): 353-461.

WEB/ONLINE

1748. "Passing and Privilege." *Bi Furious!* 7 Aug 2008. Retrieved 10 Oct 2012. http://bifurious.wordpress.com/2008/08/07/passing-and-privilege.

Anderson-Minshall, Diane. "Ending Bi Erasure—on TV and in Our LGBT Worlds." *Advocate.com.* 23 Sept 2011. Retrieved 12 Nov 2012. www.advocate.com/news/daily-news/2011/09/23/ending-bi-erasure-tv-and-our-lgbt-worlds.

Andre, Amy. "Adrienne Williams, Bi Social Network Founder, Talks 'I Am Visible' Campaign and Snagging Alan Cumming." *Huffpost: Gay Voices.* 24 Jan 2012. Retrieved 12 Nov 2012. www.huffingtonpost.com/amy-andre/alan-cumming-i-am-visible-campaign_b_1220156.html.

Andre, Amy. "What Does a Bisexual Look Like?" *The Bilerico Project.* 27 Sept 2011. Retrieved 10 Oct 2012. www.bilerico.com/2011/09/what_does_a_bisexual_look_like.php.

Barker, Meg. "What's wrong with heteronormativity?" *Meg Barker's Blog.* 17 Aug 2011. Retrieved 10 Oct 2012. http://learn.open.ac.uk/mod/oublog/viewpost.php?post=78518.

Bauer, Asher. "Not Your Mom's Trans 101." *Tranarchism.* 26 Nov 2010. Retrieved 30 Oct 2012. http://tranarchism.com/2010/11/26/not-your-moms-trans-101.

Bauer, Asher. "The Trans Power Manifesto." *Tranarchism*. 13 Nov 2010. Retrieved 19 Nov 2011. http://tranarchism.com/2010/11/13/thetranspowermanifesto.

Bernstein Sycamore, Mattilda. "'Community Spirit': The New Gay Patriot and the Right to Fight in Unjust Wars." *We Who Feel Differently*. Spring 2012. Retrieved 12 Nov 2012. www.wewhofeeldifferently.info/journal.php.

BiBrain.org. American Institute of Bisexuality, 2011-2012. Retrieved 30 Oct 2012.

Bigotry is Not A Mental Illness. Web log. Retrieved 9 Oct 2012. http://bigotryis notamentalillness.tumblr.com.

"Bi Men: A bi-alogue." *ron j. suresha*. 2005. Retrieved 30 Oct 2012. http://ronsuresha.com/?page_id=2351.

bisexual_community@yahoo.com. "Alan Cumming joins 'I am Visible' Campaign to combat biphobia." *BiNet USA* 22 Oct 2011. E-mail.

"Bisexuality: Myths and Realities." *Cleveland State University*. N.d. Web. Retrieved 19 Nov 2011. www.csuohio.edu/offices/odama/glbt/bisexuality.pdf.

Bi's Of Color. Web log. Retrieved 30 Oct 2012. http://bisofcolour.tumblr.com.

Blum, William. "United States bombings of other countries." *Killinghope.com*. N.d. Retrieved 12 Nov 2012. http://killinghope.org/superogue/bomb.htm.

Broadbent, Lucy. "Rape in the US military: America's dirty little secret." *The Guardian*. 9 Dec 2011. Retrieved 12 Nov 2012. www.guardian.co.uk/society/2011/dec/09/rape-us-military.

"Casualties of the Iraq War." *Wikipedia, The Free Encyclopedia*. Wikimedia Foundation, Inc. N.d. Web. Retrieved 12 Nov 2012. http://en.wikipedia.org/wiki/Casualties_of_the_Iraq_War.

"Casualties of the September 11 attacks." *Wikipedia, The Free Encyclopedia*. Wikimedia Foundation, Inc. N.d. Web. Retrieved 12 Nov 2012. http://en.wikipedia.org/wiki/Casualties_of_the_September_11_attacks.

Cedar. "Cis Privilege Checklist: The Cisgender/Cissexual Privilege Checklist." *Taking Up Too Much Space*. 10 Jul 2008. Retrieved 10 Oct 2012. http://takesupspace.wordpress.com/cis-privilege-checklist.

Chávez, Karma R. "The end of DADT, State Violence and National Belonging." *We Who Feel Differently*. Spring 2012. Retrieved 12 Nov 2012. www.wewho feeldifferently.info/journal.php.

Christina, Greta. "Five Stupid, Unfair and Sexist Things Expected of Men." *Greta Christina's Blog*. 24 Aug 2010. Retrieved 30 Oct 2012. http://greta christina.typepad.com/greta_christinas_weblog/2010/08/five-stupid-unfair-and-sexist-things-expected-of-men.html.

"Civilian casualties in the War in Afghanistan (2001–present)." *Wikipedia, The Free Encyclopedia*. Wikimedia Foundation, Inc. N.d. Web. Retrieved 12 Nov 2012. http://en.wikipedia.org/wiki/Civilian_casualties_in_the_War_in_Afghanistan_%282001%E2%80%93present%29.

Clark-Flory, Tracy. "The invisible bisexual man." *Salon*. 28 Aug 2011. Retrieved 30 Oct 2012. www.salon.com/2011/08/28/bisexuality_2.

Danios. "'We're at War!'—And We Have Been Since 1776: 214 Years of American War-Making." *Loonwatch.com*. 20 Dec 2011. Retrieved 12 Nov 2012. www.loonwatch.com/2011/12/we-re-at-war-and-we-have-been-since-1776.

David, Cory. "Monogamous Privilege Checklist." *East Portland Blog*. 15 Apr 2011. Retrieved 10 Oct 2012. www.eastportlandblog.com/2011/04/05/monogamous-privilege-checklist-by-cory-davis.

Deutsch, Barry. "The Male Privilege Checklist." *Alas! A Blog*. N.d. Retrieved 9 Oct 2012. www.amptoons.com/blog/the-male-privilege-checklist.

Feminist Epistemology. 9 Aug, 2000. In *Stanford Encyclopedia of Philosophy*. Retrieved from http://plato.stanford.edu/entries/feminism-epistemology.

Feminist Philosophy of Language. 3 Sep, 2004. In *Stanford Encyclopedia of Philosophy*. Retrieved from http://plato.stanford.edu/entries/feminism-language.

Goldsmith, Larry. "Bradley Manning: Rich Man's War, Poor (Gay) Man's Fight." *Common Dreams*. 7 Jun 2011. Retrieved 12 Nov 2012. www.common dreams.org/view/2011/06/07-6.

Hurt, Byron. "Why I Am a Black Male Feminist." *The Root*. 16 March 2011. Retrieved 30 Oct 2012. www.theroot.com/views/why-i-am-male-feminist.

"I am Visible." *Facebook*. N.d. Retrieved 12 Nov 2012. www.facebook.com/iamvisible.

Jessica. "Julia Serano – Cocky." *YouTube*. 7 Jan 2007. Retrieved 30 Oct 2012. www.youtube.com/watch?v=a95JP8i8GuE.

Medicalization. *Wikipedia, The Free Encyclopedia*. Wikimedia Foundation, Inc. N.d. Web. Retrieved 30 Oct 2012. http://en.wikipedia.org/wiki/Medicalization.

Montgomery, Cal. "A Hard Look at Invisible Disability." *Ragged Edge Online*. N.d. Retrieved 10 Oct 2012. www.ragged-edge-mag.com/0301/0301ft1.htm.

Ochs, Robyn. "Selected Quotes by Robyn Ochs: Definition of Bisexuality." Robyn Ochs. N.d. 17 Nov 2011. www.robynochs.com/writing/quotes.html.

"ORB survey of Iraq War casualties." *Wikipedia, The Free Encyclopedia*. Wikimedia Foundation, Inc. N.d. Web. Retrieved 12 Nov 2012. http://en .wikipedia.org/wiki/ORB_survey_of_Iraq_War_casualties.

O'Riordan, Aoife. "In Defense of Barsexuals and Faux-Mos." *Consider the Tea Cosy*. 23 Nov 2011. Retrieved 15 Oct 2012. http://considertheteacosy.word press.com/2011/11/23/in-defense-of-barsexuals-and-faux-mos.

Pepper Mint. "Bisexuals and straight privilege." *freaksexual*. 11 May 2007. Retrieved 10 Oct 2012. http://freaksexual.wordpress.com/2007/05/11/bisexu als-and-straight-privilege.

Perceful, Kaley. "In Defense of 'Party Bisexuals.'" *Delusions of Grandeur*. 3 Oct 2011. Retrieved 15 Oct 2012. http://s1utever.tumblr.com/post/10999636110/in-de fense-of-party-bisexuals.

Pulcifer, Ash. "America Has Always Been At War." *Rense.com*. 3 Mar 2012. Retrieved 12 Nov 2012. http://rense.com/general46/atwar.htm.

Pully, Anna. "9 Stupid Myths About Bisexuals That Will Make You Laugh." *AlterNet*. 27 Jan 2011. Web. Retrieved 19 Nov 2011. www.alternet.org/sex/149710/9_stu pid_myths_about_bisexuals_that_will_make_you_laugh.

Queers United. "The Cisgender Privilege Checklist." *Queers United*. 15 Aug 2008. Retrieved 10 Oct 2012. http://queersunited.blogspot.co.il/2008/08/cisgender-priv ilege-checklist.html.

Queers United. "The Heterosexual Privilege Checklist." *Queers United*. 12 Oct 2008. Retrieved 10 Oct 2012. http://queersunited.blogspot.co.il/2008/10/heterosexu al-privilege-checklist.html.

Rogers, Simon, and Amy Sedghi. "Afghanistan civilian casualties: year by year, month by month." *The Guardian*. 12 Mar 2012. Retrieved 12 Nov 2012. www.guardian. co.uk/news/datablog/2010/aug/10/afghanistan-civilian-casualties-statistics.

Rosario, Michael. "Phallocentrism and bisexual invisibility." *The Dissident View*. 6 Jul 2012. Retrieved 30 Oct 2012. http://sapphiretrance.wordpress .com/2012/07/06/phallocentrism-and-bisexual-invisibility.

Rubenstein, Andrea. "FAQ: What is 'slut-shaming'?" *Finally, A Feminism 101 Blog*. 4 April 2010. Web log. Retrieved 15 Oct 2012. http://finallyfeminism101 .wordpress.com/2010/04/04/what-is-slut-shaming.

Scalzi, John. "Straight White Male: The Lowest Difficulty Setting There Is." *Whatever*. 15 May 2012. Retrieved 30 Oct 2012. http://whatever.scalzi .com/2012/05/15/straight-white-male-the-lowest-difficulty-setting-there-is.

Serano, Julia. "Bisexuality and Binaries Revisited." *Whipping Girl*. 19 Nov 2012. Retrieved 16 Feb 2013. http://juliaserano.blogspot.co.il/2012/11/ bisexuality-and-binaries-revisited.html

Serano, Julia. "Bisexuality does not reinforce the gender binary." *The Scavenger*. 10 Oct 2010. Retrieved 19 Nov 2011. http://masculineheart.blogspot .com/2011/01/julia-serano-bisexuality-does-not.html.

Serano, Julia. "Rethinking Sexism: How Trans Women Challenge Feminism". *AlterNet*. 5 Aug 2008. Retrieved 19 Nov 2011. www.alternet.org/reproductivejustice/93826/ rethinking_sexism:_how_trans_women_challenge_feminism.

Simpson, Mark. "Bisexual Men Exist! But Does Scientific Sex Research?" *Marksimpson. com*. 23 Aug 2011. Retrieved 30 Oct 2012. www.marksimpson .com/blog/2011/08/23/bisexual-men-exist-but-does-scientific-sex-research.

Simpson, Mark. "Curiouser and Curiouser: the Strange 'Disappearance' of Male Bisexuality." *Marksimpson.com*. 26 Apr 2006. Retrieved 30 Oct 2012. www .marksimpson.com/blog/2006/04/26/curiouser-and-curiouser-the-strange-disappearance-of-male-bisexuality.

STFU Biphobia. Web log. Retrieved 9 Oct 2012. http://stfubiphobia.tumblr.com

Strauss, Vinny. "5 things I hate about being a bi guy." *YouTube*. 10 May 2011. Retrieved 30 Oct 2012. www.youtube.com/watch?v=-XT-UAxXSl8.

"Things bisexuals aren't." *Pink Panthers* N.d. Web log entry. Retrieved 19 Nov 2011. http://pinkpanthers.tumblr.com/post/7961671976/things-bisexuals-arent.

"This is Our Community: Bisexual Anti-stigma Poster Campaign." *Re:searching for LGBTQ Health*. N.d. Retrieved 12 Nov 2012. http://lgbtqhealth.ca/community/ bisexualantistigmacampaign.php.

"Trigger warning." *Geek Feminism Wiki*. N.d. Retrieved 15 Oct 2012. http://geekfemi-nism.wikia.com/wiki/Trigger_warning.

TSB. "Mad, Bad & Dangerous to Know, or: 'how I came to stop worrying and like the word bisexual,' Part 2". *The Only Bi in The Village* 30 Nov 2010. Web log entry. Retrieved 19 Nov 2011. http://suburbanbi.blogspot.com/2010/11/mad-bad-danger-ous-to-know-or-i-came-to.html.

V. "But you'll leave me for men! (Or: Don't make your penis envy my problem)." *Bi Furious!* 22 Aug 2008. Web log entry. Retrieved 19 Nov 2011. http:// bifurious.wordpress.com/2008/08/22/but-youll-leave-me-for-men-or-dont-make-your-penis-envy-my-problem.

V. "The 'two' in 'bisexual.'" *Bi Furious!* 7 May 2009. Web log entry. Retrieved 17 Nov 2011. http://bifurious.wordpress.com/2009/05/07/the-two-in-bisexual.

"WHAT DOES BIPHOBIA LOOK LIKE?" *Lani Ka'ahumanu*. Retrieved 9 Oct 2012. http://lanikaahumanu.com/looklike.shtml

Footnotes

1. "Primitive" is a word used in psychoanalysis to describe early developmental stages, though it also certainly draws its sources from colonialist discourses.
2. For (unchecked) descriptions of biphobia in pre-Stonewall lesbian communities, see: Davis, Madeline and Elizabeth Kennedy. *Boots of Leather, Slippers of Gold: The History of a Lesbian Community*. Penguin (Non-Classics), 1994.
3. In the 1980s the bisexual community, along with all the other LGBT communities, was mainly busy dealing with AIDS.
4. For more about the idea of bisexual temporality, see: Ku, Chung-Hao. (See Further Reading List)
5. As opposed to asexual.
6. Note that Queen was writing in the '90s, when language describing transgender identities was even more tricky than it is today, with no standardized forms at the time.
7. In doing so, I am in many ways following in the footsteps of Kenji Yoshino's article "The Epistemic Contract of Bisexual Erasure" as well as some of the critical ideas put forth by the Bi Academic Intervention group.
8. For an idea of "appropriate" sex, see: Rubin, Gayle. (see Further Reading List)
9. Note that not all bodies with penises are male, and that not all male people have penises.
10. For the sake of fairness, I will mention that I too once subscribed to this approach.
11. This interest, of course, has to do with the other reasons for bisexual erasure. Specifically, Clare Hemmings theorizes that much of queer theory's presumptions about sexuality and its workings rely on the repression of bisexuality.
12. I realize that for some communities, this may not be true. However, this has been my experience with communities I've been involved with or exposed to.
13. The rest were uncategorizable or repeated links.
14. Other criticisms of the term point out that equating prejudice with a mental illness constitutes ableist language.
15. Note that Friedan's main effect was limited to white middle-class heterosexual cis women.
16. Yoshino here seems to ignore the gap between the treatment of heterosexuality as "not explicitly sexual" and that of of queer sexualities as "always explicitly sexual" (including when they are not necessarily so).
17. No one is ever really out. Society builds closets all around us.
18. Yoshino himself uses the terms "populations" and "communities," thereby insinuating personal(ized) interests or efforts. I intentionally changed the terminology so as to speak about discourses and structures, not about people.
19. Note that both homosexuality and heterosexuality rely on the structure of gender binary—an accusation often heard against bisexuality, yet oddly silent concerning homo- and heterosexuality.
20. Yoshino uses the term "sex"; however, I prefer to use "gender" so as to uncouple the social structure of gender from the (also gender-charged) field of human anatomy.
21. This is the first and so far only time that an LGBT organization in Israel/Occupied Palestine acted with physical violence toward activists from the community.
22. During the writing of this book, another report of the same kind was published, this time in the U.K., called *The Bisexuality Report*. Please see the "Further Reading" list for more information.

23. The two exceptions to this are Sarah's *Bi Furious!* blog post, which tries to work out the mechanisms of privilege; and "Bisexual *Women*, Feminist Politics" by Tamara Bower (in *Bisexual Politics*), which questions the notion of heterosexual privilege using statistical information about women's condition in marriage.

24. That butches, femmes, kinksters, and poly people have somewhat escaped this stigma over the years owes to the hard and relentless struggles of activists from these groups who worked and insisted on acceptance and inclusion. That the rest of us have (largely) not, testifies to the power hierarchies at work in lesbian and other queer communities, and in particular to monosexism and cissexism's widespread character and enormous influence in our communities.

25. Only when concerning sexual orientation, of course. Transgender people are far worse off than any other LGBT population.

26. While also echoing nineteenth century inversion theory, presuming that trans men are necessarily attracted to cis women, and that trans women are necessarily attracted to cis men.

27. It's worth mentioning that bisexuals and bi-spectrum people share this status with asexuals, as well as several other groups.

28. This example, by the way, is intentional: Douglas's research is about racialized cultures, and it suffers from considerable streaks of white and Christian ethnocentrism. My example is meant to somewhat counter these racist tendencies.

29. There are incidents in which society fails to gender certain people. This "noncomplicity" is met with social punishment in a way that reinforces how much weight society puts into the gender binary.

30. Note that by "female" and "male" I do not mean people's bodies, but identities. See chapter 6 for more about this.

31. The study neglects to mention transgender people in general, among whom experience of these types of violence might be even more prevalent.

32. According to the U.S. Health Department study, almost 90 percent of the bi women reported only male perpetrators.

33. "Fighting for their country" is in quotations since in the great majority of cases, men do not in fact fight "for their countries," but for the narrow interests of their country's ruling classes.

34. It's important to remember that lack of physical sexual response is not the definition for asexuality. Many asexual people do experience physical arousal but are nevertheless uninterested in being sexual.

35. In Hebrew, language is gendered and masculine pronouns are default. Using feminine pronouns is associated with feminism.

36. I use the word "biphobia" and avoid "monosexism" intentionally. In my experience, trans communities are often specifically biphobic, but rarely monosexist.

37. The message was transphobic for four reasons: First, because it presumed that trans women are a type of men (which means that a straight man fantasizing about a trans woman might be bisexual); second, it objectified trans women and treated them as a sexual fetish rather than as actual people; third, the author saw fit to state that he might find trans women "disgusting"; and fourth, he used the hate word "tranny."

38. Note that here too, bisexuality means the originary state of the fetus, which begins its development without distinctive sexual features but develops them throughout the pregnancy. Likewise, monosexuality here means clear sexual differentiation between two biological sexes.

39. Yosef himself does not use the word "bisexual," nor does he address the biphobic element in Marito's character.

40. "Homosexual" is in quotations because at least one of the characters participanting in the sexual act was not necessarily homosexual.

41. Writing "sex" and not "gender" is deliberate. Being rigidly cissexist, what matters to this legal proposal is the sex one has been assigned at birth.
42. The connection between women's oppression and the oppression of animals is too broad for elaboration here. I encourage my readers to learn more about this topic.
43. I am indebted to my partner, Lilach Ben-David, for her indispensable knowledge and help in writing this section.
44. Note that the fact that the It Gets Better campaign has a catchy name still doesn't mean that its content lacks problems. Indeed, this campaign is far more problematic than the one discussed above.
45. Note that my use of gendered descriptions relies on these people's gender presentation and not identity. Except for the trans man, whose gender was the topic of his poster, no gender identity was mentioned for anyone. In the framework of cissexism, this usually denotes cisgender. I do acknowledge, however, that they may not identify as cis.

Index

Acknowledgments

Without the help and encouragement I received from the people around me, this book would have remained an idea in my head.

First and foremost, I need to thank my predecessors in bisexual movements. I owe my thanks to Elad Livneh, Daniel Hoffman, Dana G. Peleg, and other past and long-time bi activists in Israel/Occupied Palestine, for planting the seeds of the movement that became my life project these last three years. If Elad Livneh hadn't founded the first bisexual support group in Tel Aviv, this book might very well had not been written.

I thank the many activists and writers in bisexual movements around the world, and in particular in the United States. Thank you to Loraine Hutchins and Lani Ka'ahumanu for editing the first bisexual anthology in the United States, *Bi Any Other Name.* Thank you to Naomi Tucker, Liz Highleyman, and Rebecca Kaplan for editing the anthology *Bisexual Politics.* Thank you to Elizabeth Reba Weise for editing *Closer to Home: Bisexuality & Feminism.* Special thanks to Robyn Ochs not only for editing *Getting Bi,* but also for reaching out to bi communities around the world. The piece I wrote for that book was my first writing on bisexuality. Thank you to all the people and activists who contributed to these books. These books gave me inspiration, language, and thought. They made me happy, angry, interested, outraged, and overjoyed. By providing me with food for thought, they made this book happen.

Likewise, thank you to bisexual theory scholars for giving me the critical and analytical tools with which to radicalize bisexuality. The world of knowledge I discovered within their pages has literally altered my point of view about bisexuality and its potentials. Thank you to the (now inactive) Bi Academic Intervention group from the U.K. for editing the anthology *The Bisexual Imaginary*. Thank you to Maria Pramaggiore and Donald E. Hall for editing the American anthology *RePresenting Bisexualities*. A huge thank you to Clare Hemmings for writing *Bisexual Spaces*, my bisexual theory bible.

My friends Y. Gavriel Ansara, Lisa Millbank, and Meg Barker have all taken the time to read and review each chapter as I was writing. I am indebted to Gavi for his suggestion of the term "minority world." In addition, his well-informed and thoughtful comments provoked me to think about issues that previously seemed obvious, adding depth to the topics I discussed. Lisa was one of the people who convinced me to make the final decision to write; she provided me with much needed feedback, and has been a wonderful friend to me besides. Meg Barker, the fairy godmother of this book, accompanied me from start to finish, gave her advice, feedback, and help when needed. She also made me blush without end. Without her advice on how to write a book, I might just have remained too confused and scared to begin.

Tanya Rubinstein and Alon Zivony have both, in different periods of time, allowed me to use their university usernames and passwords, and in so doing allowed me to reach many an academic journal and article while researching the book. I also owe thanks to Alon for his feedback on chapter 5, and for being the one person in my life who *never* grows tired of talking to me about bisexuality.

My partner, Lilach Ben-David, made this book happen in so many different ways that listing them would take up another book. From convincing me to write it, through feedback and encouragement to making food for me, cleaning the house and taking care of the cats while I sit and write, I could not have written this book without her. Thank you for being the most wonderful thing in my world.

Thank you to Brooke Warner, Laura Mazer, Elizabeth Kennedy, and everyone else at Seal Press for believing in this book and helping me bring it to the world.

Thank you to blogger V. of *Bi Furious!* for writing (back in 2008): "No one has yet written the book I want to read about bisexuality."

Finally, I'd like to thank my bisexual community, and especially my fellow activists at Panorama and the members of the bisexual consciousness-raising group. Seeing this awesome and radical community grow around me in only three years has been one of the most amazing experiences of my life. Thank you for your love, politics, wisdom, friendship, and support. You make me believe in the revolution.

With love, rage, and pride.

© LILACH BEN-DAVID

About the Author

Shiri Eisner is a feminist bisexual and genderqueer activist, writer and researcher. She resides in Tel Aviv, Israel/Occupied Palestine, where she founded and currently heads the grassroots bisexual organization, Panorama—Bi and Pansexual Feminist Community. She is currently pursuing her MA in gender studies while keeping involved with various political movements, including Mizrahi, feminist, queer, disability, animal liberation, and Palestine solidarity work. She hopes to incite the revolution very soon.

CPSIA information can be obtained
at www.ICGtesting.com
Printed in the USA
BVOW08s0515050318
509617BV00001B/1/P